# State Insurance Regulation

# *State Insurance Regulation*

**_Kathleen Heald Ettlinger, CPCU, AIC, CPIW_**
*Insurance Education Consultant*
*Heald/Ettlinger Enterprises*

**_Karen L. Hamilton, Ph.D., CPCU_**
*Director of Curriculum*
*Insurance Institute of America*

**_Gregory Krohm, Ph.D., CPCU, ARM_**
*Editor*
*Journal of Insurance Regulation*

*First Edition • 1995*

*Insurance Institute of America*
*720 Providence Road, Malvern, Pennsylvania 19355-0770*

First Edition • July 1995
Library of Congress Catalog Number 95-77157
International Standard Book Number 0-89462-088-6
*Printed in the United States of America on recycled paper.*

# Foreword

The American Institute for Chartered Property Casualty Underwriters and the Insurance Institute of America are independent, nonprofit, educational organizations serving the needs of the property and liability insurance business. The Institutes develop a wide range of programs—curricula, study materials, and examinations—in response to the educational requirements of various elements of the business.

The American Institute confers the Chartered Property Casualty Underwriter (CPCU®) professional designation on those who meet the Institute's experience, ethics, and examination requirements.

The Insurance Institute of America offers associate designations and certificate programs in the following technical and managerial disciplines:

Accredited Adviser in Insurance (AAI®)
Associate in Claims (AIC)
Associate in Underwriting (AU)
Associate in Risk Management (ARM)
Associate in Loss Control Management (ALCM®)
Associate in Premium Auditing (APA®)
Associate in Management (AIM)
Associate in Research and Planning (ARP®)
Associate in Insurance Accounting and Finance (AIAF)
Associate in Automation Management (AAM®)
Associate in Marine Insurance Management (AMIM®)
Associate in Reinsurance (ARe)
Associate in Fidelity and Surety Bonding (AFSB)
Associate in Insurance Services (AIS)
Certificate in General Insurance
Certificate in Insurance Regulation

Certificate in Supervisory Management
Certificate in Introduction to Underwriting
Certificate in Introduction to Claims
Certificate in Introduction to Property and Liability Insurance
Certificate in Business Writing

The Institutes began publishing textbooks in 1976 to help students meet the national examination standards. Since that time, we have produced more than seventy-five individual textbook volumes. Despite the vast differences in the subjects and purposes of these volumes, they all have much in common. First, each book is specifically designed to increase knowledge and develop skills that can improve job performance and help students achieve the educational objectives of the course for which it is assigned. Second, all of the manuscripts of our texts are widely reviewed before publication, by both insurance business practitioners and members of the academic community. In addition, all of our texts and course guides reflect the work of Institute staff members. These writing or editing duties are seen as an integral part of their professional responsibilities, and no one earns a royalty based on the sale of our texts. We have proceeded in this way to avoid even the appearance of any conflict of interests. Finally, the revisions of our texts often incorporate improvements suggested by students and course leaders.

We welcome criticisms of and suggestions for improving our publications. It is only with such constructive comments that we can hope to improve the quality of our study materials. Please direct any comments you may have on this text to the Curriculum Department of the Institutes.

Norman A. Baglini, Ph.D., CPCU, CLU
President and Chief Executive Officer

# Preface

IR 201, Insurance Regulation, is a course offered by the Insurance Institute of America that is designed to provide information and foster learning in the area of insurance regulation that is valuable to students on a professional level. Many insurance professionals deal with regulatory issues. Information in this text will prepare students to handle those regulatory issues.

State insurance regulation is the primary form of insurance regulation to which the insurance industry is subjected. Students should be aware of the different types of state regulatory constraints and requirements with which they could be faced. Having this knowledge will help them understand and appropriately deal with the insurance regulation imposed on them.

*State Insurance Regulation* is one of the texts used for the IR 201 curriculum. It describes the various types and aspects of state insurance regulation and the effect of that regulation on the insurance industry. The text covers insurance regulation regarding formation, licensing, and marketing of an insurance company; underwriting and ratemaking; claims settlement; solvency; agent and broker activities; and receiverships and guaranty fund operation.

Many reviewers contributed a substantial amount of time and effort to develop a text that is accurate, up-to-date, and readable. The following reviewers' constructive comments and suggestions are greatly appreciated:

Gary Amerine, CPCU, ARM
Director of Compliance
American Continental Insurance Company

W. Bradford Connor, CIE, CPCU, ARP
Director of Market Regulation
State of Missouri Department of Insurance

Darren Cook
Director of Financial Services
National Association of Insurance Commissioners

Lindell Crump
Audit Manager
State of Missouri Department of Insurance

Sid J. Gauthreaux
License Bureau
California Department of Insurance

Vanna Hunter, CPCU
Property & Casualty Analyst
State of Utah Insurance Department

C. Clarke Imbler
Executive Vice President, Secretary, and Treasurer
Alliance of American Insurers

Stewart Kier, CPCU, CFE, CIE
Assistant Deputy Superintendent and Chief Examiner
Property & Casualty Insurance Bureau
State of New York Insurance Department

Robert W. Klein, Ph.D.
Director of Research
National Association of Insurance Commissioners

Claude C. Lilly, III, Ph.D., CPCU, CLU
The Joseph F. Freeman Distinguished
Professor of Risk Management and Insurance
Appalachian State University

Richard Lynde, CPCU, CFE, CIE
Property & Casualty Insurance Bureau
State of New York Insurance Department

Jerome J. McAvoy, Jr.
Executive Director
Insurance Committee
Pennsylvania House of Representatives

Gary W. Meyer
Audit Manager
State of Missouri Department of Insurance

Patrick Musick, CPCU
Deputy Commissioner
Property and Casualty Insurance—Rates & Contracts
State of Washington Insurance Department

Eric C. Nordman, CPCU, CIE
Senior Regulatory Specialist
National Association of Insurance Commissioners

Kathleen Parsons
Director
Company Admissions Division
Insurance Bureau of the State of Michigan

Patrick Pawlowski
Filing Licensing Administrator
Westchester Specialty Group

Raymond E. Rathert

Carol Selleck, CPCU, ARM
Director, Regulatory Compliance
Scottsdale Insurance Company

Damian V. Sepanik
Director & Counsel
Law Department
CNA Insurance Companies

Michael E. Surguine
Insolvency Counsel
National Association of Insurance Commissioners

Barbara L. Sutherland, CPCU
Vice President, Internal Corporate Counsel
Northland Insurance Companies

Thomas W. Tomlinson
Director, Rate Development & Filings
Bituminous Insurance Companies

Jerome Trupin, CPCU, CLU, ChFC
Trupin Insurance Services

Special thanks go to Michael W. Elliott, Assistant Vice President, Insurance Institute of America; James Fryer, Director of Continuing Education, Insurance Institute of America; Connor M. Harrison, Director of Underwriting Education, Insurance Institute of America; Warren Hope, Vice President, Insurance Institute of America; Daniel P. Hussey, Director, Western Region, Insurance Institute of America; Christine L. Lewis, Vice President—Curriculum, Insurance Institute of America; James J. Markham, Vice President—Personnel, Insurance Institute of America; Everett D. Randall, Director of Examination Evaluation, Insurance Institute of America; and Lowell S. Young, Director of Curriculum, Insurance Institute of America, for their useful suggestions and assistance.

Special thanks also go the Executive Committee for the Regulatory and Legislative Section of the CPCU Society, the National Association of Insurance Commissioners staff, and members of the Society of State Filers. The text has benefited from their interest, support, and guidance.

Our goal is to help develop an understanding of this material that will sufficiently prepare students for the future. In order to reach this goal, we must pay close attention to reader responses. Your comments regarding this text are welcome and extremely valuable. In preparation for the next edition, we need any suggestions or advice you might offer. Please write or call the Curriculum Department of the Insurance Institute of America to give your input.

Kathleen Heald Ettlinger
Karen L. Hamilton
Gregory Krohm

# Contributing Authors

The Insurance Institute of America and the authors of this text acknowledge, with deep appreciation, the work of the following contributing authors:

Justin L. Brady, CPCU
Vice President & Manager
Government and Industry Services
Factory Mutual Service Bureau

Joyce Hall Mellinger, JD, CPCU, CLU, ChFC, AFSB
Vice President and Associate General Counsel
The Maryland Insurance Group

Kenneth N. Scoles, Jr., Ph.D.
Assistant Director of Curriculum
Insurance Institute of America

# Contents

# Chapter 1

# Introduction

State insurance regulation is viewed by some people in the insurance industry as an ogre on their backs. Regulatory pressure is felt but ignored until it interferes with a particular industry activity or product choice. Many others in the insurance industry argue that state insurance regulation is part of the insurance market and, as such, should be considered in each decision made by insurance industry participants. Insurance regulation should not be ignored until an activity is already planned and about to be implemented or until a product is developed and ready for sale.

One of the goals of this text is to provide those in the insurance industry with a basic understanding of regulation as enforced by state insurance departments. The industry needs to understand how insurance regulation works and how it relates to insurance markets and the insurance industry. Such knowledge can lead to strategic advantages for those industry participants who use it wisely.

Consider the following hypothetical example. Wise Insurance Company (WIC) and Unwise Insurance Company (UIC) both developed a new insurance product for a particular state's insurance market. They both analyzed the insurance market and determined that no other insurer was offering a particular product that would meet the needs of many insurance consumers in the state. WIC also considered how the state's regulators might view the new product. WIC's president assigned a manager in the company's Compliance Department to the project and charged the manager with determining what regulatory conditions might be imposed for the product to gain the state's approval. UIC chose to ignore the regulatory perspective.

WIC's manager discovered that for such a product to be approved by the state's insurance regulators, the product must include three specific clauses and be submitted for prior approval. In addition, WIC must file rates for the new product under the state's prior approval law. Finally, certain information about the new product had to be provided to the insurance consumers before any sales were finalized. WIC developed the product with the required clauses and went through the regulatory rate and product approval processes with little trouble. WIC also developed the necessary consumer information and provided it with each policy issued. The product was successful and by the second year had generated three times its development costs in premiums written.

UIC developed its product and began to sell it to the targeted insurance consumers. The state's insurance regulators, discovering that UIC had not met the regulatory requirements, forced UIC to withdraw the product from the market until all regulatory requirements had been fulfilled. UIC spent an additional nine months revising the product to meet the regulatory specifications and developing the required consumer information. By the time UIC met all the regulatory requirements, WIC had cornered the market and UIC was unable to generate the amount of sales needed to recoup its development costs.

Although this example is simplistic, it stresses the need for insurance companies, agents, brokers, and others in the insurance industry to consider insurance regulation from the beginning of any development process. In so doing, strategic advantages can be obtained.

Beyond strategic advantages, knowledge of insurance regulation is important so that the company remains in compliance with regulatory requirements. By continually being out of compliance, a company can earn a poor reputation with regulators, which can impede its operations. For example, such a company might be examined frequently and be subject to regulatory intervention in its management. The general marketplace also would not hold such a company in high esteem.

# Organization of the Text

This text focuses on state insurance regulation as it applies to property-liability insurers. In some areas, regulation from other sources might also be covered. For example, in claims, while the state insurance department enforces the state's unfair claims settlement practices act, the threat of a lawsuit for acting in bad faith might be the principal control that prevents a claims adjuster from acting unfairly when settling claims.

In detailing state insurance regulation as it applies to property-liability insurers, this text loosely follows the typical life cycle of an insurance company. Thus, topics appear in the following order:

- Formation requirements for insurers
- Licensing requirements for insurers
- Regulation of marketing by insurers
- Regulation of insurers' underwriting practices
- Regulation of rates charged by insurers
- Regulation of insurers' claims practices
- Regulation of insurer solvency
- Regulation that applies to agents and brokers and other representatives of insurers
- Liquidation and rehabilitation of insurers
- Guaranty fund operation

The text's concluding chapter presents case studies that tie much of the content of the other chapters together in applied situations.

# The Two Sides of Insurance Regulation

In general, in insurance regulation, regulatory activities are divided into two broad categories: those that concern insurers' solvency and those that apply to insurers' market conduct. **Market conduct regulation** focuses on the treatment by insurance companies of insureds, applicants for insurance, and claimants, with oversight in four areas of insurance company operations: sales and advertising, underwriting, ratemaking, and claims settlement. **Solvency regulation** focuses on detecting insurers that might become insolvent, identifying the problems that have led to the insurers' financial impairment, and addressing those problems, thereby hopefully averting the actual insurer insolvencies.

Solvency regulation and each of the areas under market conduct regulation are discussed in this text. However, since the text is organized around the life cycle of an insurance company, market conduct regulation shows up in four different chapters, while solvency regulation and regulation addressing insolvencies are covered in two chapters. Because of this split coverage throughout the remainder of the text, market conduct regulation and solvency regulation are briefly described below.

## Market Conduct Regulation

Market conduct regulation, as described above, is concerned with consumer protection. By overseeing insurers' sales and advertising, underwriting, ratemaking, and claims settlement procedures and activities, insurance regulators can help protect insurance consumers from such events as unfair discrimination, insurer fraud, excessive rates, and poorly developed insurance coverages. Market conduct regulation promotes competition within the insurance marketplace. A key regulatory tool for market conduct regulation is market conduct examinations.

Market conduct examiners must often rely on complaint information and analysis or information from other jurisdictions and other indicators (such as financial examinations) in identifying insurers that should be subjected to market conduct examinations. A market conduct annual statement is available only in Illinois.

Market conduct examinations tend to be more locally focused than do financial examinations. Insurance regulators are concerned with the insurance market in their own states, and thus, market conduct examinations are generally conducted on a state-by-state basis. However, state-by-state regulation has created a situation in which an insurer can be subjected to one market conduct examination after another, which is disruptive and inefficient because insurers must continually supply the same records and devote time to the examination that could be spent doing their business. Market conduct examiners are considering how to move to *association examinations* similar to those used for financial regulation. (In association examinations, or zone examinations, several states join together to examine an insurer.)

As mentioned above, market conduct examinations look at four areas of insurers' operations: sales and advertising, underwriting, ratemaking, and claims settlement. Sales and advertising market conduct concerns are described in Chapter 2, underwriting market conduct concerns are detailed in Chapter 3, market conduct regulation with respect to rates is mentioned in Chapter 4, and market conduct regulation that applies to claims settlement is discussed in Chapter 5.

## Solvency Regulation

Solvency regulation, as mentioned above, is concerned with preventing insurance company insolvency. If financially troubled insurers are identified early enough, regulators can generally rehabilitate the insurers or find other companies willing to acquire the financially troubled insurer or its book of business. A key insolvency detection device used by insurance regulators is the financial examination.

Each year insurers file Annual Statements with the insurance departments in the states in which they are authorized to do business. Financial examiners can use those Annual Statements to determine whether insurers require more in-depth financial analysis through financial examination. Insurers are also targeted every three to five years for financial examination. Financial examinations are generally concerned with the overall financial strength of the insurers and, therefore, are conducted on a regional or national level. Furthermore, since many insurers operate in many or all states, several states might join together in conducting a financial examination—a process coordinated by the National Association of Insurance Commissioners (NAIC) and referred to as association examinations or zone examinations as mentioned above. The level of detail, the scheduling and coordination, and the prioritization of financial examinations will be discussed in Chapter 6 of this text.

In some cases, financial examiners do not detect financially troubled insurers early enough, and the insurers are placed under state supervision. State insurance regulators try to rehabilitate insurers or find other insurers that can acquire the failing insurers' books of business. If that cannot be arranged, the insurers are liquidated and guaranty funds help to cover the claims and reimburse the unearned premiums of the failed insurers. The rehabilitation and liquidation processes and the use of guaranty funds are discussed in Chapter 9 of this text.

# Uniformity Among the States

Because states are the primary regulators of the insurance industry, each state has an *insurance code* (a set of laws that pertain to insurance) and insurance regulations and rules. State insurance regulators impose their state's insurance code, regulations, and rules on insurance activities in their states. Therefore, an insurer operating in fifty states is subject to fifty sets of state insurance laws. One of the complaints about the state system of insurance regulation is that the laws in the various states are not uniform. The regulatory requirements of each state often differ from those of the other states. Thus, not only is the insurer that operates in fifty states subject to fifty insurance codes, the insurer is subject to fifty *different* insurance codes.

Historically, states have developed insurance regulation on an ad hoc basis. As a problem occurs in the state's insurance market, the state legislature enacts legislation designed to correct the problem. Thus, each state has arrived at its own unique solutions, which are incorporated into its insurance laws, regulations, and rules. However, that trend is changing because of the influence of the NAIC.

One of the goals of the NAIC is to increase uniformity among state insurance laws, and it has in some cases. For example, the financial examination process discussed above is uniform. In fact, for national insurers and some regional insurers, the NAIC coordinates the financial examinations of different states so that insurers are subjected to one exam instead of to many independent financial examinations.

Unfortunately, the NAIC came into existence after many states already had extensive insurance codes. Furthermore, in the early years of the NAIC, states often chose to enact their own insurance laws, which might have been loosely based on the NAIC's recommended model laws. The NAIC cannot mandate that its models be enacted.

The NAIC's influence over the uniformity of state insurance laws increased with the passage of the McCarran-Ferguson Act (McCarran). The threat of federal intervention instilled a spirit of cooperation in state insurance regulators. States were more likely to enact legislation that followed more closely the NAIC's recommendations, which were in the form of model laws or model regulations. For example, shortly after McCarran was enacted, the NAIC developed its Unfair Trade Practices Model Act. The model was approved by the NAIC in 1947, and by 1949 most states had enacted the model or a substantially similar version.[1]

In the current regulatory climate, the influence of the NAIC on the uniformity of state insurance laws has increased. As insurance market problems appear, state insurance regulators from all states work together through the NAIC to address the problems, and that cooperation often results in a uniform response among the states. In 1989, the NAIC approved its accreditation program to further increase the uniformity of state solvency regulation. The accreditation program, which is discussed in greater detail in Chapter 6, has increased uniformity in several areas by requiring that the model laws or substantially similar laws be enacted and enforced in each state that is accredited.

As of the end of 1994, forty-four states had been accredited. Thus, the uniformity of insurance laws among the states is increasing. However, a great deal of variation is still evident in the details of the laws, regulations, and rules under which each state regulates insurance. This text focuses on the similarities with examples of how insurance regulation might differ from state to state. Each reader must take care to learn the specifics of insurance regulation in the states for which he or she does business.

## The Importance of Understanding State Insurance Regulation

As discussed at the beginning of this introductory chapter, knowledge and understanding of state insurance regulation are vital to success in the insurance industry. If the insurance industry can communicate with insurance regulators and can understand their concerns, the relationship between the insurance industry and insurance regulators can be enhanced. Furthermore, understanding the regulatory perspective might help the insurance industry to develop and promote improved regulation. And, as indicated in the first paragraphs of this chapter, knowledge of insurance regulation and of how it applies to the insurance industry can result in strategic advantages for insurance industry participants who choose to use their knowledge wisely.

## Chapter Note

1. National Association of Insurance Commissioners (NAIC), "Unfair Trade Practices Model," *NAIC Model Laws, Regulations, and Guidelines*, vol. IV, 1993, pp. 880-14 to 880-17.

# Chapter 2

# Regulation of the Formation, Licensing, and Marketing of Insurance Companies

As the influence of the NAIC increases and states adopt more of their model acts and regulations, we see increased uniformity among the states in how they regulate the business of insurance. The process of licensing insurers, however, is one topic the NAIC has not touched. Thus, there are a number of differences among the states in the process for seeking a certificate of authority and the requirements the applicant must fulfill to gain that certificate of authority. One fact is uniform among the states—no one can form and operate a traditional property-liability insurance company without gaining state approval and being subject to the regulation of the state granting the license.

## Formation

In the formation stages of a property-liability insurance company, the persons involved in forming the company typically define why they are undertaking such a project and what leads them to believe they will be successful. For purposes of discussion, the company organizers are referred to as the **promoters**. The retention of legal counsel, independent actuaries, and other outside experts or consultants is often prudent in this process. Before submitting an application to be licensed, the promoters of a new insurance company should be exploring many issues:

- *Name of the company*. If the promoters have decided on the insurer's name, they should conduct a search to verify that it is not already taken or too similar to another insurer's name. A state insurance department will not approve the use of a company name that is identical to or deceptively similar to the name of another insurer licensed in the state. In some states, if the name appears to pass this test, the promoters can reserve the name for future use, following the appropriate corporate procedure.
- *Choice of domicile*. For a new company, the world is open to the choice of where the business will start. In some cases, the choice is logical. If the promoters and key prospective employees reside in one state, they might begin there. Others review the business climate, taxation structure, and state insurance regulatory requirements of several states and base their choice of domicile on the results of those investigations. Whether a state's insurance department is accredited by the NAIC is becoming an important factor to weigh in the equation as well, especially if the company will want to seek licenses in other states. This is a concern because a nonaccredited state insurance department's financial or other regulation of an insurer might not be given great weight by other state insurance departments, which might increase the supervision of those states over the insurer.
- *Product selection*. Identifying what insurance products the company plans to sell is important. To the extent that there are distinguishing features that might give the insurer a competitive advantage, this can improve the chances of market penetration (and ultimate success). Further, the products selected by the prospective insurer might actually aid in receiving regulatory approval if a state has a market poorly serviced by existing insurers, but that the applicant seeks to service.
- *Market identification*. The promoters should be confident that the products they have selected appeal to the market(s) they have identified to target. They should verify that the markets they have targeted have a need for the products they have selected and that their products are priced competitively.
- *Distribution*. The promoters need to consider how their products will be sold by selecting a marketing and distribution system. The options range from using independent agents to sending direct mailings.
- *Capital requirements*. Although minimum capital and surplus requirements are discussed in more detail below, the promoters need to consider the amount of capital they have (or can raise reasonably), the source of

capital, whether they are in range with anticipated state requirements, and whether they expect business needs to exceed the minimum requirement. How much capital they put at risk depends on *net retention* (that is, the amount of risk the company will retain as opposed to reinsuring) and other underwriting factors.

- *Reinsurance support.* Even before the license application is submitted, the promoters should be defining what reinsurance the company will need and what reinsurers they will use. Most start-up companies do not have such sizable capitalization that they can retain large percentages of risk. Reinsurance support can be a vital component to company stabilization and to the attractiveness of the license application package.
- *Company structure.* Early on, decisions need to be made regarding the legal formation and ownership structure of the insurance company because, in some states, capitalization requirements and other licensing issues are dependent on company structure.
- *Directors, officers, key personnel.* Initial work needs to be done in deciding who will run the day-to-day operations of the new company and who will be the initial officers and directors of the company. Since most, if not all, states require biographical affidavits of such persons, it is important that those persons have the requisite expertise and experience to satisfy state insurance regulators.
- *Key outside advisors and experts.* In the early stages of formation, the promoters should be interviewing anticipated key outside advisers and contractors—banks, investment managers, legal counsel, accountants, and actuaries. Most license application packages ask that some or all of these parties be identified, so it is never too early to begin the selection process.

This is certainly not a complete list of all issues that need to be explored early in the process. But the more issues that are defined early, the more complete the application for a certificate of authority can be—which makes for a better application.

At some point in the initial formation process, some promoters hire an outside party (such as an actuarial firm) to conduct a feasibility study of the proposed company. The **feasibility study** takes the plans of the promoters and runs actuarial and financial projections to determine whether the assumptions are justified and the projected results are reasonable. It is at this juncture that the best-laid plans of many insurance entrepreneurs have been stopped in their tracks! When the results are not as good as expected, redefining the company's plan of operations before submission of an application package might be necessary.

## License Application Package

Once the preliminary plans are thought through and the promoters are ready to seek authority for the insurance company to be formed and operated in the state they have selected, they must submit for the insurance department's review the department-required application package. When done, it will look like a book. The requirements that states impose regarding the information and documents that must be submitted vary widely, but several general themes emerge in license packages for start-up insurance companies seeking to be licensed as a domestic property-liability insurer:

- *Application for Certificate of Authority form.* Typically, the **Application for Certificate of Authority** is a preprinted form in which the name of the insurer, its intended home address, its corporate organizational form (that is, stock, mutual, reciprocal, or other), and the lines of business it seeks authority to write must be set forth. The purpose of this application is to solicit information that typically is set forth on the Certificate of Authority, should one be issued. The information also serves as the basis for the annual license renewal information. Further, by noting the line(s) for which authority is sought, the state insurance department can calculate the minimum capitalization requirements.
- *Power of attorney.* The insurer designates, through the **power of attorney document**, the highest executive of the state's insurance department to accept service on its behalf in all lawful process or legal process against it. For example, if a lawsuit is served on an insurer at its office and is not accepted there, the department of insurance can accept service on the insurer's behalf.
- *Business plan or plan of operations.* The **business plan** or the **plan of operations** document is the most important ingredient in the application process. In this document, the promoters describe why they are seeking a certificate of authority and describe their business plan in as much detail as possible. Many states do not specify particular topics that should be addressed in the plan. This gives the promoters complete freedom in drafting. Other states give a list of items that have been designated as the key information components they want addressed.
- *Feasibility study and pro forma financial projections.* The feasibility study supporting the applicant's business plan is submitted along with pro forma financial projections for the number of years required by the state (typically ranging from two to five years). The **pro forma financial projections** indicate to the state insurance department the time at which the promoters anticipate that the insurer will reach the *break-even point* (the point at which premiums and investment earnings equal the costs of doing business).

- *Other legal documents*. The proposed **articles of incorporation** indicate to the state insurance department the legal scheme chosen for the company, and **bylaws** indicate the powers given for operations to officers, directors, and the company's board of directors and officers collectively. These documents must comply with state requirements on legal structure and powers, such as the number of directors and the age of the incorporators. In some states, the insurance commissioner incorporates the insurance company. In most states, however, the articles are accepted by the corporations or financial division of the state after approval to do so is given by the insurance department.
- *Holding company information*. Any proposed holding company position must be disclosed, including identification of all controlling persons and affiliates and any proposed transactions (such as management or reinsurance agreements) with affiliates.
- *Insuring documentation*. Many states want to review draft policy forms and rate materials to verify the coverages the insurer intends to offer and how it is pricing those products. However, some states wait for these materials to be filed in final form after the company is licensed. Waiting can expedite the licensing process, but the insurer knows it cannot begin operations (even with a license) until its policy forms and rates are filed (and approved by the state insurance department, if the state has such a requirement).
- *Source of funding*. Insurance regulators will want to review documentation regarding the source of capitalization. For example, if borrowed money will be the source of funds, a copy of the loan agreement and any security agreements will be evaluated. In a public or private offering, copies of the prospectus or private placement memorandum will be reviewed. If another corporation will contribute funds, many regulators will want to review recently audited financial statements that verify the existence of these funds.
- *Biographical affidavits*. As stated earlier in this chapter, it is important that the insurance regulators are comfortable with the caliber and experience of the directors, officers, and key persons who will run and oversee the newly-created company. The NAIC has promulgated a **biographical affidavit** used by many state insurance departments to solicit key background information. An excerpt from the NAIC's biographical affidavit is shown in Exhibit 2-1. Other departments have adopted their own forms based on the NAIC model to satisfy their own particular review. Essentially, the affidavit form is designated to solicit the following information for each director, officer, and other key person (referred to as an **affiant**):

**Exhibit 2-1**
Excerpt from the NAIC's Biographical Affidavit

Full Name and Address of Company (Do Not Use Group Names). ____________________
____________________

In connection with the above-named company, I herewith make representations and supply information about myself as hereinafter set forth. (Attach addendum or separate sheet if space hereon is insufficient to answer any question fully.) IF ANSWER IS "NO" OR "NONE," SO STATE.

1. Affiant's Full Name (Initials Not Acceptable). ____________________
2. a. Have you ever had your name changed?____ If yes, give the reason for the change.
____________________
b. Other names used at any time. ____________________
3. Affiant's Social Security Number. ____________________
4. Date and Place of Birth. ____________________
5. Affiant's Business Address. ____________________
Business Telephone. ____________________
6. List your residences for the last ten (10) years starting with your current address, giving:
DATE ADDRESS CITY AND STATE
____________________
7. Education: Dates, Names, Locations and Degrees.
College ____________________
Graduate Studies ____________________
8. List memberships in Professional Societies and Associations. ____________________
9. Present or Proposed Position with the Applicant Company. ____________________
10. List complete employment record (up to and including present jobs, positions, directorates or officerships) for the past twenty (20) years, giving:
DATE EMPLOYER AND ADDRESS TITLE
____________________

. . .

19. Have you ever been an officer, director, trustee, investment committee member, key employee, or controlling stockholder of any insurer which, while you occupied any such position or capacity with respect to it, became insolvent or was placed under supervision or in receivership, rehabilitation, liquidation or conservatorship? ____________
20. Has the certificate of authority or license to do business of any issuance company of which you were an officer or director or key management person ever been suspended or revoked while you occupied such position? ____________________
If yes, give details. ____________________

Dated and signed this ________ day of ________ at ________. I hereby certify under penalty of perjury that I am acting on my own behalf, and that the foregoing statements are true and correct to the best of my knowledge and belief. ____________________
(Signature of Affiant)

State of ____________________
County of ____________________

Personally appeared before me the above named ____________________ personally known to me, who, being duly sworn, deposes and says that he executed the above instrument and that the statements and answers contained therein are true and correct to the best of his knowledge and belief.
Subscribed and sworn to before me this ________ day of ________, 19____.

____________________
(Notary public)

(SEAL)

My Commission Expires: ____________________

- General name and principal identification features such as Social Security number and place of birth
- Educational background
- Ownership of insurer stock
- Employment records for twenty years
- Address records for ten years
- Licensing information on any professional, occupational, or vocational licenses held by the individual
- Criminal and civil records
- Regulatory, criminal, and civil adjudications of insurers with which the affiant was employed

Some states now require the submission of fingerprint cards for the purpose of criminal history checks.

Once the application package is compiled, the package and the check for the application fee are ready to be mailed. The fees can amount to as much as a couple of thousand dollars.

If the license application package is acceptable to the state insurance department, the promoters should seek a meeting with the insurance department staff to discuss their application. After all, it is usually easier to expand on the business plan and to answer questions the regulators have in person. The meeting also gives the regulators the opportunity to meet and evaluate the key persons who will run the insurance company. And, if nothing else, requesting and having a meeting can produce two additional benefits:

1. It will force the department to give the application priority attention.
2. If the meeting indicates that the application has serious problems, it might be prudent to voluntarily withdraw it from consideration. If the promoters intend to embark eventually on a multistate licensing project, most applications for a foreign certificate of authority will ask whether the company has ever had a license request denied. It is better to withdraw a troubled application and rework it than to have the request for an application denied outright. No one wants to have to explain repeatedly why a previous application did not pass regulatory muster.

## Minimum Capital and Surplus Requirements

It takes a large sum of capital to be able to convince state insurance regulators that a proposed insurer has the financial stability to survive in the competitive marketplace. Further, a marginally capitalized company without proper reinsurance support could become insolvent because of one catastrophe—leaving insureds unpaid and state guaranty funds to cover insured's losses.

However, states vary widely in the stated minimum capital and surplus requirements. Increasingly, the trend has been to increase the statutory minimums. Current insurers (formed under lower minimum requirements) are often given a period of time in which to meet the new minimum requirements. Sometimes they are "grandfathered in" and, thus, are not subject to the new requirements. The purpose behind this trend is to ensure insurer solvency and thereby protect the interests of the companies' insureds. An indirect effect of this action has been that certain states are hard to enter. When minimums are high, the small start-up insurer might not be able to obtain a certificate of authority in that state.

In the property-liability insurance industry, the states of New York and California have the highest statutory minimum requirements. Insurers seeking multiple-line authorities will need in excess of $5 million in total capitalization just to meet the minimum statutory levels in these two states.

Minimum capital requirements and minimum surplus requirements are stated separately. Furthermore, minimum surplus requirements for new insurers are usually stated separately from minimum surplus requirements for existing insurers. For stock insurers, **initial free surplus requirements** specify the amount of surplus a new insurer must provide, above the minimum capital required and the **minimum required basic surplus** is the amount of surplus existing insurers must hold to continue writing insurance. For mutual insurers, minimum required basic surplus is treated as for stock insurers. However, initial free surplus requirements specify the amount of additional surplus new insurers must provide over the minimum required basic surplus.

## Differences by Line Authority

Some states set forth capitalization requirements for each line of business for which authority is sought. Thus, an insurer that does not intend to write certain property-liability lines will benefit from a lower minimum capitalization requirement. Using the state of Arizona statutory minimum requirements shown in Exhibit 2-2 as an example, a stock insurer seeking to write casualty, multiple-line, and vehicle coverages would find the following requirements:

| | Minimum Capital | Initial Free Surplus |
|---|---|---|
| Casualty | $ 600,000 | $300,000 |
| Multiple Line | $1,000,000 | $500,000 |
| Vehicle | $ 600,000 | $300,000 |

**Exhibit 2-2**
Arizona's Capital, Surplus, and Deposit Requirements for Domestic Insurers
(Title 20, Arizona Revised Statutes)

SECTION 20-210.

Capital Funds Required

A. Except as provided in subsection B, to qualify for authority to transact any one kind of insurance or combinations of kinds of insurance as shown below, an insurer shall possess and thereafter maintain unimpaired minimum required capital stock, if a stock insurer, or unimpaired minimum required basic surplus, if a mutual or a reciprocal insurer, and free surplus not less than fifty per cent of the initial free surplus, and when first so authorized shall possess initial free surplus, all in amounts not less than as determined from the following table:

| | **Stock Insurers** | | **Mutual Insurers** | | **Reciprocal Insurers** | |
|---|---|---|---|---|---|---|
| **Kind or Kinds of Insurance** | Minimum Required Capital Stock | Initial Free Surplus | Minimum Required Basic Surplus | Initial Free Surplus | Minimum Required Basic Surplus | Initial Free Surplus |
| Casualty | $ 600,000 | $300,000 | $ 600,000 | $300,000 | $ 600,000 | $300,000 |
| Disability | 300,000 | 150,000 | 300,000 | 150,000 | 300,000 | 150,000 |
| Life | 300,000 | 150,000 | 300,000 | 150,000 | N/A | N/A |
| Life & Disability | 400,000 | 200,000 | 400,000 | 200,000 | N/A | N/A |
| Marine & Transportation | 600,000 | 300,000 | 600,000 | 300,000 | 600,000 | 300,000 |
| Property | 600,000 | 300,000 | 600,000 | 300,000 | 600,000 | 300,000 |
| Surety | 1,000,000 | 500,000 | 1,000,000 | 500,000 | 1,000,000 | 500,000 |
| Multiple Line | 1,000,000 | 500,000 | 1,000,000 | 500,000 | 1,000,000 | 500,000 |
| Vehicle | 600,000 | 300,000 | 600,000 | 300,000 | 600,000 | 300,000 |
| Title | 500,000 | 250,000 | N/A | N/A | N/A | N/A |

Confusion often occurs at this point. Does the insurer total these line minimums to get the total minimum requirement, which for this insurer is \$2.2 million minimum capital and \$1.1 million free surplus? Or does the insurer work with the highest minimum, which in this case is \$1 million minimum capital and \$500,000 free surplus? The general rule is the former: add the line minimums to get the total. Thus, this insurer would be required to possess at least \$2.2 million minimum capital and \$1.1 million in free surplus if it is applying for casualty, vehicle, and multiple-line authority in Arizona.

Typically, the more-hazardous lines demand larger capital because of the potentially significant adverse loss exposure. For example, as indicated above and shown in Exhibit 2-2, Arizona requires new casualty insurers to show proof of at least \$600,000 in capital and \$300,000 in free surplus. However, Arizona requires new surety insurers to have at least \$1 million in capital and \$500,000 in free surplus.

## *Differences by Ownership Form*

The capitalization structure of an insurer depends on the corporate form it takes, as explained in the following paragraphs.

### *Stock Companies*

By definition, stock companies issue stock. Stated capital is based on the par value of the shares issued. If 600,000 shares with \$1 par value are issued and outstanding, the corporate books would reflect a capital account of \$600,000. The amount paid by the purchasers for the shares above the \$1 par value would be allocated to the surplus account. Using the Arizona example again, an insurer seeking only casualty authority and intending to issue 600,000 shares of stock with \$1 par value for a price of \$2 per share, would fulfill the stated minimum requirements of \$600,000 capital and \$300,000 free surplus. It would raise \$1,200,000 (\$600,000 in capital and \$600,000 in surplus).

In some states, however, the allocation is crucial. The total is not the issue. Insufficient capital with an abundance of surplus is not adequate to meet the requirements nor vice versa. For example, if the stock discussed above had a par value of \$.75 but the insurer still issued and sold 600,000 shares for \$2, the minimum capital requirement of \$600,000 would not be met because only \$450,000 of the \$1,200,000 raised would be allocated to capital.

### *Mutual Companies*

By definition, mutual insurers do not issue stock. Therefore, there is no capital account. Minimums are stated by the amount of minimum surplus needed.

### *Reciprocal Insurers*

**Reciprocal insurers** or **insurance exchanges** are systems of individuals, corporations, and other entities similarly engaged in business who agree to indemnify one another for certain kinds of losses by way of the exchange of insurance contracts. These systems have no stock and no capital as viewed traditionally and are managed by common attorneys. They do have the contingent liability of the subscribing members to make payments beyond their premiums in the place of capital.[1] In some states, such as in Arizona, separate capitalization requirements are established for reciprocals. In other states, minimum surplus requirements for mutual insurers and reciprocals are the same.

### *Captive Insurers and Risk Retention Groups*

Captive insurers, typically special purpose companies, can have lower capitalization requirements. States that seek to attract captive business are under fire from fellow state insurance regulators to increase minimum capitalization requirements—which for risk retention groups can be as low as $600,000 to $1 million.

### *Discretion of State in Setting Requirements*

Although it is a good practice for promoters to research the statutory minimums in the state in which they intend to set up their company before filing the license application, in fact and practice, the capital requirements are set by the state insurance department. Promoters are frequently surprised by the fact that they might need to raise total capital in excess of the statutory minimums. Regulators set the capitalization minimums; they are not limited to the statutory minimums. They can adjust their requirements based largely on the risk of the lines to be insured. Thus, an insurer planning to write environmental impairment liability coverage could face minimums in the $50 million range even though the statutory minimum might be only $1 million.

## *Licensing—Domestic Insurers*

State insurance departments often impose specific requirements on applicants seeking to become domestic insurers. In satisfying these requirements, certain issues, including the following, must be addressed:

- *Location of books and records.* The domiciliary regulator usually seeks assurances that the books and records of the company are to be retained in the state. One of the principal reasons behind this requirement is to facilitate the regulators' ready access to records. If an out-of-state administrator is to handle the insurer's operations, special arrangements might need to be made, such as by maintaining duplicate records so that one set is in the state of domicile or by giving the regulator computer access to records.

- *Principal office.* If an applicant chooses a state as its intended domicile, many state insurance departments require that an office—if not the principal office—be maintained in the state. The hope is, of course, that this will generate jobs in the state. But, more importantly from a regulatory perspective, this gives the regulator close access to the insurer under its primary (if not sole) supervision.

Once the state insurance regulators are satisfied that the company is acceptable and they are prepared to issue a license to the applicant, they often schedule an organizational examination preceding license issuance. An **organizational examination** can be as simple as the domiciliary regulator verifying that the minimum capitalization is on deposit in an approved financial institution. However, the process usually goes beyond this scope of review. Often, one or more examiners go to the principal office of the company to verify that the management team is in place, the corporate records are in good order, the policy forms and rates are evidenced by department approval (if needed), and the banking and financial records are in place. Essentially, the examiners seek assurance for themselves that the company is set to operate in the manner disclosed in the license application. This organizational examination also provides an important resource to the company because it gives key personnel a chance to review with the examiners the various expectations and requirements of the insurance department for financial and other reporting.

# Licensing—Foreign and Alien Insurers

Insurers, once established in their domiciliary state or country, often seek to operate in another state, and possibly another country. In the United States, an insurer domiciled in one state that seeks to operate in another state is a foreign insurer in the second state. An insurer domiciled in another country that seeks to operate in a state is an alien insurer. The licensing requirements for each of these categories is discussed below.

## Foreign Insurers

In some respects, a licensed insurer seeking to expand operations into other states has an advantage over start-up companies when it submits its license application package. If it has been a strong performer with solid financials, the prospective regulatory body is likely to be more comfortable with approving the company for license. Further, the company has already gone through the rigors of the domiciliary jurisdiction's review and regulations.

The application process is similar to that of domestic insurers. Many of the same general requirements discussed above apply to them. Some differences exist, however, in the types of information solicited and the documents that must be provided in the package. Once again, the states differ in their requirements, but some general requirements emerge that are added to the requirements discussed regarding a domestic application:

- *Charter and bylaws*. Since this company has been in operation in at least one jurisdiction, the regulators want to review certified copies of the charter and bylaws so they can evaluate the terms of its operations as a legal entity.
- *Annual Statements*. The insurance department reviews the results of the insurer's recent operations by requesting to see the company's Annual Statements, which are filed with each jurisdiction in which it is already licensed. Typically, the department asks for statements for the past two or three years. It would likely also request quarterly statements covering the current year-to-date so that it has an accurate picture of the company's recent performance.
- *Examination report*. The applicant needs to file its most recent report of financial examination performed by its state of domicile, usually within the past two to three years. This gives the reviewing insurance department important insight as to how the company has been operating and whether it is keeping in compliance with the domiciliary jurisdiction's laws and regulations. When a recent financial examination report is not available because an examination has not been performed, some jurisdictions (such as Florida) accept, in lieu thereof, an audited certified public accountant's report prepared on a basis that is consistent with the insurance laws of the state of domicile and is certified by the state of domicile. For those states that insist on a recent financial examination report and do not waive the requirement, an applicant might either have to withdraw its application or not file at all until an examination is performed. This illustrates how important the examination report of the domiciliary regulator can be in the process to obtain a foreign license.
- *Financial statements*. In addition to the Annual Statements, the applicant will also have to submit its most recent audited statutory and, in certain instances, GAAP financial statements for evaluation.
- *Certificates of compliance*. The prospective regulatory authority seeks evidence that the applicant is in compliance with its domiciliary jurisdiction and that it is duly organized and authorized to transact insurance in its domiciliary state for the stated lines of authority. The certificate that satisfies this evidentiary requirement is called a **certificate of compliance**.

To be acceptable evidence, it should be issued within thirty days of the date of the license application.

- *Holding company registration statement.* If the applicant is a member of an insurance company holding system (which consists of two or more affiliated entities, one or more of which is an insurer), a statement must be provided, typically certified by the state of domicile. Most states require that the registration statement include audited financial statements for the ultimate controlling entity.

In addition to those requirements listed above, some states place an additional requirement on a company that is seeking to be licensed in a state where an affiliate under common ownership is already actively writing business. In such cases, the insurer's comprehensive underwriting criteria must accompany its Certificate of Authority. States make this a requirement to ensure that the parent company does not shift business back and forth between the affiliated companies depending on the market.

In the context of licensing foreign insurers, the issue of *seasoning* often arises. The insurance department can use a criterion whereby only experienced operations (or **seasoned companies**) are acceptable candidates for licensing. The seasoning requirement generally ranges from two to five years of operational experience, and often this requirement is an administrative guideline not disclosed in the statutes or regulations. Unless the requirement is mandated by law, it can traditionally be waived if the company has substantial capital, if it is owned by an insurer with a lengthy operational history, or if the department is otherwise comfortable with the applicant.

Seasoning requirements weed out start-up companies from engaging in multistate licensing projects in their initial years of operation. Instead, the new insurers must focus their efforts on gaining sound operational experience before they can interest other states in their expansion plans.

## Alien Insurers

When an alien insurer seeks its first license in the United States and it does not choose to do so by establishing a subsidiary incorporated in the United States, it must choose a state to act as its *port of entry* for establishing its U.S. branch. To date, few states have laws that provide for the port of entry mechanism. Briefly, the applicant would have to submit the data, described earlier in this chapter, for foreign insurers as well as the following documentation:

- *Appointment of United States manager.* Most states will require a form or other evidence that indicates the appointment and authority of the applicant's United States manager.

- *Trust agreement.* The trust agreement must be provided.
- *Certificate of alien funds on deposit.* Most states will require a deposit of substantial funds in trust to be retained in the United States (or even in the state of the port of entry).

# Licensing—Notes on Priority and Process

Promoters seeking their first certificate of authority and licensed insurers seeking to add more states in which to conduct business commonly comment (or complain) about how long the licensing process can take. Even if a complete and acceptable application is submitted, it still could take months or even years in some jurisdictions before the license is forthcoming. Increasingly, the process is becoming more lengthy and expensive. One of the key reasons for this state of affairs is the low priority given to insurer licensing.

Licensing is a low priority to state insurance regulators. Solvency regulation takes the primary spotlight in most state insurance departments. As the economy has forced employers, in general, to constrict the size of the workforce, the same phenomenon has impacted state insurance departments. These departments now have greater responsibilities than ever, but they also have fewer employees. When allocating the resources of the workforce, the greatest resources must be focused on solvency issues, not licensing. With few staffers available to work on licensing, the process necessarily becomes protracted.

On balance, however, it probably takes less time for an applicant seeking to become a domestic insurer to work through the application process than for a foreign insurer. Domestic insurers hold out the promise of bringing jobs to the state and premium tax revenue. State governments seek industry for their states, including the insurance industry. When a governor tells the state's insurance commissioner to work on facilitating the domestic market, domestic applications take on a new priority. Vermont provides a good example of this situation. Vermont has a small economy and few industrial bases. It has, however, an attractive captive insurer law (including comparatively low premium tax rates), and a portion of the state's insurance department is devoted solely to the regulation of captive insurers. In Vermont, a captive insurer applicant is assured prompt attention to the application and can likely expect a result in thirty to sixty days. In this favorable climate, captives have been attracted to the state, and the tax revenues have become a large portion of the state's budget. Further, the captive market has brought jobs to the state.

As an example, the insurance law requires each licensed captive insurer to have a resident Vermont manager; thus, management firms have sprung up across the state.

The methodology of state insurance department consideration of a license application is quite varied. Typically, the rules are unstated. Set forth below are examples of the varieties an applicant might encounter:

- *Domestic*. Domestic insurer applications receive priority attention over foreign insurer applications.
- *First in/first out*. This is probably the most equitable method of application consideration. The applicant waits its turn in line based on date and time of the department's reception of its application. The applicant moves through the line as the applications that were received ahead of it are processed.
- *Volume quotas*. Based on available staffing, the insurance department might decide on the number of applications it will accept for consideration for the year. Once the quota is met, either the application is returned or the application is scheduled for consideration for the next year. Volume quotas are not popular in the insurance industry, so the fact that they exist is usually not advertised. They are never stated in the insurance laws or regulations.
- *Priority lines*. When a state insurance department determines that its consumers are lacking access to insurance in certain lines (also known as being **underserved**), it might give high priority to applications seeking authority to write such lines of business. In such cases, the applications in these lines will be processed before those in lines that are adequately served are processed.
- *Licensing cycles*. Some states only accept applications during a certain time frame. The states of Connecticut, Maine, and Vermont, for example, accept applications up until October 1 of each year. If the package is received after that date, it is returned, and the applicant has no choice but to wait another year until the submission period opens again.
- *Moratorium*. Occasionally, a state insurance department imposes a moratorium on license applications whereby none (or those seeking certain line authorities) are accepted for consideration. There are many reasons for moratoriums. Sometimes the state has an excessive backlog of license applications. Or, the department concludes that there is an abundance of competition for certain lines and there is no need for additional carriers in the state. This, too, is an unpopular methodology to the insurance industry. Luckily, it is used sparingly.

# Marketing

Once the license is in hand, operations can begin. But this involves having insurance policy forms that have been approved by the state insurance department or using those that can be filed and used (without prior approval). Whatever the case, the language of the insurance policy is often prescribed by state law. Thus, the insurer does not have total freedom in developing its products. The state can mandate standard contract wording or, at the minimum, the standard provisions that must be set forth in the policy of insurance. A close review of state requirements is necessary. Some states mandate the use of a standard form but permit the addition of other terms. Policies are more standardized in the life and health insurance industry, but in the property-liability insurance arena, fire insurance policies are typically standardized. (These topics are further discussed in Chapter 3.)

Assuming that the insurer's policies meet state contract wording requirements, the next hurdle for the insurer is to ensure that its marketing efforts do not violate the states' unfair trade practices laws. Every state has adopted either the NAIC model Unfair Trade Practices Act or similar or related legislation. Usually, states do not give aggrieved persons a private cause of action against an insurer, but an insurer violating these laws can be penalized monetarily by a state insurance department or even have its license revoked for egregious conduct. Through the influence of the NAIC, the tenets of the model act have become standard guidelines for insurers in how they should *not* conduct their businesses.

Although the NAIC model Unfair Trade Practices Act sets forth fifteen practices that are defined as unfair trade practices in the business of insurance, only four of the practices are germane to marketing. The following are the practices that should be guarded against:

1. *Misrepresentations and false advertising of insurance policies.* Insurers cannot make, issue, circulate, or cause to be made, issued, or circulated any estimate, illustration, circular or statement, sales presentation, omission, or comparison that misrepresents (among other things) the benefits, advantages, conditions, or terms of an insurance policy; policy dividends; or the financial condition of the issuing insurer.
2. *Defamation.* Insurers cannot knowingly circulate or disseminate false information about another insurer or information that is maliciously critical of or derogatory to the financial condition of any other insurer that is calculated to injure the insurer.
3. *Boycott, coercion, and intimidation.* Entering into an agreement to commit

or committing any act of boycott, coercion, or intimidation that results or tends to result in unreasonable restraint of or monopoly in the business of insurance is prohibited.

4. *Unfair discrimination*. A long list of prohibited practices that are considered to be unfair discrimination can be drawn up. The list includes redlining (the refusal to insure or refusal to renew property-liability insurance solely because of the geographic location of the risk) and underwriting practices resulting in the refusal to insure or renew coverage solely because of an applicant's sex, marital status, race, religion, or national origin or his prior cancellation by another insurance carrier.

# Summary

From their very formation, insurance companies are subject to state insurance regulation. Insurance regulators must approve and license new insurers before the insurers can start to write insurance coverages. Insurance regulators must be shown that prospective insurers will be successful and will meet the insurance needs of their intended markets before insurance regulators will approve the insurers for formation and licensing. This is not an easy task—it is complex and time-consuming.

When individuals or entities (the promoters) determine that they want to form and license an insurance company in a state, they must first thoroughly describe the prospective insurer and investigate its feasibility. The promoters must establish such items as the insurer's name and ownership form, the insurer's business plan, and the board of directors and the officers for the insurer. The complete details of the insurer must then be submitted to the state insurance department in the state in which the insurer is to be domiciled. The state regulators will examine such items as the initial capital and surplus sources, the pro-forma financial statements, and the biographical affidavits of the proposed board members, officers, and key employees of the insurer. If the state regulators approve the insurer, the insurer is then incorporated and licensed in the state as a domiciliary insurer. The insurer can begin to write insurance coverages.

Insurance companies often branch out to other states. To write business in other states, however, most insurers must be licensed in those states. Again, insurers must apply for the licenses and submit detailed information to the state insurance department in each state in which the insurer wants to write business. Among other items, insurers generally must show that they are successful in their domiciliary states and other states in which they are licensed. Once approved for licenses, insurers can begin to write insurance coverages in those states.

When insurers are ready to write insurance, they must market their coverages. Insurers must also conform to state regulation in marketing. Unfair trade practices acts are often the principal regulation that applies to insurers's marketing.

# Chapter Note

1. See, generally, *Couch on Insurance*, 2d (rev. ed.), (Rochester, NY: The Lawyers Cooperative Publishing Co., 1984), pp. 18:11-18:16.

# Chapter 3

# Regulation of Underwriting

Underwriting is the process an insurer uses to select and classify the loss exposures for which it is willing to provide insurance coverage. Proper underwriting is essential to the solvency of an insurer and to the fair and equitable treatment of insureds and potential insureds.

Of concern to insurance regulators is that improper underwriting can result in the following consequences:

- *An insurer could become insolvent.* Underwriting allows the insurer to analyze loss exposures to determine the likelihood and ultimate cost of any losses that might occur. Loss exposures can then be denied if they are too risky for the insurer to assume. Acceptable loss exposures are placed in the appropriate risk classification and charged the appropriate premium. If insurers often accept loss exposures when they should have denied coverage or if they frequently classify risky loss exposures as lower-risk loss exposures, insurers face financial loss, because the premiums collected might be far below the amount needed to cover the losses that are incurred, and policyholders' surplus will have to be used to pay the claims. If improper underwriting occurs frequently, an insurer's surplus can be drained to the point of insolvency for the insurer.
- *An insured or potential insured could be improperly discriminated against.* In insurance, discrimination is not necessarily a negative term so much as a descriptive one. For insurance, *fair* discrimination is not only permitted

but necessary. For example, an insurer can charge higher auto insurance premiums for insureds with poor driving experience than for those with excellent driving records. However, *unfair* discrimination is not permitted. **Unfair discrimination** occurs when an underwriting decision is based on certain characteristics deemed unacceptable for such purposes—such as race, or, in some states, sex. For example, in a state that does not allow discrimination based on sex, an insurer cannot charge a higher premium for a male driver than it does for a female driver who is otherwise at the same level of risk. Unfair discrimination also occurs when there is no statistical support for an underwriting decision. For example, an insurer cannot deny coverage to drivers of blue cars, because there is no data suggesting that the color of cars affects their level of risk.

Insurance regulators want to prevent insurers from becoming insolvent and to protect insurance consumers against unfair discrimination. Thus, insurance regulation as it applies to the underwriting function imposes the following limitations:

- *Constraints on insurers' ability to accept, modify, or decline loss exposures.* State insurance statutes require insurers to provide coverage for some loss exposures that insurers might prefer not to cover as a means to provide insurance consumers with access to insurance coverage. For example, an insurer is usually not allowed to refuse to insure an otherwise acceptable auto liability loss exposure because the auto's owner lives in a low-income neighborhood.
- *Requirements for policy wording.* Insurance regulators often specify the types of clauses and possibly the wording of the policy clauses that must be included in insurance policies. Many state insurance departments require that insurance policies be approved before they can be used. These requirements protect both the insurers and the insureds. Insurers are protected from offering coverage that is too risky and thus might cause financial harm to the insurers. Insureds are protected from policy wording that is misleading or, in some cases, fraudulent.
- *Promulgation of allowable classifications.* In assigning loss exposures to classifications, insurers are increasingly subject to constraints. For example, unisex rating is required in several states for personal auto insurance. *Unisex rating* prohibits underwriters from using sex as a classification factor in those states. Another example pertains to Proposition 103, which was passed in California in the late 1980s. One provision of this law removes territory as a classification factor in auto insurance. Thus, in California, an underwriter is not allowed to consider where a vehicle is principally used.

- *Restrictions on the timing and conditions of cancellations and nonrenewals of coverages*. All states require insurance companies to provide insureds with an adequate advance notice of cancellation or nonrenewal so that the insureds can obtain replacement coverage. In addition, insurers are typically allowed to cancel or nonrenew only for a limited number of reasons—such as nonpayment of premium or a material increase in the loss exposure. These policy restrictions are designed to protect the insurance consumer.

This chapter discusses the ways in which underwriting is regulated. Laws and regulations that place limitations on underwriters (such as cancellation laws) and that give regulators the authority to police underwriters' activities (such as unfair trade practices acts) are dealt with first. The second part of the chapter describes the market conduct examination procedures for examining insurers' underwriting practices, and the final section of the chapter discusses the relationship of underwriting regulation to other areas of insurance regulation, such as the regulation of rates and claims.

# Laws That Apply to Underwriting

The underwriting function is subject to several types of laws. Most states restrict the underwriters' ability to decline, cancel, or nonrenew most lines of property-liability insurance coverage, including personal and commercial auto, workers compensation, homeowners, and general liability, among others. In addition, most states regulate an underwriter's activities under unfair trade practices laws. These types of laws define certain activities, such as unfair discrimination or collusive underwriting, as unfair trade practices. Many states also review and approve policy wording and policy forms for most lines of insurance.

## Declination, Termination, and Disclosure Laws

Before declination, termination, and disclosure laws were introduced, insureds and prospective insureds could have their coverage canceled or nonrenewed or could be denied coverage without any explanation and without much notice. Although these laws are discussed separately from unfair trade practices laws to emphasize their importance, many states incorporate the declination, termination, and disclosure provisions into their unfair trade practices laws.

Declination, termination, and disclosure laws are based on the principle that consumers should know why they are denied insurance coverage or why their insurance coverage has been canceled or nonrenewed. Consumers should also be given enough notice of such actions that they can find alternative means of insuring the loss exposures for which they are losing coverage. For these reasons, declination, termination, and disclosure laws specify the terms under which an underwriter can decline an applicant or can cancel or nonrenew a policy. The laws also establish requirements for providing declined applicants or terminated insureds with notice of the denial or termination, including the insurers' reasons for such actions.

## Definitions

Declination, termination, and disclosure laws typically define the terms declination and termination as follows:

- **Declination** means that the insurer refuses to provide coverage to an applicant who has made a written request to the insurer or its agent or a broker, or it means that an agent or broker refuses to forward such a written request to an insurer. Declination also means (1) that the insurer that provides the coverage differs from the one to which the request for coverage was made or (2) that the terms of the insurance policy differ significantly from the terms requested in the submitted written application.
- **Termination** means canceling the policy during the policy term or nonrenewing coverage at the end of a policy term.

## Notification

**Notification requirements** provide guidelines about when notice of declination or termination must be delivered and what information such notices must include. The requirements differ, depending on whether the notice follows a declination, cancellation, or nonrenewal of coverage.

When applicants are denied coverage, the insurers servicing the applicants must provide written explanation directly to the applicants or must inform the applicants that written explanation is available on request. However, in some states, if applicants are represented by agents or brokers and do not deal directly with insurers, the insurers are required to provide written notice of declination only to the agents or brokers with the agents or brokers forwarding the declination to the applicants. In either case, the National Association of Insurance Commissioners (NAIC) recommends that insurers, agents, or brokers provide requested written explanations within twenty-one days of receiving those requests.[1] However, states vary in the number of days insurers have to provide written explanation.

When insureds' policies are canceled, notices must be personally delivered to the named insureds or mailed to the named insureds at their last known address. The notices must explain the insurers' decisions to cancel the policies. Notices must be sent within a certain time frame. The NAIC recommends the time periods indicated in Exhibit 3-1.[2]

**Exhibit 3-1**
NAIC's Recommendations for Number of Days' Notice in the Event of Policy Cancellation

| Type of Insurance Policy | Conditions | Days' Notice |
|---|---|---|
| Property[1] | In force ≤ 60 days | 14 |
| | In force > 60 days | 30 |
| Auto[2] | Cancel for nonpayment of premium | 10 |
| | Cancel for other reason | 20 |

1. Source: National Association of Insurance Commissioners (NAIC), "Property Insurance Declination, Termination and Disclosure Model Act," *NAIC Model Laws, Regulations, and Guidelines*, vol. IV (NAIC, July 1992), p. 720-2.
2. Source: National Association of Insurance Commissioners (NAIC), "NAIC Automobile Insurance Declination, Termination and Disclosure Model Act," *NAIC Model Laws, Regulations, and Guidelines*, vol. IV (NAIC, July 1992), p. 725-2.

States can vary from these recommendations. For example, Pennsylvania has the following notification requirements for personal auto policy cancellations:

- Fifteen days' notice for:
  - Nonpayment of premiums
  - A policy in effect for sixty days or less and not a renewal policy
  - Suspension or revocation of the named insured's driver's license during the policy period
  - Issuance of the policy based on material misrepresentations
- Sixty days' notice for all other reasons[3]

When insurers decide not to renew insureds' policies, notices must be mailed to named insureds at their last known address or be delivered to named insureds in person and must include written explanations of the nonrenewal decisions. The NAIC recommends that at least a thirty-day notice be given to insureds whose coverage will not be renewed.[4]

States often vary from the NAIC recommendation. For example, New York requires that notice of nonrenewal for commercial insurance be sent at least sixty days and no more than 120 days before the end of the policy period.[5] Florida requires at least a forty-five-day notice for nonrenewal of personal auto policies unless the policy is nonrenewed for nonpayment of premium, which does not require notice.[6]

## Allowable Terminations and Declinations

Declination, termination, and disclosure laws generally allow insurers to cancel insurance policies for only the reasons specified in the laws. These reasons can differ depending on the state law that applies and the type of insurance purchased.

If a policy has been in effect for less than a certain period of time (usually sixty days) and it is not a renewal policy, cancellation is often allowed for any reason. This is generally true for all lines of insurance.

Typically, insurers are allowed to cancel personal and commercial property-liability insurance policies (other than auto, which is discussed below) for the following reasons if the policy has been in effect for a certain period of time (usually sixty days) or after the renewal date has passed:

- The premium is not paid.
- Fraud or material misrepresentation is made by or with the knowledge of the named insured when applying for coverage, while continuing coverage, or when presenting a claim.
- Willful and reckless acts or omissions committed by the named insured increase the insurer's risk.
- The risk insured against increases substantially.
- The insured property violates local fire, health, safety, building, or construction regulations or ordinances, thus substantially increasing the insurer's risk.
- The insurance commissioner determines that if the insurer were to continue to insure the risk, the insurer would be in violation of a law.
- The real property covered by the insurance is subject to property taxes that are at least two years delinquent at the time the notice is issued.[7]

Under personal and commercial auto insurance laws, insurers can usually cancel auto insurance policies for the following reasons if the policy has been in force for more than sixty days or the policy is up for renewal:

- The premium is not paid.

- Fraud or material misrepresentation is made by or with the knowledge of the named insured when applying for coverage, while continuing coverage, or when presenting a claim.
- The named insured or, for personal auto insurance, any driver within the same household fails to satisfy an insurer's written request for his or her driving record for the previous thirty-six months.
- The named insured's license or, for personal auto insurance, the license of any driver residing in the same household is suspended or revoked.
- Conviction or forfeiture of bail results from actions arising out of or in connection with the operation of an auto that could result in suspension or revocation of the license of the named insured or, for personal auto insurance, any driver within the same household.
- The insured motor vehicle is in any of the following categories:
    - Mechanically defective and endangers public safety
    - Used to carry passengers for hire
    - Used to transport flammables or explosives or used for illegal purposes
    - An authorized emergency vehicle
    - Altered during the policy period, which substantially increases the risk
- The named insured relocates to a state in which the insurer is not licensed.
- Dues or fees that are required to acquire or maintain coverage are not paid.
- The commissioner determines that if the insurer were to continue to insure the risk, the insurer would be in violation of a law.[8]

States do, however, vary from the reasons listed above for canceling property-liability and auto insurance. For example, Arkansas allows cancellation of commercial auto policies in effect for more than sixty days for only three reasons:

1. Nonpayment of premium
2. Fraud or material misrepresentation
3. Material change in risk[9]

States can also limit an insurer's ability to nonrenew or to decline coverage. For example, New York allows an insurer to nonrenew only 2 percent of the auto insurance policies it has in force each year. However, for every two new auto insurance policies the insurer voluntarily sells, it is allowed to nonrenew an additional (over the 2 percent limit) auto insurance policy.

In Massachusetts, an insurer cannot deny coverage for autos. An insurer must provide coverage for at least a year. At renewal, insurers can nonrenew only for limited reasons, as discussed earlier in this chapter.

### Terminations and Declinations That Are Not Allowed

In addition to specifying the conditions on which cancellation can be based, the declination, termination, and disclosure laws often define those reasons for declination and termination that are expressly *not* allowed. These reasons include the following:

- The race, religion, nationality, ethnic group, age, sex, or marital status of the applicant or named insured or, for personal auto policies, other occupants within the same household. Regarding auto insurance, however, rating differentials can be based on age, sex, and marital status in many states.
- Solely due to the lawful occupation or profession of the applicant or named insured or, for personal auto policies, other occupants within the same household.
- Previous declination or termination of the applicant or named insured.
- Use of residual market mechanisms by the applicant or named insured.
- Age or location of the insured residence or the residence to be insured, unless such decision is made for acceptable business reasons (for example, the moral hazard is too great).
- Principal location of the insured motor vehicle, unless such decision is made for acceptable business reasons (for example, the insurer is not licensed in the state).[10]

### Enforcement

If an insurer, agent, or broker violates the law regarding the timing and content of the notification or regarding the reasons for termination or declination, the state insurance departments can sanction the violator. An insurer might be required to accept an applicant or reinstate or renew an insured's policy at rates and terms offered to other, similar risks. If the violation is determined to be a business practice, the insurer, agent, or broker might be ordered to cease and desist. In addition, the violator might be assessed significant monetary fines and penalties, such as suspension or revocation of the violator's license, by insurance regulators.

## Unfair Trade Practices Acts

The purpose of unfair trade practices acts is to regulate the trade practices of the business of insurance as required under the McCarran-Ferguson Act

(McCarran). Before McCarran, the Federal Trade Commission Act provided regulatory supervision over insurance trade practices along with other businesses. With the passage of McCarran, states needed to develop and implement their own laws that defined and provided a means for determining and prohibiting insurance business practices that constituted unfair methods of competition or unfair and deceptive practices. Failure of the states to enact such legislation could result in federal intervention in these areas. Thus, the NAIC developed the model Unfair Trade Practices Act and states began to adopt it.[11] Currently, all U.S. jurisdictions but the District of Columbia and Guam have unfair trade practices acts.[12]

Unfair trade practices acts apply to several different functions of insurers. This section, however, focuses on the acts as they apply to underwriting.

### Definition of Unfair Trade Practices in Underwriting

Unfair trade practices acts prohibit an insurer from using unfair methods of competition and unfair acts or practices as defined in the acts (and discussed below). Most acts also give the insurance commissioner the authority to decide whether an insurer's activities result in unfair competition or qualify as unfair trade practices if such activities are not included in the list of unfair activities in the state's unfair trade practices act.[13]

The NAIC had initially suggested that an **unfair trade practice** be defined as a specific activity described in an unfair trade practices act that an insurer commits with such frequency as to indicate a general business practice.[14] For example, if an insurer regularly performs a particular prohibited activity—such as providing only five days' notice of cancellation—an unfair trade practice has been committed. However, such a definition of unfair trade practice failed to prohibit activities that were listed in an unfair trade practices act but that were committed only once or twice and thus were not general business practices. Such a case was heard in Connecticut. In Mead v. Burns, the court found that a single act of misconduct by an insurer did not violate Connecticut's Unfair Trade Practices Act because the act referred only to general business practices.[15]

To address the issue, the NAIC recommended that a second definition of an unfair trade practice—the commission of an activity specified in an act in a flagrant manner with conscious disregard for the law—be added to unfair trade practices acts. With this additional definition, if an insurer knows that an activity is banned under the law—such as discriminating unfairly—and does it anyway, an unfair trade practice is committed, even if the insurer discriminates unfairly only once. Most states have not yet incorporated this second definition into their unfair trade practices acts.

As mentioned, certain prohibited activities are described in unfair trade practices laws. The prohibited activities with respect to life underwriting, accident and health underwriting, and property-liability underwriting are listed in Exhibit 3-2. However, this section focuses on property-casualty underwriting.

Property-liability companies sometimes commit underwriting unfair trade practices. The following are examples of underwriting violations of unfair trade practices acts:

- In Pennsylvania, the insurance commissioner determined that sex-based auto insurance rates were unfairly based on actuarial and other relevant factors because they did not treat "equals equally." The court supported the commissioner's determination and required the insurer to use unisex rates. (This was overruled by the state legislature and has been further challenged in courts.)[16]
- In Florida, a rule prohibited the use of sex as a rating factor in personal auto insurance. A rating organization challenged the rule in court. The court in this case decided in favor of the rating organization by concluding that while the unfair trade practices law in Florida prohibits unfair discrimination, sex is an actuarially sound rating factor.[17]

## Enforcement

If an insurer allegedly commits an unfair trade practice, the commissioner of the state in which the activity is alleged can hold a hearing to allow the insurer to present proof of why the activity does not violate the state's unfair trade practices act. Before the hearing, however, the commissioner will most likely issue a cease-and-desist order to bar the insurer from continuing the activity alleged to be in violation. If the insurer proves that the activity is not an unfair trade practice, the commissioner removes the cease-and-desist order. But, if an insurance company is found in violation of the unfair trade practices act, the insurer is subject to one or both of two forms of penalty:

- *Fine per violation.* The fine is often significantly increased if the activity is considered to be flagrant with conscious disregard for the law.
- *Suspension or revocation of license.* This usually occurs if the insurance company's management knew or should have known that the activity was an unfair trade practice.

If an insurer disagrees with the commissioner's findings, generally the insurer can file for judicial review by the county court within a specified time period after the commissioner's findings have been imposed. However, if the judicial review finds with the commissioner, the insurer must obey the commissioner's orders.

**Exhibit 3-2**
Unfair Trade Practices With Respect to Underwriting

- Making or permitting unfair discrimination under the following conditions:
  - Among individuals of the same class with equal life expectations in any terms and conditions of a life insurance policy
  - Among individuals of the same class with similar health characteristics in any terms and conditions of an accident or health insurance policy
  - Among individuals or risks of the same class with similar characteristics by refusing to insure or renew or by canceling or limiting the amount of insurance on property-casualty loss exposures solely based on the geographic location of the risk unless such action was necessary for sound underwriting and actuarial principles related to actual or reasonably expected loss experience
  - Among individuals or risks of the same class with similar characteristics by refusing to insure or renew or by canceling or limiting the amount of insurance on residential property, or personal property contained within, solely based on the age of the residential property
- Refusing to insure or to continue to insure or limiting the amount of insurance available to an individual because of his or her sex, marital status, race, religion, or national origin. However, marital status can be considered with respect to eligibility for dependent coverage
- Terminating, changing, or refusing to issue or renew a property-casualty policy solely based on the applicant's or insured's physical or mental impairment. However, this does not apply to accident and health insurance sold by property-casualty insurers. Furthermore, this provision does not change any other provision of the law with respect to termination, modification, issuance, or renewal of a policy
- Refusing to insure a risk solely because another insurer has refused to insure or has canceled or nonrenewed an existing policy on the risk. This does not prevent termination of an excess insurance policy due to failure of the insured to maintain underlying coverage.
- Failing to maintain books, records, documents, and other business records so that data is accessible and retrievable by insurance regulators for examinations.

Source: National Association of Insurance Commissioners (NAIC), "Unfair Trade Practices Act," *NAIC Model Laws, Regulations, and Guidelines*, vol. IV, Section 4, (NAIC 1993), pp. 880-4 to 880-6.

## Form Regulation

Policy forms, both new and revised and including applications for insurance, insurance binders, policy jackets, declarations pages, and insurance policies and endorsements, typically must be approved by a state's insurance department for such forms to be issued in that state. To get state approval, forms must generally be **filed** (submitted in the proper format and with the appropriate supporting information) with the state insurance department. Forms must be filed in accordance with form filing laws in each state in which insurers expect to issue them. States can have one or more of the following form filng laws:

- **Prior approval**, under which the forms must be filed and approved before they can be issued by insurers.
- **File and use**, under which forms must be filed a certain number of days before they are issued. If the insurance department does not disapprove filings within a certain period of time established in the state's form filing law, the filed form can be used.
- **Use and file**, under which insurers can issue forms before they are filed. However, the forms must be filed within a certain number of days of their initial use (specified in the state's form filing law). The insurance department then has a reasonable period of time to disapprove the forms (also specified in the state's form filing law).
- **No-file**, or **open competition**, under which forms can be issued without ever being filed with the state insurance department.
- **State-mandated**, under which the state insurance department requires certain forms to be used. If the forms are not used, any forms issued in their place will be interpreted as if they were the state-mandated forms.

Some states specify the reasonable time periods allowed for form review as deemer provisions. **Deemer provisions** state that if the state insurance department does not disapprove of filed forms within the time period specified in the deemer provision, the forms are *deemed* approved and can be issued by the insurance companies that have filed the forms.

The type of form filing law that applies to a form depends on the state in which the form is to be issued and the type of insurance coverage to which the form applies. For example, a state might have a prior approval law for personal property-liability forms and have a file and use filing law for commercial property-liability forms. In this state, insurers would be required to file any new or revised personal property-liability forms and wait for them to be approved before they could issue the forms. Insurers would also have to file commercial property-liability forms before they were issued. However, once the period in which the regulators were required to respond had passed without the forms being disapproved, the insurers could use those commercial forms.

The type of form filing law that applies can also be determined by the size or type of the risk covered by the form or by the type of form itself. For example, a Texas form filing rule exempts policies and endorsements used for large risks from its filing requirements. *Large risks*, according to the Texas filing law, are those risks that meet at least one of the following:

- The insured has total insured property of at least $10 million.
- The insured received engineering or inspection services meeting the standards approved by the Texas Department of Insurance.
- The insured has total annual gross revenue of at least $20 million.
- The insured has a total property insurance premium of at least $25,000, a total general liability insurance premium of at least $50,000, or a total multiperil insurance premium of at least $75,000.

Some states exempt from form filing requirements policies used to insure highly protected risks (HPRs) and special risks that are odd and difficult to insure. In addition, states often exempt manuscript policies from form filing requirements.

State insurance regulators check filed forms to make sure provisions, such as the following, are included in the forms as specified by state law:

- Policy cancellation provisions
- Loss reporting requirements
- Claims settlement provisions
- Subrogation provisions
- Fraud and dishonesty definitions and penalties
- Dispute resolution procedures

Insurance regulators also use form filings to determine whether policy forms meet the requirements imposed by the state regarding readability of the included provisions. Most states have a *readability requirement* that policies be in "plain English" as measured by the Flesch reading ease scale or some similar tool. Such readability requirements specify the minimum acceptable reading score a policy must meet to be approved.

When forms are required to be filed, property-liability insurers generally must complete a document similar to that represented in Exhibit 3-3. This document shows the type of information regulators require, in addition to the new or revised forms.

Insurers often hold informal discussions with insurance regulators regarding form filings before the filings are made. This helps insurers understand what is required on the filing and in the supporting information. Such preparation increases the efficiency and effectiveness of the form-filing process.

**Exhibit 3-3**
Property-Liability Forms Filing Supplement

1. Company name:
2. Company identifier:
3. Type of liability coverage, if applicable:

   [ ] Claims-made or [ ] Occurrence
4. Is there a corresponding rate filing: Yes [ ] No [ ]

   If yes, give date and file #
5. List of forms: Use an additional sheet for multiple form filing, if necessary.

   (a) Form title:

   (b) New form number and edition date:

   (c) Replaced form number and edition date:

   (d) Type of form:

   (e) Give a brief description and purpose of forms:
6. I certify that I am authorized to make this form filing on behalf of the Company, further that to the best of my knowledge and belief the information contained in these transmittals and the filing is true, complete and correct and in compliance with all applicable laws of your state, including applicable policy readability standards.

   ____________________________
   Signature
7. ____________________________
   Type Name—Title

- - - - - - - - - - - - - - - - - - - - - - - - - -

**Sheet for Multiple Form Filing**

| Form Title | New Form # | Replaced Form # | Type of Form | Description of Form |
|---|---|---|---|---|
| | | | | |

Source: NAIC Property-Casualty Forms Transmittal Supplement, December 1989.

# Market Conduct Examinations of Underwriting

Much of what market conduct examiners look for when examining underwriting departments of insurers revolves around the laws discussed in the previous sections: declination, termination, and disclosure laws and unfair trade practices laws. Specifically, market conduct examiners might look for one or more of the following activities during a market conduct examination of underwriting:[18]

- Unfair discrimination in underwriting practices
- Improper cancellations and nonrenewals
- Failure to file rates or forms or both
- Inaccurate application of filed rating plans
- Improper classes of risks
- Inaccurate application of risk classifications
- Anticompetitive practices

As discussed in Chapter 1, market conduct examinations might be general or specific. If a particular type of complaint continually arises about a particular insurer, such as unfair discrimination based on sex of an insured, a targeted market conduct examination might be arranged to look specifically at the underwriting guidelines of the insurer and its conformance to the guidelines and to state laws and regulations. Or, the company might not have been subjected to a market conduct examination for a period of years, and, thus, market conduct examiners might be interested in studying all of the areas listed above.[19]

Given the desired scope of the market conduct examination in the underwriting department, an examiner could look at the insurer's following underwriting details:[20]

- *The policy population by line of business.* By pulling a statistically selected and random sample from the company's entire policy population, an examiner can study the company's compliance with its manual rules, the company's use of proper forms, and the company's proper licensing of agents and brokers.
- *The underwriting criteria.* In studying this area, the examiner might look at all relevant underwriting information, including underwriting guidelines (for each geographic area and regional office), underwriting bulletins, declination procedures, agency agreements, correspondence with produc-

ers, interoffice memos, and company minutes. With this information, examiners can determine whether the insurer is being unfairly discriminatory and whether the insurer is engaging in other anticompetitive practices. By comparing the results from this area of the insurer's examination with the results of market conduct exams of other insurers in the same market, the examiner can also get an indication of general industry underwriting practices.

- *The application of underwriting rules to risks insured.* Again, an examiner can study a statistically selected, random sample of policies to determine whether the proper underwriting rules are applied to the insured risks. This process can include looking at premiums charged, new business, the use of endorsements, and termination procedures. In conducting his or her part of the examination, the examiner is concerned (1) about trends that indicate underwriting rules that are not written and (2) with the application of the insurer's written underwriting rules.
- *The company's cancellation and nonrenewal practices in general or by line of insurance.* The examiner can determine whether the company is complying with applicable statutes, rules, and regulations by studying its cancellations and nonrenewals of policies. The examiner can also ensure that the company is following its own underwriting rules and guidelines. Furthermore, by studying different lines of insurance, the examiner can determine whether the company is involved in inappropriate underwriting in one particular line, a fact that might be missed by looking at general trends.

The typical violations discovered under market conduct examinations of an insurer's underwriting function include the following:

- Discriminating unfairly according to the applicable laws and regulations in the selection of risks
- Misclassifying risks
- Canceling or nonrenewing policies contrary to statutes, rules, and policy requirements
- Using underwriting rules or rates that are not on file with or approved by the insurance departments in the states in which the insurer does business
- Failing to use mutually exclusive underwriting guidelines for each program
- Failing to apply newly implemented underwriting and rating factors to renewals
- Failing to use correct forms and rates
- Failing to use rules that are state specific

# Underwriting Regulation's Relationship to Other Areas

Underwriting is affected by regulation in other functional areas, such as ratemaking, and underwriting regulation affects other insurer functions, such as claims. Regulators and industry participants should be aware of the influence of and on these areas in the regulation of underwriting.

## Rate Regulation and Underwriting

Rate regulation affects underwriting most directly. If rates are improper, inadequate, or politically biased, underwriters cannot be sure that the classification system will properly or adequately distribute the costs of insurance coverage. And proper distribution of costs is key to achieving equity among insureds—one of the goals of underwriting and underwriting regulation. However, equity has a different meaning for different people. Insurers generally want to achieve actuarial equity, in which each insured pays only for the risk he or she represents to the insurer. Underwriters help to achieve actuarial equity in conjunction with ratemakers, because underwriters assign insureds to the appropriate classification, which results in the appropriate premium being paid by the insured. Rate regulation ensures that the rates for each class are adequate, fair, and not excessive; and underwriting regulation ensures that insureds are assigned to the correct classification.

The concept of actuarial equity is founded in cost-based pricing. Cost-based pricing attempts to identify and control for every variable that will have a significant impact in quantifying differences between otherwise identical risks. However, insurance regulators must balance insurers' desire for actuarial equity with the consumers' requests for social equity—ensuring that all consumers have equal access to insurance at affordable rates. To help achieve social equity, legislators and the public have identified certain rating variables that are socially unacceptable—including, in virtually every state, the use of race, religion, and national origin for pricing decisions. Thus, in these cases, even if loss experience differs based on these factors, they cannot be reflected in rating plans, and this can affect underwriters' decisions. For example, in some jurisdictions, sex has been eliminated as a rating factor for auto insurance—although insurers have gathered historical loss information that detects a difference in loss experience between youthful male operators and youthful female operators. In those jurisdictions where sex has been eliminated as a rating factor, youthful males and youthful females pay the same rates. Underwriters might be tempted to avoid underwriting youthful male operators and seek out youthful female operators to insure. When this occurs, underwriting regulation is often necessary to override underwriters' natural risk selection tendencies.

Insurers and regulators sometimes disagree on the appropriate rate level for a particular classification, which can affect underwriting decisions. If an underwriter perceives that a given rate for a particular classification is inadequate, the underwriter might tend to shy away from insuring risks that fall within that classification. If an underwriter perceives that a given rate for another classification is excessive, the underwriter might tend to seek to insure risks that fall within this second classification. Thus, regulators and insurers work to achieve the optimal rate for each classification so that the phenomenon described is avoided.

## Solvency Regulation and Underwriting

Underwriting is indirectly influenced by solvency regulation. For example, underwriters are limited by the amount of surplus required in relation to premiums written. Surplus requirements stipulate a ratio of premiums to surplus that cannot be exceeded, and new business cannot be written when the surplus requirement is exceeded. Suppose a surplus requirement states that the ratio of premiums to surplus cannot exceed 3 to 1—that is, premiums written cannot be more than three times the surplus. If the ratio is already at this 3-to-1 limit, the underwriter cannot accept new business.[21]

Furthermore, because of this premium to surplus limitation, the availability of reinsurance can become an issue for underwriters and insurance regulators. Primary insurers can use reinsurance to free up surplus so that new business can be underwritten. If reinsurance is not available for this purpose, the insurers cannot take on new business, thereby reducing the availability of insurance for consumers. This concerns insurance regulators who try to protect consumers by ensuring that insurance is available. Thus, the insurance regulators have to get involved to help the insurers and reinsurers reach a solution. For example, suppose that a reinsurer refuses to insure commercial liability policies that do not contain a specific pollution exclusion. Even though pollution is not a problem in the primary insurer's market, it can no longer write commercial liability policies because it no longer has access to reinsurance. Thus, the availability of commercial liability insurance in the regulator's jurisdiction is reduced. To improve the availability of commercial liability insurance, the insurance regulator must approve the primary insurer's revised commercial liability policy with the pollution exclusion.

## Other Regulation and Underwriting

Compulsory auto insurance and financial responsibility laws affect the underwriters in the auto insurance line. Underwriters must provide auto insurance at specified limits to risks that they would otherwise not accept. This affects the classification system and the spread of costs among insureds.[22]

The ICC and state public utility commissions often specify requirements for coverage regarding public autos. Thus, underwriters for these risks must abide by established regulations.[23] For example, the Federal Motor Carrier Act specifies that policies covering vehicles subject to the act must meet the following requirements:

- Provide blanket coverage for all owned or hired autos
- Meet the notification requirements regarding (1) the timing of notices and (2) the names of those to whom notices are sent
- Provide the required limits of liability based on the vehicle covered
- Satisfy policy and endorsement wording requirements[24]

Underwriters are also influenced by the residual markets for auto insurance and property insurance. Insurance companies are often required under residual market mechanisms to accept risks at inadequate rates. This affects the underwriting losses of the insurer and usually results in standard insureds being charged a rate that is excessive so that the insurers can subsidize the loss experience of the residual market risks. Thus, since the residual market risks are not charged the true cost of their protection, even though they are correctly classified as high risk, standard insureds are paying more than the true cost of their protection. In other words, standard drivers subsidize the costs of supplying insurance protection to high-risk drivers.[25]

## Underwriting Regulation's Effect on Other Areas

Not only are underwriters influenced by other types of regulation, underwriting regulation indirectly influences rates, claims, and solvency regulation. Each of these functions depends to some extent on the ability of underwriters to adequately perform their jobs. For example, if the underwriters consistently misclassify risks, current and future rates will not be accurate. If underwriters accept risks that are fraudulently submitted, the claims function will be affected and rates will be inflated. Furthermore, the solvency of the insurance company could be impaired if too many poor risks are accepted and misclassified. Thus if underwriting regulation leads to proper underwriting, the insurer's solvency is protected and rates and claims are likely to be minimized.

# Summary

Underwriting regulation involves the policing of policy declinations and terminations and the means by which insurers achieve fair discrimination. Underwriting regulation is performed under the authority of three principal areas of legislation: (1) declination, termination, and disclosure laws, (2) unfair trade practices acts, and (3) form regulation. In many states, (1) and (2) are combined under the unfair trade practices acts. Form regulation varies by state and by line, and is divided into five general categories: prior approval, file and use, use and file, no file, and state-mandated.

Market conduct examiners are one group of the enforcers of underwriting regulation. They study various activities performed by insurance company underwriters to determine whether the insurers are discriminating fairly and following the laws, rules, and regulations regarding classification, declination, cancellation, and nonrenewal of coverage on various risks.

Underwriters are not influenced by underwriting regulation alone. Other areas of regulation influence how underwriters operate, including rate regulation, compulsory auto insurance laws, financial responsibility laws, laws that apply to public autos, residual market mechanisms, and solvency regulation. Although the primary emphasis of each of these areas is not underwriting, the underwriter must be aware of the regulation of these areas.

Underwriting regulation also ensures that other areas of insurer operations, such as ratemaking, claims settlement, and solvency, are not adversely affected by underwriters. Improper underwriting can cause insurers' rates to be inaccurate, can increase insurers' claims to unacceptable levels, and can cause insurers financial distress. By preventing improper underwriting, underwriting regulation also prevents these problems.

# Chapter Notes

1. National Association of Insurance Commissioners (NAIC), "NAIC Automobile Insurance Declination, Termination and Disclosure Model Act," *NAIC Model Laws, Regulations, and Guidelines*, vol. IV (NAIC, July 1992), p. 725-2; and "Property Insurance Declination, Termination and Disclosure Model Act," *NAIC Model Laws, Regulations, and Guidelines*, vol. IV (NAIC, July 1992), p. 720-2.
2. National Association of Insurance Commissioners (NAIC), "NAIC Automobile Insurance Declination, Termination and Disclosure Model Act," *NAIC Model Laws, Regulations, and Guidelines*, vol. IV (NAIC, July 1992), p. 725-2; and "Property Insurance Declination, Termination and Disclosure Model Act," *NAIC Model Laws, Regulations, and Guidelines*, vol. IV (NAIC, July 1992), p. 720-2.
3. Pennsylvania Insurance Code §§ 40-73-104, 106, 107.

4. National Association of Insurance Commissioners (NAIC), "NAIC Automobile Insurance Declination, Termination and Disclosure Model Act," *NAIC Model Laws, Regulations, and Guidelines*, vol. IV (NAIC, July 1992), p. 725-3; and "Property Insurance Declination, Termination and Disclosure Model Act," *NAIC Model Laws, Regulations, and Guidelines*, vol. IV (NAIC, July 1992), p. 720-3.
5. New York Insurance Code § 3426.
6. Florida Insurance Code § 627.728.
7. National Association of Insurance Commissioners (NAIC), "Property Insurance Declination, Termination and Disclosure Model Act," *NAIC Model Laws, Regulations, and Guidelines*, vol. IV (NAIC, July 1992), p. 720-3.
8. National Association of Insurance Commissioners (NAIC), "NAIC Automobile Insurance Declination, Termination and Disclosure Model Act," *NAIC Model Laws, Regulations, and Guidelines*, vol. IV (NAIC, July 1992), pp. 725-3 to 725-4.
9. Arkansas Insurance Code §§ 66-4007 to 66-4010.
10. National Association of Insurance Commissioners (NAIC), "NAIC Automobile Insurance Declination, Termination and Disclosure Model Act," *NAIC Model Laws, Regulations, and Guidelines*, vol. IV (NAIC, July 1992), p. 725-4; and "Property Insurance Declination, Termination and Disclosure Model Act," *NAIC Model Laws, Regulations, and Guidelines*, vol. IV (NAIC, July 1992), pp. 720-3 to 720-4.
11. National Association of Insurance Commissioners (NAIC), "Unfair Trade Practices Act," *NAIC Model Laws, Regulations, and Guidelines*, vol. IV (1993), pp. 880-1, 880-20.
12. National Association of Insurance Commissioners (NAIC), "Unfair Trade Practices Act," *NAIC Model Laws, Regulations, and Guidelines*, vol. IV (1993), pp. 880-15 to 880-18.
13. *CalJur: Insurance Companies to Insurance Contracts and Coverage*, vol. 39, 3d ed. (Bancroft-Whitney Co., 1977), § 40, pp. 49-50; Fla. Stat. Ann. § 626.9521 (West 1994); N.Y. Insurance Law § 2403 (McKinney 1985); Titles 40-41 Insurance Pa. Cons. Stat. Ann. § 1171.4 (1992).
14. National Association of Insurance Commissioners (NAIC), "Unfair Trade Practices Act," *NAIC Model Laws, Regulations, and Guidelines*, vol. IV (1993), p. 880-2.
15. Mead v. Burns, 509 A.2d. 11 (Conn. 1986).
16. Hartford Accident and Indemnity Company v. Insurance Commissioner of Commonwealth of Pennsylvania, 442 A.2d 382, 65 Pa. Cmwlth. 249 (1982); affirmed 482 A.2d 542, 505 Pa. 571 (1984).
17. State Department of Insurance v. Insurance Services Office, 434 So.2d 908 (Fla. App. 1983).
18. National Association of Insurance Commissioners (NAIC), *Market Conduct Examiners' Handbook*, p. V-1.
19. National Association of Insurance Commissioners (NAIC), *Market Conduct Examiners' Handbook*, pp. V-2 to V-3.

20. National Association of Insurance Commissioners (NAIC), *Market Conduct Examiners' Handbook*, pp. V-8 to V-10.
21. J. J. Launie, J. Finley Lee, and Norman A. Baglini, *Principles of Property and Liability Underwriting*, 3d ed. (Malvern, PA: Insurance Institute of America, 1986), pp. 439-440.
22. G. William Glendenning and Robert B. Holtom, *Personal Lines Underwriting*, 2d ed. (Malvern, PA: Insurance Institute of America, 1990), pp. 214-218.
23. Larry D. Gaunt, Numan A. Williams, and Everett D. Randall, *Commercial Liability Underwriting*, 3d ed. (Malvern, PA: Insurance Institute of America, 1990), p. 305.
24. Gaunt, Williams, and Randall, p. 175.
25. Glendenning and Holtom, pp. 218-220.

# Chapter 4

# Rate Regulation

*Ratemaking*, the setting of insurance prices, or *rates*, is vital to an insurer. Rates are set to recover prospective costs of operations and covered losses. In addition, rates and underwriting practices are the core strategic tools in competition for markets. An insurer meets corporate goals or counters competitive threats by setting the correct rates.

Insurance consumers have a keen interest in the cost of their insurance. They want their rates to be affordable and fair, yet they also need sufficient rates to keep insurers sound enough financially to pay their claims. Without insurance, individuals and businesses are restricted in the range of economic pursuits and can suffer undue hardship from fortuitous loss. For this reason, the U.S. Supreme Court said that insurance is "affected with the public interest."[1] As such, one might expect the public to create special government powers to protect consumers from being charged improper rates for insurance.

Regulating rates is government's attempt to control what insurers charge for coverage since under- or overcharging is contrary to the public interest. Defining the public interest with respect to rate regulation is a great challenge to regulators. Numerous groups see the role of regulation in different ways. The following items illustrate a few of the common conflicts that regulation must balance:

- Rural drivers (who have low loss experience) do not want territorial auto insurance rates blended to include urban areas (where loss experience is greater), but drivers from large cities want blended territorial rating. This was one of the controversial issues in the debate over California's Proposition 103.

- Small businesses (which often have comparatively higher losses and policy expenses) want to pay the same rates for health insurance as larger businesses. Doing so would increase the rates for larger businesses, which was a central issue in the debate over state and federal health insurance reform.
- Employers in high-loss industries want to be pooled for workers compensation rates with employers with fewer claims. This would increase rates for the lower-risk classes they were merged into while decreasing rates for high-risk employers.

# Introduction to Rate Regulation

Insurance regulation affects almost every aspect of an insurer's operations. Originally, concern over the solvency of insurers led early regulators to focus on reserves and investments. However, one of the primary targets of today's regulators is pricing. Unlike financial regulations that deal with abstract issues like financial standards and reserving, insurance premiums hit people in their pocketbooks. When people start to complain about the "fairness," "equity," or "affordability" of insurance, policymakers start to look for remedies through regulation.

The regulation of insurance rates is unique in four respects:

1. Insurance rates are set before the actual cost of the product can be determined. Unlike that of a manufactured product, the actual cost of insurance can take years to determine, because losses might occur long after the policy expires.
2. State legislatures have chosen a variety of rate regulatory environments under which insurers can operate. Some states allow insurers considerable flexibility to charge the rates they see fit. Others impose a variety of requirements that must be met by insurers in order to receive approval to sell their products.
3. The insurance industry has developed a variety of information-sharing and joint-product-development mechanisms that would be considered antitrust violations if practiced in any other industry.
4. The formula for regulating rates has been—until recently—quite different from the return-on-equity emphasis of utility regulation.[2]

The degree of regulatory scrutiny varies markedly by line of insurance. Some lines of insurance have never been regulated, although markets for other lines of insurance were developed by legislative mandate or with close government involvement. The different degrees of regulation and their possible rationale are shown in Exhibit 4-1. Ocean marine insurance, for example, has traditionally been free of regulation because of the competitive nature of the marketplace and the presence of sophisticated purchasers.[3]

Paradoxically, even within the same state, rate regulation is frequently active and prescriptive for one line of insurance yet passive for other lines. For example, Idaho is unusually strict in regard to title insurance rates, has a relatively relaxed rate review policy for workers compensation insurance, and requests that companies file information within thirty days of the effective date of the new rate for other property-liability insurance lines.

The rate regulatory system is partly explained by the political theory of regulation, which says that regulatory attention is greatest for issues that have "salience" to voters and can be conceptually grasped by policymakers.[4] Ocean marine insurance attracts no regulatory interest because it directly affects few voters and is difficult to understand. Workers compensation insurance, on the other hand, affects almost every business in a state, constitutes a large business expense, and has a well defined rate manual and experience rating system. An increase in workers compensation rates immediately affects thousands of employers when they open their renewal notices.

The remainder of this chapter reviews the history and current practice of rate regulation. The chapter reviews the development of competing philosophical and policy approaches. Then it outlines the content of a rate system for an insurance product, first from the perspective of the actuary who prepared it and then from the perspective of the regulator who must evaluate and approve it. This is followed by a comparative analysis of the four main forms of regulatory review of rates. Special consideration is given to the evolving role of rate advisory organizations and antitrust policy. The chapter concludes with an assessment of how rate regulation affects the operation of insurers and the price and availability of insurance products.

# The Mechanics of Ratemaking

A **rate** is the price per exposure unit for a given level of insurance coverage. Casualty actuaries broadly agree on principles that should govern rate setting. These principles are codified in the "Statement of Principles Governing Property and Casualty Ratemaking" of the Casualty Actuarial Society (CAS). These principles are worth discussing, since they represent a consensus of both regulators and the regulated. The principles, as stated by the CAS, are as follows:

**Exhibit 4-1**
Differing Degrees of Rate Regulation by Line of Insurance and Possible Explanations

| Line | Degree of Regulation | Rationale |
|---|---|---|
| Ocean Marine | Nil | • Highly individualized risks<br>• No statistical information<br>• Sophisticated buyers and sellers |
| Inland Marine | Generally only pro forma filings | • Highly individualized risks<br>• No statistical information<br>• Diverse coverages and classifications |
| Surety | • Rate manuals developed and filed<br>• Relatively little regulatory review | • Less detailed statistical plan and ratemaking data<br>• Fewer statistically-based rating factors<br>• Judgmental risk evaluation<br>• Less credible loss experience |
| Title | Similar to surety | • No statistical plan or ratemaking data<br>• Few rating or risk evaluation factors<br>• Underwriting and exposure identification key to controlling loss<br>• Expense versus loss driven |
| Commercial General Liability | Only general regulation, except during tight markets | • Sophisticated buyers |
| Private Passenger Auto | Often regulatory review of overall rates and details of rating plan | • Legally required or socially desirable for consumers to purchase<br>• Uninformed consumers<br>• Highly uniform statistical plan with credible rate data<br>• Complex rates and classification system |
| Workers Compensation | Close regulation including prior approval of rates and classification system | • Legally required of most employers<br>• Large cost of business<br>• Complex rating and classification system |

| | |
|---|---|
| Principle 1: | A rate is an estimate of the expected value of future costs. |
| Principle 2: | A rate provides for all costs associated with the transfer of risk. |
| Principle 3: | A rate provides for the costs associated with an individual risk transfer. |
| Principle 4: | A rate is reasonable and not excessive, inadequate, or unfairly discriminatory if it is an actuarially sound estimate of the expected value of all future costs associated with an individual risk transfer.[5] |

These principles, particularly principle four, echo language found in many state statutes: rates should not be inadequate, excessive, or unfairly discriminatory. These principles seem fair and straightforward but in practice are sometimes difficult to meet. Many hours of hearings and expert testimony are sometimes spent sorting out opposing actuarial opinion on what makes an "actuarially sound estimate" of cost. Moreover, as shown later, classification systems are embroiled in controversy over what constitutes "unfair" discrimination.

## Rate Filings

There is no generally accepted format for a rate filing, nor is there consensus on what type of information should be attached to a filing. The insurance industry uses a wide assortment of styles in developing rates and presenting them to regulators. Rate filings (the presentations made to regulators) range from simple memoranda declaring the company's intentions to detailed justifications. A few of the biggest personal lines insurers use ratemaking principles found in the actuarial literature. Some insurers use unique methods to justify rates. Filings can either brim with loss and expense data or be almost numberless. For example, the following is the lead-in to a rate filing using competitive conditions, not actuarial analysis, to justify a 6.2 percent rate increase:

> . . .[company] writes a very small volume of private passenger automobile in Wisconsin, with only about 0.2% of the private passenger market written in 1990. Therefore, we cannot rely totally on our own experience, but must consider the experience underlying the rate of other insurers. This filing contains the following changes based partly on conditions in the marketplace. . . .

NAIC model acts offer general guidelines on the content of rate filings, but each state is free to define its preferred format and the degree of latitude it is willing to give to insurers in supporting rates. Exhibit 4-2 is an excerpt from the NAIC Property and Casualty Model Rating Law (file and use version) dealing with rate filings.

**Exhibit 4-2**

Excerpt from NAIC Property and Casualty Model Rating Law (File and Use Version)

Section 6. Rate Filings

A. (1) Every insurer shall file with the commissioner, except as to inland marine risks which are not written according to manual rates or rating plans, every manual, minimum premium, class rate, rating schedule or rating plan and every other rating rule, and every modification of any of the foregoing which it proposes to use. An insurer may file its rates by either filing its final rates or by filing a multiplier and, if applicable, an expense constant adjustment to be applied to prospective loss costs that have been filed by an advisory organization on behalf of the insurer as permitted by Section 14. Every such filing shall state the effective date, and shall indicate the character and extent of the coverage contemplated.

(2) Every insurer shall file or incorporate by reference to material which has been filed with or approved by the commissioner, at the same time as the filing of the rate, all supplementary rating and supporting information to be used in support of or in conjunction with a rate. The information furnished in support of a filing may include or consist of a reference to:

(a) The experience or judgment of the insurer or information filed by the advisory organization on behalf of the insurer as permitted by Section 14;

(b) Its interpretation of any statistical data it relies upon;

(c) The experience of other insurers or advisory organizations; or

(d) Any other relevant factors.

A filing and any supporting information shall be open to public inspection upon receipt of the filing.

(3) When a filing is not accompanied by the information upon which the insurer supports such filing, the commissioner may require such insurer to furnish the information upon which it supports such filing and in that event the waiting period shall commence as of the date such information is furnished. Until the requested information is provided, the filing shall not be deemed complete or filed nor available for use by the insurer. If the requested information is not provided within a reasonable time period, the filing may be returned to the insurer as not filed and not available for use.

(4) After reviewing an insurer's filing, the commissioner may require that the insurer's rates be based upon the insurer's own loss, special assessment and expense information. If the insurer's loss or allocated loss adjustment expense information is not actuarially credible, as determined by the commissioner, the insurer may use or supplement its experience with the information filed with the commissioner by an advisory organization.

(5) Insurers utilizing the services of an advisory organization must provide with their rate filing, at the request of the commissioner, a description of the rationale for such use, including its own information and method of utilization of the advisory organization's information.

The requirements for rate filings vary considerably. Many states require their own transmittal forms, special certifications, compliance checklists, or other unique filing requirements. It is not unusual for states to require an officer of the filing company to "certify" compliance with all of the laws of that state. The bulk of the documentation required by regulators consists of the loss experience underlying overall rates or classification systems rates. The larger the state, the more likely that it will require evidence of the insurer's loss experience for that line of insurance. The information that is typically required as part of a rate filing is discussed below.

Through the NAIC, regulators have been working toward standardization and electronic filing of rates and forms. This includes standard transmittal forms and acceptance acknowledgments from regulators. Electronic filing and standardization is an increasing trend that insurers and trade associations support.

## Rate

The new rate must, of course, be included in the rate filing. The rate should be set just high enough to cover expected losses and expenses for insuring a particular exposure. Expenses include an allowance for profit and contingencies. Filings should provide an actuarial indication of both losses and expenses through exhibits and narrative. An **indication** is what the loss experience suggests that the insurer should charge to cover costs. Often, the rate filing's actuarial memorandum will state that the company is not "taking the indication" because of "competitive" or "market" conditions. This implies that the insurer is charging less than its fully allocated costs for that class of policyholders. It also implies that other classes of customers must be charged more if overall costs are to be recovered by the rate.

Actuarial and regulatory principles demand that the indicated rate be supported by data. Rate filings typically include such components as the following:

- One or more years of loss data for the state, and, if state data are not large enough to be statistically credible, regional or countrywide data.
- Incurred losses for each experience year *developed* to their ultimate cost, when all claims for that year are finally closed.
- Projection of patterns of losses over the historic experience years into the policy year being rated.
- Historic accounting of costs and expectations for future changes in the insurer's expenses for issuing and administering the policy and paying claims.

## Classification Systems

**Classification systems** have been developed for rating purposes in order to group similar loss exposures into homogenous classes. Actuaries justify such classification because it reduces adverse selection. Classification also avoids cross subsidies by charging each member of a group of insureds his or her or its share of the expected losses and administrative expenses for the group. Economists add that equating rates to expected losses provides group members the proper incentive to invest in loss control and safety.

In theory, classifications should be so detailed that each member of each class presents the same expected loss. Unfortunately, if this were to be done, classes of one would be formed. Such a classification system is ineffective and inefficient because losses cannot be accurately predicted and the costs to administer the system would be astronomical. In practice, an economically efficient classification system balances actuarial and economic gains against the incremental cost of collecting and processing rating information.

The justification for the highly complex classification system used in many lines has not satisfied many regulators. They have significantly restricted classifications based on age, sex, marital status, and location or territory.[6] Exhibit 4-3 contains examples of the many constraints that states have placed on rating classifications.

The regulatory response is partly driven by a disbelief that certain classification systems are based on verifiable loss experience. Insurers will freely admit that some rate classifications and rate relativities are based on educated guesswork. For example, discounts for good student drivers, cars with air bags, or houses with smoke detectors are based on judgment and competitive pressures. Some smaller insurers' rating plans follow the rating plans of larger predominant insurers. Others do not charge the actuarially indicated rates because they believe that the market cannot bear that rate or that the rate would be deemed unfairly discriminatory against minority groups.

Even if a classification system were actuarially supported, the system might be opposed by regulators because it imposes a socially undesirable outcome. One such outcome is that rates might be increased to such levels for some that they would elect to go without coverage. Financially irresponsible drivers inflict higher costs on other drivers, who pay more for uninsured motorists coverage. Another socially undesirable outcome would be inflicting "regressive" rates on low income households for basic coverages.

### Experience Modification

Most rating plans have some means of adjusting rates upward or downward for

**Exhibit 4-3**
Selected Classification Systems That Have Been Restricted or Banned by Regulators

| Line of Insurance | Classification | Limitation |
|---|---|---|
| Automobile | Health condition | No restrictions if applicant holds driver's license (WI) |
| Automobile | Territories | No use of ZIP Codes (CA)<br>No territories smaller than a city (MI)<br>Chicago cannot be subdivided (IL) |
| Automobile | Gender | Gender cannot be used for rating purposes (MT) |
| Health | Blindness | Cannot be used without actuarial justification (NAIC Model) |
| Homeowners | Age of construction | Outlawed without clear business reason (NAIC) |
| All lines | Race, religion, ethnicity | Absolute ban (widespread in U.S.) |

individual risks, depending on the claims experience in the previous policy period—that is, **experience modification**. Rates are set for an *average* policyholder. **Experience rating** is a way to adjust rates for risks that are not average. In business insurance, experience rating is responsive to loss experience, largely because business risks have more exposure units covered and are, therefore, statistically more reliable (credible). Personal insurance makes limited use of experience rating.

Experience rating that is too sensitive to bad loss experience generates complaints from insureds whose rates are increased. Those insureds reason that they are being unfairly penalized because insurance is supposed to protect them against the adverse financial consequences of fortuitous events. Insurers point out that experience rating promotes loss control and equity across insureds with different expected losses. Experience rating rewards those risks that have good loss experience with lower rates. Furthermore, risks with good loss experience object to being combined with risks that have bad loss experience—the good risks' rates increase and the bad risks' rates decrease.

## Rate Rules

A typical filing includes pages of rate rules that govern the application of rates to real-world risks and conditions. **Rate rules** (also known as **rate guidelines**) are procedures that reflect an insurer's underwriting posture for a given line of insurance. Occasionally, rate rules create problems. The following are examples of controversial rules that are illegal in some jurisdictions:

- This product is not available to circus performers or clergy.
- The minimum value for this homeowner's policy is $45,000.
- Binders cannot be issued for applicants for auto insurance over the age of seventy-five without a medical examination.

Rate rules appear only in agent and company manuals. They are little known to the buying public. When problems are discovered by regulatory staff in the course of rate reviews or market conduct examinations, "unfairly discriminatory" rules can be the source of controversy and possible disciplinary actions by regulators.

Some lines of property-liability insurance have developed their own traditions and practices, which do not seem to resemble those of other property-liability lines. For example, surety and title insurance use highly judgmental methods for determining manual rates.

## Effects of Rate Elements

The rate itself often has less effect on consumers than the other elements of the rating system do. How insurers classify businesses frequently causes friction. For example, under Wisconsin's workers compensation program cheese makers were rated at $4.50 per hundred dollars of payroll versus $8.90 per hundred dollars in payroll for milk product producers. Businesses that want to capitalize on lower rated classifications do not appreciate the differences in hazards and losses considered by the insurer, especially when they appear subtle or arbitrary, like the difference between cheese makers and milk product producers.

Experience modification factors almost always apply to commercial insurance and can cause swings of 20 percent from year to year for a given business, even though the rate and exposures have not changed. Finally, rate rules will determine whether an applicant is eligible for a special discount. For example, most auto insurers offer a 10-15 percent "good student discount" for youthful drivers who are still in school and maintain a grade point average above some standard set by the insurers or "package policy discounts" to individuals who buy both homeowners and automobile coverage.

## Rate Advisory Organizations

One of the features of the property-liability insurance industry is its heavy reliance on statistical agents and rating bureaus to assist in the ratemaking process. While the terms are often used interchangeably, **statistical agents**, which collect and report loss experience, are different from **rating bureaus**, which prepare all or part of a rate filing and submit it to regulators on behalf of their members. The largest of those two types of organizations and their services are described in Exhibit 4-4. In this section, the terms "statistical agent" and the more current term, "advisory organization," are used to encompass such entities.

**Exhibit 4-4**
Range of Services Provided by Statistical Agents

| Organization | Lines of Insurance | Services |
|---|---|---|
| Insurance Services Office (ISO) | Auto, homeowners, commercial fire and general liability, inland marine, malpractice, boiler and machinery, farm/ranchowners, crime, other commercial lines | • Statistical agent<br>• Prospective loss filings<br>• Policy form filing<br>• Actuarial services |
| National Council on Compensation Insurance (NCCI) | Workers compensation | • Statistical agent<br>• Prospective losses and final rates<br>• Actuarial services |
| National Association of Independent Insurers (NAII) | Auto and homeowners | • Statistical agent<br>• Some loss development<br>• Trade association |
| American Association of Insurance Services (AAIS) | Auto and homeowners<br>Commercial lines | • Statistical agent<br>• Prospective loss filing |
| Surety Association of America (SAA) | Surety<br>Fidelity | • Statistical agent<br>• Final rate filing |

Both statistical agents and rating bureaus are licensed and regulated to varying degrees by the states (for antitrust reasons discussed below). Their role is in transition. While they once set and filed final rates, they now simply provide statistical information on losses and loss trends to regulators. These are usually filed as **loss costs**—that is, the expected losses for insuring a given exposure. Individual insurers can then use the loss costs by adding their own expense costs to set their own rates.

## *Statistical Agents and Statistical Plans*

The concept of a statistical agent is unique to the property-liability insurance industry. No other industry collects data on costs from its members and shares this data with its members for purposes of price setting. In fact, it is considered a per se violation of the Sherman Act for any firm, other than an insurance firm exempted from this part of the Sherman Act by McCarran, to share its cost data with a competitor or to in any way coordinate pricing.

What is the rationale for allowing insurers to do this? Single insurers often cannot reliably set the price for a coverage, because their data is not statistically credible. Individually, insurers cannot accurately project the true probability of loss. Aggregate industry loss data, however, provides enough statistical information to accurately estimate the probability of loss facing individual insurers writing contracts of insurance. (The underlying concept is the law of large numbers.)

Without industry-wide data gathering and loss dissemination, individual insurers would be forced to resort to guesswork in pricing. Consumers would probably pay an extra charge for the uncertainty and would possibly see some products and insurers disappear.

A **statistical plan** is a formal set of directions for recording and reporting losses, and sometimes expenses, to a statistical agent. Traditionally, statistical agents developed their own plans to support ratemaking. Since 1986 the NAIC and individual states have been more aggressive in defining statistical requirements and periodic reports. During 1986-87, many states mandated special reports on commercial insurance losses and premiums collected for purposes of understanding the extreme volatility in rates. In response to public pressure to monitor the fairness of rates charged in minority communities, the NAIC is working on defining new statistical elements to be collected on automobile and homeowners insurance by rating territory.

## *Rating Bureaus*

Rating bureaus are statistical agents that go a step beyond merely collecting data. They perform actuarial analysis on the data to provide insight into future losses. At one time, rating bureaus developed final rate manuals for agents. Now their rate development services are largely limited to the following items:

- **Loss development** refers to estimating the ultimate liability for loss payments for policies written in any given time.
- **Loss trending** refers to forecasting the trend in losses from the middle of the experience period (period covered by actual loss statistics) to the middle of the policy period being rated.

In addition, rating bureaus offer other actuarial and analytical services. Examples include developing classification systems and class relativities for rates and establishing rate rules. **Relativities** are the numerical estimates of losses in one classification relative to losses in a base classification. The base class is usually the class that generates a large volume of premium. For example, the relativity of a twenty- to twenty-five-year-old male driver to the thirty-year-old male base driver is 1.4, or 140 percent of the base driver's rate.

Regulators are increasingly involved in the formulation of statistical plans because these plans are the means by which classifications are justified. In addition, regulators are more likely than ever to limit the services of rating bureaus to avoid coordination of pricing. The current regulatory view seems to be that collecting and sharing pure loss data are the only functions that can be done in a coordinated way among many insurers. Individual insurers should determine how much these losses should be marked up to reflect individual insurer costs or what kind of loss trend to assume.

## Other Services of Advisory Organizations

Advisory organizations also perform other services, such as the following, for member or client insurers:

- Making filings to insurance departments
- Developing policy forms
- Producing statistical reports required by regulators

The NAIC has relied on advisory organizations to perform a variety of special studies for regulatory purposes. For example, statistical agents performed a major study for the NAIC to assess the probable effect of various tort reform proposals. The NAIC has also encouraged statistical agents to work in concert with the industry to provide industry-wide statistical reports. One such report is the "Fast-Track" series, which shows industry loss and premium information for use as an early warning of possible rate trends in auto, homeowners, and general liability insurance.

### Antitrust Concerns

The services of rating bureaus continue to be closely examined for their anticompetitive effects. In 1989, under criticism by state and federal policymakers and a major lawsuit by nineteen state attorneys general, Insurance Services Office (ISO) voluntarily began phasing out the filing of final rates.[7] That phaseout began a trend in other rate service organizations to discontinue the preparation of final rates.

## Regulatory Practices

Insurance rate regulation commonly uses one of the filing approaches described in Chapter 3 regarding form filing. The filing approaches are addressed to rate regulation as follows:

- *Prior approval*. Prior approval generally means that the rate and supporting rules must be approved by the regulator before they can be used in that state. In some cases, a deemer provision in the law says that a filing is deemed approved if the insurer has not heard from the regulator within a given time period (usually thirty to ninety days).
- *File and use*. Under file and use systems, the insurer must file rates and rules within a specified time before use (usually thirty to ninety days). That time period gives the regulator a minimal opportunity to uncover violations of law or other practices that might be challenged.
- *Use and file*. Under use and file laws, the insurer can use any rate it wants, provided that the insurer files the rate with the regulator within thirty to sixty days after the rate is put into use. The regulator then has a reasonable period in which to review the rate and to request a hearing to disapprove the rate.
- *Open competition*. Open competition, also called no file, allows insurers to develop and use rates without having to get approval or to file with state regulators. Open competition is officially the regulatory practice in only a handful of states and then only for some lines of insurance.
- *State mandated*. Some states set the rates insurers use. If insurers do not use the mandated rates, they can be paralyzed.

Hybrids of these filing approaches exist. For example, open competition might apply as long as certain tests are met, such as evidence of competitive markets or rate increases of less than 25 percent per year. Failing these tests means that prior approval or another regulatory review might apply. Kentucky provides an example of this approach.

Exhibit 4-5 classifies several states according to which filing approach they employ for different lines of insurance. As explained in Chapter 3, policy form regulation follows a parallel process. However, rate and form regulation can be different by line of insurance within a state.

Distinctions among the filing approaches are often misleading. Some jurisdictions can nominally require prior approval of rates in particular lines of insurance but in practice can exercise almost no scrutiny over rates. Other jurisdictions might not challenge overall rate increases but take an activist role protecting assigned risk pool rates.

California is a good example of a state employing sharply contrasting forms of rate regulation. With the passage of Proposition 103 in 1988, property-liability rate regulation veered sharply from open competition toward government controls. Before Proposition 103, California's regulatory philosophy relied heavily on open competition. The exception was workers compensation, which was a prior approval line. California's Proposition 103 allowed not only prior approval of new rates; it called for a 20 percent rollback in existing rates. At about the same time, the workers compensation line went the other way. In 1989, California began a phased shift to open competition for governing all rates and rating plans for workers compensation.

## History of Rate Regulation

Before discussing current rate regulatory practices, a brief history of rate regulation can help students understand how rate regulation has developed. There is no single history of rate regulation. Each line of insurance has undergone its own market and regulatory development. Ocean marine, the oldest line of insurance, has remained relatively unchanged over centuries, while relatively new insurance products, such as commercial general liability and professional liability have experienced periods of regulatory turmoil. These regulatory developments have a few common themes discussed below.

### Cutthroat Competition

In 1752 Benjamin Franklin organized the Philadelphia Contributorship, the first incorporated fire insurance company,[8] which set rates with limited statistical data on losses. As dozens of local fire companies sprang up, the lack of a sophisticated approach to ratemaking was compounded by cutthroat competition among carriers for business. Excessive competition led to low rates followed by the failure of many insurers and, in turn, a return to higher rates. For decades this fledgling industry went through boom-and-bust cycles. The lack of stability and confidence in the industry led business and government leaders to call for more coordination of insurers' operations.[9] Regulators, by and large, supported this call for greater coordination.

**Exhibit 4-5**
Regulatory Laws on Rates in Selected States

| State | Filing Method | Lines | Comments |
|---|---|---|---|
| Alabama | Prior approval | Property and inland marine | In effect, prior approval because rate can be withdrawn at any time by regulator |
| | Prior approval | Casualty, surety, workers compensation | |
| | Exempt from filing | Title | |
| Arizona | File and use (15 days) | Medical malpractice, workers compensation, title | |
| | Use and file (30 days) | Other property-liability lines | |
| Florida | File and use (60 days) | Auto | If rate found excessive, return of premium allowed |
| | Use and file (60 days) | Other lines, except workers compensation and title | |
| | Prior approval | Workers compensation | |
| | Rate set by Florida Department | Title | |
| Idaho | File and use (60 days) | Workers compensation | NCCI makes filings |
| | No file | Other property-liability | |
| | Prior approval | Title | Ask insurers to file rates |
| Kentucky | Use and file (15 days) in competitive market<br><br>File and use (30 days) in noncompetitive market; prior approval for large rate increases | All lines | Filing method depends on findings on the degree of competition |

For a full listing of state laws see NAIC *Rate Filing Methods for Property/Casualty Insurance, Workers' Compensation, Title* (Kansas City, MO: NAIC, 1993).

## The Emergence of Rating Bureaus

Rating bureaus were established to use the umbrella of government to protect coordinated rating. The stated purposes of this were to stabilize the industry and to promote solvency. Their original functions, including rate and form development and handling regulatory filings, were broad. Rating bureaus included fire and allied lines, but not marine, life, and surety. The rating bureaus, organized by insurers, enforced the pricing consensus of specific lines of insurance, such as fire, crop-hail, surety, fidelity, and title. For example, in the late 1940s, the South-Eastern Underwriters Association (SEUA) had a membership of nearly 200 insurers that represented 90 percent of the fire and allied lines sold by stock insurers in its six states. Like other rating bureaus, this association set premiums and commissions and actively enforced these terms on member and nonmember insurers. Companies that were not members of the SEUA were denied the opportunity to reinsure their business. Nonmembers were publicly criticized if they rebelled against coordinated pricing.[10] Regulators tacitly approved or encouraged these bureau tactics in the hope of improving financial and rate stability. The potential for higher insurance prices was thought to be a lesser threat than insolvent insurers and unstable prices.

Indeed, the number of insurer failures decreased after rating bureaus were established. However, this came at a hidden cost to consumers, because letting rating organizations "coordinate" pricing was essentially permitting them to create a monopoly.

Insurers in associations like SEUA had to police each other's loyalty to the agreed prices. Most insurers wanted to increase profits by selling more policies at new and higher prices. Moreover, since the prices set by monopolistic combinations were generally above one or more of the members' production costs, those insurers had an additional incentive to discount their prices below the agreed industry prices to attract more market share. The desire to undercut association prices led to coercive tactics and to enlisting regulators' support for cartel price enforcement.[11]

## The South-Eastern Underwriters Decision and Its Aftermath

In 1944, a landmark decision by the U.S. Supreme Court declared that insurance was interstate commerce subject to federal regulation. As such, the antitrust provisions of the Sherman, Clayton, and Robinson-Patman Acts applied to the "business of insurance." In effect, this decision outlawed the coordinated rating that associations like SEUA were doing unless states actively supervised rating.

The SEUA decision caused insurers and regulators to lobby Congress to protect the system of state regulation of insurance. The McCarran-Ferguson Act of 1945 (McCarran) did just that. McCarran shielded the insurance industry from federal antitrust laws to the extent that states actively regulated the conduct of insurers. McCarran altered the character of state rate regulation.

With help from the insurance industry, the National Association of Insurance Commissioners (NAIC) approved a model rate regulation act in 1947. This model act called for prior approval of a wide class of rates with specific criteria that should be used to approve rates. After McCarran, every state passed some form of rate regulation statute. To preempt federal antitrust law, an explicit state regulatory policy displacing competition was needed. Therefore, states specified the limits to which insurers could cooperate in data gathering and form filing. In those lines of insurance in which the state would establish a single rate, a ceiling rate, or limits on how insurers could compete, the public policy objective for this noncompetitive pricing had to be established by law.[12]

## Competitive Rating

During the late 1960s, many regulators began to question the effectiveness of regulatory rate reviews. The growing burdens on state regulators to review rates were too high a price to pay for consumer protection, especially since it appeared that regulatory review did not systematically change rates or loss ratios relative to *competitive rates* (rates established through competition among insurers).

Many states adopted open competition as the objective for rate regulation. The NAIC Model Property and Casualty Model Rating Law (File and Use Version), first adopted in 1981, shows preference for competition as a means to control excessive rates. The law states, "[a] rate in a competitive market is not excessive." Only in the absence of competition were regulators to seek justification for insurer rate change requests. Some states, like Illinois, embraced open competition, while others were more tentative. Kentucky law, for example, says that property-liability rates do not require prior approval (only filing) unless an absence of competition is shown to exist, in which case the insurance commissioner's prior approval is required.

## The Return to Supervision

The *excesses* of open market competition, like those that occurred a hundred years ago, are justification for restricting insurers' competitive behavior. The justifications have changed over the years, but the end result is the same: less competition and more central coordination and intervention in industry decision making. Today rate regulation is likely to be defended on the grounds that socially undesirable competition creates availability or affordability problems for protected classes. Prior approval of rates is intended to protect consumers from excessive pricing.

## Current Evaluation of Rates

Very broadly speaking, insurers must often justify their rates to regulators in two areas. First, are the rates based on realistic and factual estimates of cost? Second, is the level of profit associated with the rate reasonable? The older mode of regulation was devoted almost entirely to determining what expected losses and administrative expenses could reasonably be expected for the policy period being rated. Recently, regulators have become more concerned about whether the profit being earned by insurers is reasonable.

### Loss Based

Actuarial techniques seek to set rates by projecting covered losses into the policy period being rated. A **loading** for the insurer's administrative expenses is added, generally based on historic ratios of expenses to premium. The rate is increased by a fixed *profit and contingency percentage*. This percentage for profit is set more by tradition than by sophisticated financial criteria. For example, the traditional actuarial practice for many personal lines has been to use a 3.5 percent factor for profit and contingency, regardless of expected investment earnings, cash flow, or changes in the expected payout period for claims. Profit was treated as if it were part of the expense load.

### Investment Return

Using a fixed percentage of premium for profit is being increasingly rejected by regulators. A new set of models has sprung up from the regulatory community to evaluate the rate needed to make an adequate, though not excessive, profit or return on investment. To be sure, these models also use prospective losses and administrative expenses. However, they seek to determine what rate of return on equity is implicit in a given rate proposal. Insurers and regulators agree in principle that the return on investment or profit should be high enough to maintain the insurers' willingness and financial solidity to serve the market in the long run. They disagree on what that level of profit should be.

Many variations exist within each of these models. Arguably, there should be a third class for financial models that set rates to maximize the present value of the firm. This model, while commonplace in financial analysis in other industries, is seldom discussed in insurance circles.[13]

Consumer complaints influence how regulatory power is applied with regard to investment return. Regulators implement changes to stem the tide of criticism and minimize further government intervention. The shift from fixed profit factors to esoteric investment models is a good example. The traditional 3.5 percent profit factor was applied by actuaries and was not challenged by regulators for many years. Only when a price increase distressed consumers was it challenged. The new investment models are more sophisticated than the old ones. They compare an insurer's return on equity with other similarly risky industries. If the models are applied correctly, the insurer gets neither more nor less of a return than is necessary to keep an active supply of insurance capacity in the market.

Another recent trend in rating is to reconsider the rate loading for catastrophic losses such as Hurricane Andrew or the Northridge, California, earthquake. This contingency loading is distinct from profit because it is designed to fund a cost likely to be paid by insurers. Sophisticated models used today estimate the maximum exposure from such natural catastrophes to be in the $20-100 billion range. In many credible scenarios, the losses from a natural disaster could exceed the entire net worth of the carriers writing in a state. Both insurers and regulators want to ensure that an adequate provision is being made in the insurer's capital reserves for catastrophic losses. Whether catastrophes are funded through carrying extra surplus or through greater reinsurance, the primary insurer must charge enough to pay for these prefunding mechanisms.

## Antitrust Issues

Insurance rate setting and market conduct regarding rating plan development are not governed by the same antitrust laws applicable to other industries. The Sherman Act, Clayton Act, and Federal Trade Commission Act, from which insurers are currently exempt under McCarran, establish strict standards for conducting business regarding pricing and marketing. In general, those acts prohibit any coordination of pricing and marketing activities among businesses that are likely to be competitors. The courts have strictly enforced price-setting standards in many industries and situations.

The courts have attempted to define the bounds between what Congress intended to exempt from the federal antitrust laws under McCarran and activities related to insurance. Regarding rates and rate regulation, the rule of case law is that for the exemption of McCarran to apply to an insurer, a two-part test must be met:

- The state in which an insurer is doing business must have a clear law displacing some aspect of competitive insurance markets in favor of coordinated pricing and marketing.
- The state must actively supervise the conduct of the insurers it allows to coordinate their own business.[14]

*Active state rate supervision* means that the state must have a definite program in place to review rates for their compliance with public policy objectives. Active state rate supervision has become an increasingly important issue in regulation. Insurers have run afoul of federal and state antitrust laws for coordination or collaboration on various aspects of rating and other operations. Federal courts have applied antitrust laws when state regulators conducted only minimal reviews of filings and disciplinary procedures.[15]

Congress, the NAIC, and individual states have become increasingly wary of immunizing the insurance industry against all federal antitrust laws. Some in the industry are largely in favor of changes that would open up its conduct to more antitrust scrutiny. Indeed, some large countrywide carriers are on record favoring the abolition of special antitrust protection in favor of open competition to govern rate setting.

Instead of blanket protection against federal laws, the insurance industry will likely have only "safe harbors" of immunity for specifically described conduct. One such safe harbor will be the coordinated collection of loss statistics and the sharing of statistical and actuarial data for purposes of ratemaking. That safe harbor allows some degree of collective data gathering and analysis and is a concession to the needs of smaller insurers that might find it difficult to survive (at least in the commercial lines) without some indicators of expected losses.

Developments in case law and changes in public attitudes have placed new requirements on regulators as supervisors of insurer conduct. Only active, detailed review of every aspect of rate setting can protect insurers from possible antitrust actions. The industry is increasingly aware of this shift in the ground rules. Insurers are changing their use of statistical agents, coordinated development of policy forms, and information sharing about marketing plans. Insurers might seek a regulatory review of decisions to shield them from expensive suits by antitrust regulators.

# The Underwriting Cycle and Rate Regulation

Property-liability insurance pricing, especially in the commercial liability lines, has been volatile. Part of this instability comes from a tendency for property-liability pricing to move in cyclical patterns. The typical pattern is a few years of low rates, relaxed underwriting, and underwriting losses (*soft market*) followed by a few years of high rates, restrictive underwriting, and strong underwriting gains (*hard market*). This pattern is known as the **underwriting cycle**.

During 1985, one of the longest and steepest declines in insurance pricing since World War II suddenly reversed itself. Many commercial rates increased by 100 percent or more in one renewal period. In addition, many insurers nonrenewed marginal accounts and withdrew entirely from some markets. This sudden turn in the cycle placed regulators under intense public pressure to protect commercial insureds. From the consumers' viewpoint, insurer rating and underwriting seemed arbitrary and greedy. Industry experts and most financial regulators saw the need to correct years of inadequate rates and to restore the financial health of the industry.

Regulators have searched for ways to end the rating swings of the underwriting cycle. The suggested cures have been to force insurers to maintain accurate financial statements, particularly regarding their loss reserves; to impose more realistic and accurate capital and surplus requirements on insurers who engage in risky underwriting practices; and, finally, to reduce the lag time in the rate approval process. Several studies identify regulatory lags in rate approval as exacerbating the swings in the underwriting cycle.[16]

A full discussion of the causes of the underwriting cycle is beyond the scope of this text. For now, it is sufficient to know that the underwriting cycle has strong and generally undesirable effects on rate filings. Regulators have been unable to anticipate and dampen cyclical behavior; instead they try to restrict rate increases at the top of the cycle, particularly when consumers are subjected to unanticipated and sharp rate hikes.

# The Effect of Rate Regulatory Practices on Insurers

As discussed previously, the law and practice of rate regulation differ dramatically from state to state—even, within a given state, from the tenure of one commissioner to that of the next. Any insurer that does business in more than one state knows that compliance with rating laws can be a demanding task. Laws and practices vary considerably, even across neighboring states. How do insurers respond to these administrative challenges?

To begin with, insurers must maintain a working knowledge of the laws, rules, and procedures of each state. One aspect of this is maintaining a library of insurance regulations in each state, including a library of current statutes, administrative rules, official *directives* or *bulletins* from regulatory staff, and informal letter rulings. In some cases, the library would include the regulations of more than one agency—for example, the insurance commissioner, the industrial accident board (for workers compensation), rating bureau(s), assigned risk pools, and taxing authorities.

A second response to regulatory demands is to maintain one or more staff members to keep current on regulations and regulatory practices. In larger companies, the staff typically specializes by state, by line of insurance, and by functional area (such as underwriting, agent supervision, and advertising). The legal department and sometimes a government affairs department frequently share the task of monitoring the legal environment with line staff. The staff assigned to a state recognizes key individuals in a state and their regulatory philosophies. Knowing the "unwritten law" and regulatory culture of an insurance department is essential to the smooth handling of rate filings.

An insurer is expected to keep current with the law, even laws that change suddenly, such as emergency rules. Every state publishes its nonemergency laws (statutes and rules) before their effective dates. Most states also provide advisory notices of upcoming law changes to licensed carriers. Given the frequency of regulatory changes and the multiplicity of agencies to deal with, an insurer can easily be found out of compliance with one or more state regulations.

The most likely mechanisms for discovering an insurer's failure to comply with a rating requirement are complaint investigation or market conduct examination. While investigating a complaint, a regulator might encounter deficient premium notices, unauthorized deviations from rating plans, and so forth. Market conduct examinations can specialize in rating or can consider rates along with other aspects of company operations.

The degree of scrutiny required to administer prior approval rate regulation laws can substantially affect administrative cost. Some states focus on a few select areas, such as the allowable profit margin or return on investment. Social and political trends help focus regulatory attention, such as (1) territorial rate differences between the inner city and suburbs or (2) gender rate differences.

Does the form of rate regulation systematically affect price levels or profitability? Dozens of studies have been conducted examining differences between Noncompetitive Rating (NCR) laws and Competitive Rating (CR) laws.[17] These studies generally classify prior approval, prior approval outside of allowable changes (*flex rating*), and state or board promulgated rates as NCR laws. File and use rating laws and use and file rating laws are generally classified as CR laws. The overall findings are as follows:

- Researchers are divided on whether NCR or CR states have lower loss ratios for any given line of insurance.
- Little evidence exists of excessive pricing in the absence of an NCR law.
- Some evidence exists supporting the existence of a regulatory lag in NCR law states.

- Stronger evidence exists that NCR laws tend to narrow the range of price dispersion, at least for personal lines.

Prior approval can, in some instances, delay needed rate relief. Substantial delays provoke court challenges by insurers, leading to even longer lags in rate relief.

The rate review process directly affects the availability of insurance products and the number of companies willing to serve a market. In general, insurers are reluctant to enter markets in which they perceive a lengthy review process for rate and form filings. Insurers might withhold products they offer in some states from a state in which they are licensed because insurers cannot meet regulatory filing requirements. Finally, companies are prone to leave a state or reduce their writings of insurance if they feel the business is inadequately profitable or unduly burdensome to administer. Smaller states are especially vulnerable to being passed over by insurers if they present an unattractive regulatory image. Regulators must balance the effect of regulation on the number of products and competitors with their mission to protect consumers from unfair rates and misleading products. Regulators can maintain healthy competition by recognizing the legitimate business needs of insurers and applying reasonable demands for ratemaking information and disclosure.

The threat of federal intervention into insurance regulation has frequently modified the actions of state regulators. These episodes of federal scrutiny are driven by highly publicized problems in one part of the industry or another. For example, in the 1970s perceived inequities and failures to respond to injured workers led to the formation of the Workers Compensation Study Commission. The 1984-85 liability crisis made it appear that state regulators had failed to control rating excesses at both ends of the underwriting cycle. In the soft markets (pre-1984), rates were increasingly inadequate to cover losses, and in the hard market (1985-1989) that followed, insurers were allowed to raise rates sufficiently to compensate for previous years of inadequate pricing. However, some insurers raised rates without respect to reasonably expected costs.

# Summary

Of all the functions of regulators, rate regulation is one of the most visible and controversial. Public policy toward rate regulation has been erratic. The shifts in regulatory models since the 1944 South-Eastern Underwriters decision and the wide divergence in current practice from state to state call into question whether any generally accepted principles about how to regulate insurance rates exist. Rate regulation will continue to be shaped by complaints from the general public and by lobbying special interest groups. Consumers look for fairness, stability, and understandability in rates.

The lack of consistency among regulators is at odds with the solid consensus on the principles of ratemaking among casualty actuaries. Most professional actuaries can agree on what should ideally go into a rate filing. In practice, many rate filings differ substantially from cost-justified rating because of the insurers' need to follow the competition to avoid losing market share. For their part, some regulators appear to be more concerned with public acceptance than with adherence to actuarial principles.

The property-liability industry is unique in its reliance on statistical agents to collect and analyze loss data for ratemaking. Because of the unique role of statistical agents in the property-liability industry, federal law requires that state regulators actively supervise the ratemaking process and the role of statistical agents and rating bureaus.

Rate regulatory practices are commonly classified into five broad approaches:

- Prior approval
- File and use
- Use and file
- No file or open competition
- State mandated rates

However, these approaches might better be classified by the degree of scrutiny and challenges given to rates and rating systems. Some regulators make numerous requests for supporting data, although others just go through the motions of review. Insurers' compliance departments must understand the local culture within each regulatory commission or subdepartment.

The nature of rate regulation differs by line of insurance. Personal lines insurance, particularly auto, gets the most regulatory attention. The further removed rating and rate paying are from the general public, the lower the likelihood that any substantive attention will be given to rates.

Regulatory lags have been implicated in worsening the underwriting cycle and contributing to solvency problems in some jurisdictions. However, regulatory policies are so different from state to state and commissioner to commissioner that generalizing about the quality and effect of regulation on the underwriting cycle is difficult.

In recent years, regulators have tended to focus on three broad themes in regard to rating:

- Whether the classification systems are appropriate
- Whether provisions for profit are fair to consumers
- Whether the catastrophic loadings are adequate

Furthermore, antitrust concerns are changing the way rates are established and reviewed. The scope of services provided by rating bureaus is being sharply limited. States are under greater pressure from federal courts and Congress to actively supervise the rating practices of insurers.

The closer the degree of scrutiny, the greater the potential effect on administrative costs. Surprisingly, the degree of scrutiny has no obvious relationship with profitability. The preponderance of empirical work on regulatory approaches has shown little or no benefit from active rate supervision on the spread or consistency of prices. The timeliness, administrative requirements, and likelihood of rate approvals influence an insurer's willingness to enter or remain in a market. Regulators who try to impose extreme restrictions on insurer rates run the risk of limiting product availability and rate competition. Prolonged periods of inadequate rates threaten the solvency of insurers. Whether inadequate rates are driven by regulatory rate suppression or market forces remains a matter of debate.

# Chapter Notes

1. Paul v. Virginia, 75 U.S. (8 Wall.) 168 (1868).
2. Stephen P. D'Arcy and Neil A. Doherty, *The Financial Theory of Pricing Property-Liability Insurance Contracts*, Huebner Foundation Monograph 15, Wharton School, University of Pennsylvania, 1988.
3. In a sense the courts impose a government discipline on ocean marine insurance. Ancient rules of conduct are "cast in stone" and strictly enforced by the courts. These rules cover contract language, rating systems, and underwriting.
4. Kenneth J. Meier, *The Political Economy of Regulation: The Case of Insurance* (Albany, NY: State University of New York Press, 1988, pp. 138-142 .
5. Actuarial Standards Board, "Statement of Principles Regarding Property and Casualty Insurance Ratemaking," Promulgated May 1988, Actuarial Standards Board, Washington, DC; for a discussion of these principles and their application in state regulation, see Lee D. Barclay, "Rate Regulation for Solvency," *Journal of Insurance Regulation*, vol. 11, no. 1, Fall 1992, pp. 53-66.
6. Scott Harrington and Helen Doerpinghaus, "The Economics and Politics of Automobile Insurance Rate Classification," *Journal of Risk and Insurance*, vol. 60, no. 1, 1993, p. 59.
7. Gregory Krohm, "The Implications of ISO's Change to Loss Cost Filing for Rate Regulation," *Journal of Insurance Regulation*, vol. 8, 1990, p. 316.

8. Joe H. Murrey and John Von Fenstermaker, "Long-Run Profitability of Fire and Marine Insurance Companies: A 100-Year Study of Boston Insurers," *Journal of Insurance Regulation*, vol. 9, no. 2, Winter 1990, pp. 259-273.
9. In 1911 the Merritt Committee, appointed by the New York legislature, concluded that cooperative ratemaking under the supervision of the state was better than destructive competition. See Barbara Stewart, Richard Stewart, and Richard S. L. Roddis, "A Brief History of Underwriting Cycles" (Kansas City, MO: National Association of Insurance Commissioners, 1991.)
10. United States v. South-Eastern Underwriters Association, 322 U.S. 533 (1944), pp. 1-2.
11. For a more complete discussion see Stewart, 1991. For a complete discussion of legal issues pertaining to boycotts and coercion, see Spencer Kimball and Barbara Heaney, *Basic Source Materials on the American Regulation of Insurance* (Kansas City, MO: National Association of Insurance Commissioners, 1995).
12. For discussion of preemptive state language, see Spencer Kimball, "The Meaning of the McCarran-Ferguson Act Today," *Journal of Insurance Regulation*, vol. 10, no. 1, Fall 1991, pp. 5-22.
13. D'Arcy and Doherty.
14. Parker v. Brown, 317 U.S. 341; for a discussion of the impact of McCarran on state regulation, see Spencer L. Kimball, "The Meaning of the McCarran-Ferguson Act Today," *Journal of Insurance Regulation*, vol. 10, no. 1, Fall 1991, pp. 5-22.
15. Federal Trade Commission v. Ticor Title Insurance Co. et al., 504 U.S., 119 L. Ed. 2d 410 (1992).
16. J. Francois Outreville, "Underwriting Cycle and Rate Regulation in Automobile Insurance Markets," *Journal of Insurance Regulation*, vol. 9, no. 2, Winter 1990, p. 274.
17. For reviews of the extensive literature, see Harrington, "The Impact of Rate Regulation" and "Prices and Uncertainty Results in the Property-Liability Insurance Industry: A Survey," *Journal of Risk and Insurance* , December 1984, pp. 577-619 and Glen J. Morrow, "Regulatory Environments: Do They Matter?" *Journal of Insurance Regulation*, vol. 11, no. 1, Fall 1992, pp. 19-52.

# Chapter 5

# Claims Regulation

Because of the nature of their jobs, claims people have contact with members of the public during difficult times. Consumers' needs and continuing demands heighten an already tense atmosphere between those making claims and those whose job it is to settle them. Thus, claims people and consumers might find themselves in adversarial positions over a claim. The temptation for either party to misstate facts or values makes claims handling challenging for everyone.

Claims activities, therefore, are heavily regulated. The primary purpose for claims regulation is to achieve consumer protection while promoting good business practices in insurance. Most claims laws are generated by the individual states, with many states' regulations differing substantially. New claims regulations are developed as needed, and existing regulations are revised occasionally.

This chapter covers the state regulation and private regulation of claims, which together include adjuster licensing requirements, Unfair Claims Settlement Practices Acts, market conduct examinations, arbitration, and appraisal procedures. It also includes a section on fraud detection and antifraud efforts from the state and industry levels and addresses the effects of claims regulation on consumers.

## State Regulation of Claims

Claims activities are regulated by state insurance departments. Many states follow the model acts of the National Association of Insurance Commissioners (NAIC). Because of the degree of regulation, it is important to understand the work of claims adjusting. Also, laws and regulations can vary for insurance company adjusters, independent adjusters, public adjusters, and insurance agents who are involved in claims activities. For these reasons, licensing requirements, the Unfair Claims Settlement Practices Act, service standards, and market conduct examinations are addressed in this section.

## The Work of Claims Adjusting

Anyone who has a loss will file an insurance claim and expect someone to take care of it. Regardless of the type of claim and surrounding coverage issues, the claim will be handled by an adjuster.

In many states, insurance adjusters (those representing insurance companies and those representing insureds) must be licensed. Many requirements stem from the responsibilities of the adjusters to their clients, whether the client is the insurance company, the insured, or a **claimant** (third party who is presenting a claim to an insurance company with which he or she is not insured). Licensing and prelicensing programs are required because of the technical nature of claims adjusting.

### Who Are Claims Adjusters?

A **claims adjuster** receives, reviews, and handles insurance claims. Most noninsurance people associate adjusters with insurance companies. Although many adjusters are employed directly by insurance companies, many other adjusters work independently.

Within the field of property and liability insurance, many people can become involved in the claims process. Company-employed adjusters can be called staff adjusters, field adjusters, claims representatives, and so on. **Staff adjusters** typically have an office job in the company. Although they can be assigned specific, limited functions, such as establishing files or taking statements, most staff adjusters handle a claim from start to finish.

#### Insurance Company Adjusters

An insurance company can employ **monoline adjusters**, who handle one line of insurance, or **multiline adjusters**, who handle several lines. For example, a monoline adjuster might handle just auto losses or property losses. A multiline adjuster might be responsible for handling auto, property, liability, and workers compensation losses.

**Field adjusters** are company adjusters who handle losses outside the office. They might take photographs, visit witnesses, take signed statements, draw diagrams, and so on. This type of function is not performed by inside staff adjusters. Field adjusters represent the company just as staff adjusters do, but they work outside the office three or four days a week. They are usually in the office one or two days each week to complete paperwork, document files, and answer phone calls.

Adjusters might be employed by primary insurers that handle the first layer of coverage, such as homeowners or auto coverages, or they might be employed by insurers writing excess layers. The major difference between primary and excess insurance is the dollar amount of loss. The losses presented to excess carriers are typically larger, might be more complex, and might involve specialists for each respective claim. Although the process of adjusting losses for a company writing excess layers can differ from the process used for a primary insurer, the basic adjusting principles, coverage concepts, and regulations still apply to both types of insurers.

### *Independent Adjusters*

**Independent adjusters** are employed by independent firms and are hired by insurance companies on an as-needed basis to handle certain specified claims on the companies' behalf. Independent adjusters' contracts and responsibilities vary according to needs.

An independent adjuster might be hired solely to determine the value of an insured's claim, while a company employee might actually determine coverage to adjust the loss accordingly. Another independent adjuster might be hired for his or her special expertise in one line of insurance, such as large, unusual property losses.

Expert independent adjusters are sometimes known as **general adjusters**. These adjusters are usually responsible for contacting all the parties involved in the loss, determining and resolving coverage issues, and evaluating the overall claim. Many independent adjusters perform all the functions of the adjustment process short of issuing a settlement check.

### *Public Adjusters*

**Public adjusters** are hired directly by the insurance consumer. They represent consumers in the reporting and settlement of their claims. Because of this direct representation, public adjusters are held to a high degree of trust by policyholders. Public adjusters typically handle fire losses (and, thus, are sometimes known as *fire loss adjusters*), but they might be involved in burglary, water damage, and other types of property losses. State laws vary regarding public adjusters' authority.

Public adjusters often approach an insured as a loss is occurring, or immediately after a loss has occurred, in an effort to obtain the insured's business. However, some state laws, such as New York's, specifically prohibit this practice. By statute, public adjusters licensed in New York cannot contact a consumer either in person or by other means of communication between the hours of 6:00 P.M. and 8:00 A.M.[1]

In addition, New York's law states that public adjusters' contracts must contain a *rescission clause* (a clause enabling the policyholder to cancel the contract with the public adjuster within a legally prescribed time period).[2] Most state laws contain a rescission requirement. Public adjusters must obtain policyholders' signatures before legally representing them. A sample contract (used by a public adjuster in Massachusetts) is shown in Exhibit 5-1. This contract contains information about the public adjuster and the client, the type of loss, the loss dates, and the date on which the public adjuster was retained. Other items contained in this contract, such as the maximum allowable charge of 10 percent of the loss, are dictated by Massachusetts statute. A public adjuster can charge less than 10 percent, and often will, to be competitive.

Most state laws indicate that the public adjuster's contract should be developed and written within the approved statutory guidelines. One such guideline is the dollar cap mentioned above. Another guideline is to include specific wording in the public adjuster's contract, such as New York's statute that requires a rescission clause in the contract.[3]

Illinois, Massachusetts, New Hampshire, and Pennsylvania are states whose statutes require public adjusters to file their contracts for approval prior to use.

By law, public adjusters should explain their responsibilities and how they can provide assistance on claims to policyholders. Policyholders must know up front that they are hiring public adjusters to work for them and that they are responsible for paying the public adjusters when their claims are settled. Public adjusters need not be hired for every property loss, but they can be of great assistance to the consumer for certain losses. The public adjuster's goal should be to assist the consumer in gathering information about the loss, properly filing a claim, and resolving the claim directly with the insurance company adjuster. However, some public adjusters might only estimate building losses while others represent clients on their business property or personal property claims.

All of the adjusters mentioned in this section evaluate covered losses. The public adjuster, however, is not responsible for determining coverage as are the adjusters who represent an insurance company. Because of adjusters' direct

**Exhibit 5-1**
Contract for the Adjustment of a Fire Loss

Joe P. Adjuster
Public Adjuster of Fire Losses
9 Newbury Street, Boston, MA
Tel. (617) 555-4321

Date ____________________

Name of Assured ____________________

Address ____________________

To the Insurance Companies interested or to whom it may concern:

____________________ hereby retains Joe P. Adjuster to advise and assist in the adjustment of ____________________

____________________

loss by fire of ____________ 19___ at ____________________

____________________ and agrees to pay him for his service ________% (not more than 10%) of the amount adjusted or otherwise recovered on account of this loss.

____________________

____________________

____________________

Witness to Assured's Signature
(Disinterested Person)

I, Joe P. Adjuster, agree to advise and assist in the adjustment of the above mentioned fire loss and will promptly, faithfully, and honestly serve the assured in the adjustment of the loss.

____________________

Notice to Assured:

The Public Adjuster does not represent any insurance company, but in consideration of the fee mentioned above, will advise and assist you in your negotiations with insurance company representatives regarding adjustment of the loss.

**EACH PARTY SHOULD RECEIVE A COPY OF THIS CONTRACT**

involvement in a consumer's claim, many states have determined that adjusters should be licensed and regulated to handle claims properly.

### *Insurance Agents' Involvement*

In addition to adjusters, insurance agents are frequently granted *draft authority* (the ability to settle and pay small claims on drafts in the agency) by insurance companies to adjust claims. Agents can adjust certain small, uncomplicated claims by using company-issued drafts. Typically, agents adjust glass, towing, and minor property damage claims that do not involve subrogation or liability issues. If the losses are more complicated, the claims are submitted to the company to handle.

## *Claims Activities and Responsibilities*

Claims adjusters, whether salaried or independent, might handle a claim from start to finish. Or, several adjusters who represent insurance companies might be involved with a claim. A claim might be paid, denied, or remain open for years. In the latter case, an adjuster might eventually compromise the value of the loss or continue to keep the claim open for investigation, particularly for fraud.

Adjusters are responsible for verifying coverage that applies to the reported claim and for investigating the claim. An investigation can take a few minutes or several years to complete. After an investigation has been completed, the adjuster should know whether a claim will be partially or fully covered or denied.

Company or independent adjusters must then determine, within their authority, what steps to take next. If no coverage or liability exists, claims should promptly be denied. If coverage applies, simple claims should be paid immediately, but complex claims should be evaluated and possibly negotiated.

Throughout the adjustment process, adjusters should remain in contact with the people who have filed a claim and keep them informed. States regulate timeliness of response and unfair claims settlement practices (discussed further in this chapter).

Public adjusters do not adjust claims, per se; they might only estimate property damage. Public adjusters are the insureds' representatives but only to the extent of the adjusters' involvement with the claims.

# *Licensing Requirements*

As of October 1994, thirty-two states[4] and Puerto Rico require adjusters to be licensed. Exhibit 5-2 shows a map indicating the states.

**Exhibit 5-2**
Continuing Education Requirements by State

■ States Requiring Licenses*

■ States Requiring Continuing Education**

The map below illustrates which states require adjusters to carry licenses, and of those states, which ones require continuing education credits to keep the license current.

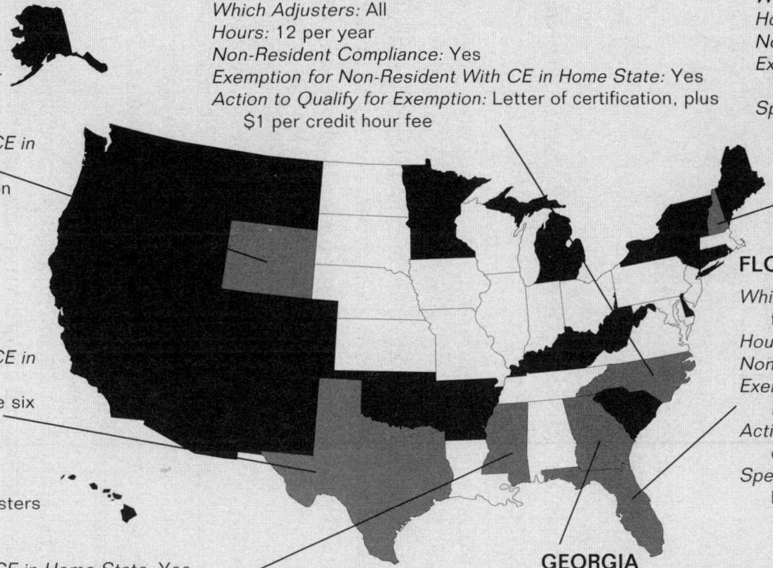

**WYOMING**

*Which Adjusters:* All
*Hours:* 10 per year (If licensed after June 30, 5 hours in first year)
*Non-Resident Compliance:* Yes
*Exemption for Non-Resident With CE in Home State:* No
*Special Requirements:* Two hours on law and ethics

**TEXAS**

*Which Adjusters:* All
*Hours:* 30 every two years
*Non-Resident Compliance:* Yes
*Exemption for Non-Resident With CE in Home State:* No
*Special Requirements:* Must include six hours of consumer protection

**MISSISSIPPI**

*Which Adjusters:* Independent adjusters
*Hours:* 12 per year
*Non-Resident Compliance:* Yes
*Exemption for Non-Resident With CE in Home State:* Yes
*Action to Qualify for Exemption:* Letter of certification
*Special Requirements:* Law to take effect January 1995

**NORTH CAROLINA**

*Which Adjusters:* All
*Hours:* 12 per year
*Non-Resident Compliance:* Yes
*Exemption for Non-Resident With CE in Home State:* Yes
*Action to Qualify for Exemption:* Letter of certification, plus $1 per credit hour fee

**NEW HAMPSHIRE**

*Which Adjusters:* All
*Hours:* 30 every two years
*Non-Resident Compliance:* Yes
*Exemption for Non-Resident With CE in Home State:* No
*Special Requirements:* Law took effect January 1994, full compliance required by 10/1/1996

**FLORIDA**

*Which Adjusters:* Workers' Compensation only
*Hours:* 24 every two years
*Non-Resident Compliance:* Yes
*Exemption for Non-Resident With CE in Home State:* Yes
*Action to Qualify for Exemption:* Letter of certification
*Special Requirements:* Must include two hours on ethics

**GEORGIA**

*Which Adjusters:* All
*Hours:* 15 every year (10 hours/year for adjusters with 20+ years' experience)
*Non-Resident Compliance:* Yes
*Exemption for Non-Resident With CE in Home State:* Yes
*Action to Qualify for Exemption:* Letter of certification and state form

* Source: *Best's Directory of Recommended Insurance Adjusters*, 1993 edition.

** Source: State Departments of Insurance, as of 1/94.

Reprinted with permission from *Claims*, February 1994, pp. 48-49.

All types of adjusters are subject to these regulations. In several states, adjusters who work within the insurance company are not required to be licensed. In most states, public adjusters must be licensed even if company or independent claims adjusters do not have to be.

Although company and independent adjusters might not have licensing requirements in their home states, those adjusters must be licensed in states that have applicable licensing statutes in which they settle claims.

Adjusters' licensing requirements can vary depending on whether an adjuster is handling auto, property, or casualty losses. Some adjusters handle only one line of business, such as property or workers compensation. Almost all public adjusters work solely within the property claims area.

## Filing for Licenses

Adjusters typically complete an application to request a license. For insurance company employees, the company generally handles the paperwork on behalf of its employees.

Since adjusters might adjust losses in their home states as well as in other states, more than one state's licensing requirements might need to be met. Some states have **reciprocal agreements** under which, once the licensing requirements of the resident state are met, other reciprocating states accept those requirements as being in compliance with their own.

Out-of-state adjusters with no licensing requirements in their home states still have to comply with the requirements of the states where they want to work, if those states license adjusters. In some states, licensing requirements will be relaxed after catastrophic events. These states want to make it easier for adjusters to get licenses in the state because of the great demand for adjusters following catastrophes.

Several states' statutes contain prelicensing education requirements. These requirements can include completing a certain number of study hours before taking an exam and possibly posting bonds. More states require people to post bonds for public adjuster licenses than for company adjuster licenses. Licensing, exam fees, and study requirements vary by state.

### Prelicensing Programs

Prelicensing programs must meet each state's particular regulations. These programs are available to all prospective licensees. Some state statutes require an applicant to satisfactorily complete a formal prelicensing program before taking the licensing exam. For example, Texas has a list of accredited schools that offer approved training courses to potential licensees. Whether or not the potential licensee is a resident of Texas, he or she must attend one of those accredited schools to be certified to take the licensing exam. The accredited schools also offer correspondence courses so that nonresidents can become certified.

Exemptions from a state's prelicensing educational requirements are often granted to applicants with a certain amount of experience in the line for which the applicant wants to obtain a license. Moreover, a few states have exemptions from prelicensing education for persons who have obtained insurance designations such as the Chartered Property Casualty Underwriter (CPCU) designation. However, although an applicant might have the CPCU designation, he or she might have no experience as a claims adjuster. Therefore, most states will only grant exemptions to those with claims experience.

For example, experienced resident adjusters in New Hampshire do not have to fulfill the prelicensing educational requirements to take that state's licensing examination. Adjusters with six months or more of experience who reside outside New Hampshire are also exempt from taking the New Hampshire licensing examination. However, New Hampshire will not issue a license to a nonresident adjuster who comes from a state requiring licensing unless the adjuster has obtained a resident license in that state.

For Maine residents, the statute requires that applicants must have one year of adjusting experience before taking the examination. Maine also approves certain entry-level courses for additional prelicensing training, but no specific educational requirements are in place.

Depending on regulations and the educational institutions available in each state, formal classes can be offered to prospective licensees. The format and length of these classes vary widely, and prospective licensees should select the classes that best meet their needs.

Usually, private schools, vendors, insurance companies, insurance agents' associations, and national organizations that sell self-study programs offer licensing preparatory courses. Most state departments of insurance provide a list of available and approved vendors for prelicensing programs.

Some seminars might last one day, while others might last five days or more. Prospective licensees should choose a program based on their needs and experience levels within the industry. In states like New Hampshire and Maine, where a certain amount of experience is necessary, applicants can pursue various training programs while learning on the job.

Examinations are offered in each licensing state at intervals specified by state regulations. Examinations are usually administered by proctors at approved sites during specified times. The examination content and length also vary by state.

Many states' regulators agree that preparing for and passing an examination does not ensure that an adjuster will maintain the required level of knowledge throughout the adjuster's career. Therefore, continuing education regulations are imposed on many license holders.

## Continuing Education

Continuing education requirements also vary by state, with some states not mandating education after the adjuster's license is acquired. As seen in Exhibit 5-2, seven states[5] currently require continuing education for adjusters to retain their licenses. For example, to comply with continuing education requirements, Texas requires all adjusters to acquire thirty hours of educational credits every two years. Florida's continuing education requirements apply only to workers compensation adjusters.

Usually, states requiring continuing education also have a requirement for nonresidents. Reciprocal agreements vary from state to state. Florida, Georgia, and Mississippi have reciprocal continuing education agreements. To verify that licensed adjusters have complied with their home state continuing education requirements, these states request a letter of certification from the adjusters' home states. Additionally, Georgia requires certification to be documented on a state form.

Some states' continuing education laws include an ethics requirement for every licensing renewal period. Florida, Texas, and Wyoming require the study of ethics or consumer protection every licensing renewal period.

Continuing education requirements occasionally change, so a licensed adjuster should always be aware of any changes within the state(s) where he or she operates.

## License Termination

States can revoke adjusters' licenses if the adjusters do not comply with the continuing education laws of those states. A state's department of insurance can issue warnings that advise adjusters of the need to accumulate additional credits to maintain their licenses. If adjusters still do not comply, the laws of the states dictate how and when the adjusters' licenses can be revoked.

Adjusters' licenses might be revoked for other statutory reasons. If adjusters violate the law, commit fraud, or act unethically, their licenses are in jeopardy. Usually, formal complaints must be filed with a department of insurance or directly with an insurance commissioner in the involved states. Depending on the state, regulations dictate the procedures for hearings before actual revocation.

## Unfair Claims Settlement Practices Acts

Unfair Claims Settlement Practices Acts probably affect claims handling practices more than any other regulation. All persons involved in handling claims should be familiar with the development, purpose, and specifics of these acts as they apply to their claims territories.

### Development of the Acts

Before Unfair Claims Settlement Practices Acts, states enforced minimal regulations on claims activities through Unfair Trade Practices Acts. The NAIC established the purpose of its Unfair Trade Practices Model Act as follows:

> The purpose of the Unfair Trade Practices Act is to regulate trade practices in the business of insurance in accordance with the intent of Congress as expressed in the Act of Congress of March 9, 1945 (Public Law 15, 79th Congress), by defining, or providing for the determination of, all such practices in this state that constitute unfair methods of competition or unfair or deceptive acts or practices and by prohibiting the trade practices so defined or determined.[6]

However, particular claims activities relating to consumer relations are not specified in the Unfair Trade Practices Model Act. The two claims-related sections of the act are section K—"Failure to Maintain Complaint Handling Procedures" and section O—"Failure to Provide Claims History." These two sections affect insurers solely with regard to their file maintenance procedures.[7]

New York was the first state to develop legislation that specifically addressed claims activities. Proponents of this legislation felt that the acts considered unfair claims handling procedures needed to be specified. They felt that New York's Unfair Trade Practices Act did not appropriately address the claims area because (1) claims activities were not described in the existing act and (2) unfair claims adjusting practices frequently occurred. Thus, the purpose for developing New York's Unfair Claims Settlement Practices Act was to establish standards for fair and equitable claims adjusting.

The NAIC was aware of New York's legislation and realized that other states would take similar action. In 1972, the NAIC decided to develop its own model law that could be used by the remaining states. The NAIC Unfair

Claims Settlement Practices Model Act was closely based on New York's Unfair Claims Settlement Practices Act. The NAIC revised its Model Act in June of 1990.

Many states have adopted the language of the NAIC Model Act almost verbatim. Other states have developed variations of the Act. Maine is an example of one variation because it uses only four paragraphs to describe unfair claims practices. For example, Section D establishes that "[f]ailing to affirm coverage, reserving any appropriate defenses, or deny coverage within a reasonable time after completed proof of loss forms have been received by the insurer" is an unfair claims practice.[8]

Many other states have used language similar to that in the NAIC Model Act but have elaborated on certain procedures, such as adjusting automobile losses. For example, part 216 of the New York Insurance Regulations is "Unfair Claims Settlement Practices and Claim Cost Control Measures." Definitions under subsection 216.1 include those of an agent, claimant, investigation, business day, and notice of claim.

New York amended Regulation 64 on June 1, 1993, to impose specific regulations surrounding motor vehicle physical damage claims involving auto body repairs. The amendment was designed to improve the quality of auto body repair by requiring insurers to use specific, approved parts on damaged vehicles and to have hazardous waste disposal costs itemized on auto repair estimates. Regulation 64 includes many pages describing the minute details about the handling of specific areas of insurance.[9]

Unfair Claim Practices Acts are often a subsection of Unfair Trade Practices Acts, which continue to apply to certain activities conducted by claims persons.

## *Unfair Claims Practices*

When the Unfair Claims Settlement Practices Acts were developed and adopted in many states, most statutes indicated that for claims activities to be considered unfair, they must occur frequently enough to indicate a business practice. The language in the NAIC Model Act proposed this standard as a guideline. Section 3 of the NAIC Model Act states the following:

> It is an improper claims practice for any domestic, foreign or alien insurer transacting business in this State to commit any act defined in Section 4 of this Act if:
>
> A. It is committed flagrantly and in conscious disregard of this Act or any rules promulgated hereunder; or

B. It has been committed with such frequency to indicate a general business practice to engage in that type of conduct.[10]

Most state statutes provide that a certain act must occur with frequency to indicate a violation of the act (Section 3B of the Model Act). Most state statutes do not include the clause 3A stated above. However, most state statutes do use the language in clause 3B, which requires that a certain act occur with frequency, to indicate a violation of the Model Act. Recent court decisions have made it possible for a policyholder or claimant to sue an insurer for violating unfair claims practices acts through private causes of action under the consumer protection statutes of the states in which the actions typically arise. The upcoming section on private regulation of claims activities discusses this in more detail.

Certain terms listed in unfair claims settlement practices statutes, such as "prompt" and "reasonable," are not defined and are therefore subject to various interpretations. An insured's idea of a prompt response to an auto claim might be different from a claims adjuster's idea of what is prompt. An insured might think a settlement is prompt only if the claim is paid the same day as the loss. This, of course, is highly unlikely because of adjusters' responsibilities, which include confirming coverage and investigating, evaluating, and concluding a claim.

Exhibit 5-3 illustrates the fourteen unfair claims settlement practices described in Section 4 of the NAIC Model Act. The following paragraphs discuss why each practice is considered unfair and provide an example of an unfair practice with respect to each type identified in the Model Act.

### *Knowingly Misrepresenting Facts or Provisions*

Claims adjusters and others involved in the claims process must be honest and explain insurance facts and policy language to consumers in an easy-to-understand manner. Adjusters must refer to specific policy language when talking to consumers about claims.

For example, a policyholder with a homeowners policy presents a claim for minor fire damage to his house. His family stayed with friends for two days following the fire because there was heavy smoke in his house. The adjuster pays the policyholder for the fire damage but does not mention that additional living expenses coverage is available for staying with the friends. This omission might constitute a violation of unfair claims laws.

### *Not Promptly Acknowledging Communications*

When a consumer presents a claim, the consumer expects acknowledgment from the claims person. Response by mail, telephone, or other method of

**Exhibit 5-3**
Unfair Claims Settlement Practices Defined

Any of the following acts by an insurer, if committed in violation of Section 3 [of the Unfair Claims Settlement Practices Model Act], constitutes an unfair claims practice:

A. Knowingly misrepresenting to claimants and insureds relevant facts or policy provisions relating to coverage at issue;

B. Failing to acknowledge with reasonable promptness pertinent communications with respect to claims arising under its policies;

C. Failing to adopt and implement reasonable standards for the prompt investigation and settlement of claims arising under its policies;

D. Not attempting in good faith to effectuate prompt, fair and equitable settlement of claims submitted in which liability has become reasonably clear;

E. Compelling insureds or beneficiaries to institute suits to recover amounts due under its policies by offering substantially less than the amounts ultimately recovered in suits brought by them;

F. Refusing to pay claims without conducting a reasonable investigation;

G. Failing to affirm or deny coverage of claims within a reasonable time after having completed its investigation related to such claim or claims;

H. Attempting to settle or settling claims for less than the amount to [which] a reasonable person would believe the insured or beneficiary was entitled by reference to written or printed advertising material accompanying or made part of an application;

I. Attempting to settle or settling claims on the basis of an application that was materially altered without notice to, or knowledge or consent of, the insured;

J. Making claims payments to an insured or beneficiary without indicating the coverage under which each payment is being made;

K. Unreasonably delaying the investigation or payment of claims by requiring both a formal proof of loss form and subsequent verification that would result in duplication of information and verification appearing in the formal proof of loss form;

L. Failing in the case of claims denials or offers of compromise settlement to promptly provide a reasonable and accurate explanation of the basis for such actions;

M. Failing to provide forms necessary to present claims within fifteen (15) calendar days of a request with reasonable explanations regarding their use;

N. Failing to adopt and implement reasonable standards to assure that the repairs of a repairer owned by or required to be used by the insurer are performed in a workmanlike manner.

communication must be made in a timely fashion. Some state laws require telephone contact within forty-eight hours and responses to letters within ten days.

For example, a policyholder might present a claim for an auto accident and expect an acknowledgment from the insurance company within a few days. If a claims adjuster knowingly takes two weeks to acknowledge the claim, the adjuster might have violated the law.

In another example, a claimant might leave a phone message for a claims adjuster requesting the status of a claim. The adjuster should acknowledge the phone call within a reasonable time. Even if the claimant who calls is not a policyholder of the insurance company, the claims adjuster is obligated to return the phone call and promptly advise the claimant of the status of the claim.

### *Not Adopting and Implementing Reasonable Standards*

If an insurance company does not provide investigation and settlement timeliness standards for adjusters to follow, some might take weeks to respond to a first notice of loss. A company that does not implement reasonable standards to promptly investigate and settle claims violates claims statutes.

Insurers often establish their own standards for conducting claims investigations. For example, one standard might describe the maximum amount of time in which an adjuster might respond to a person who is filing a claim or requesting status of a claim. Insurers might publish this information in their policy and procedures manual along with certain codes of conduct and other claims rules that apply to the company staff.

### *Not Attempting in Good Faith To Settle*

This category can be interpreted subjectively. Good faith, prompt, fair, equitable, and reasonably clear can have different meanings to an insured and an insurer. Basically, an insurer must not delay paying a claim when the investigation is complete and the insurer's liability is clear. Also, the insurer must avoid making a settlement offer that is inappropriately low.

For example, a claims adjuster might offer less than a fair figure to a claimant if the adjuster knows that the claimant does not really understand the cost associated with the injury and if the claimant is not represented by an attorney. An adjuster should always offer fair settlements to all policyholders and claimants regardless of the knowledge and representation of either party.

### *Compelling Insureds To Institute Suits*

As described in the previous example, an insurer should offer fair settlement amounts on losses to policyholders and claimants. When the insured or claimant is forced to seek legal assistance and brings a suit against an insurer because of an inadequate settlement offer, an unfair claims practices act has probably been violated.

Claims adjusters must not use scare tactics to settle losses. They should offer fair settlement values. If insureds or claimants disagree with offers, they should have the right to contest and to take further action against the companies.

### Refusing To Pay Claims Without Reasonable Investigation

An insurer cannot simply deny a claim solely based on information reported on the first notice of loss. The first notice usually lacks sufficient facts to warrant denying a claim. An insurer should investigate losses, not make assumptions based on one piece of paper.

For example, when an auto claim involving the insured and a claimant is presented, both parties should be contacted for their versions of the accident. Police and operator reports should be reviewed, and witnesses to the accident should be contacted. An adjuster should take additional steps, such as getting photographs or hospital records, to investigate a claim and gather all facts before declining a claim. Without gathering this information, an adjuster does not have all the facts with which to make a proper coverage and claim decision.

### Failing To Affirm or Deny Within a Reasonable Time

Before Unfair Claims Settlement Practices Acts, some claims investigations could take unreasonable amounts of time. Some adjusters gave no explanation to those persons filing claims for the delays. No specific claims regulations stipulated that investigations were to be timely, reasonable, and fair to everyone involved.

All claims must be investigated. Some investigations last longer than others, but when the investigation is complete, a coverage decision must be made. If coverage is affirmed, insureds should be notified and their claims paid promptly. If coverage does not exist, insureds must be notified promptly.

For example, an adjuster conducted a fire loss investigation that was completed in one month. He avoided telling the insured that the loss was not covered because he did not want to explain why. The insured has been waiting for a phone call or letter to explain the next step on his claim. The longer the adjuster delays advising the insured, the bigger the problem for the insurer. The adjuster's inaction can be considered a violation of the law.

An adjuster who does not advise an insured of coverage as soon as it is confirmed might be attempting to delay payment. This inaction could be considered a violation of the law.

### Attempting To Settle for Less Than a Reasonable Amount

A claims adjuster must offer fair and equitable settlements to people with legitimate claims. An insurer's advertisements or printed materials might describe the likely value of particular types of coverage. If a loss occurs and an insured requests values as expected by the insurer's advertisements, the insurer cannot claim that the advertisement was simply an illustration and not based on reality. Likewise, an insured might expect certain coverage based on an insurer's printed materials. If the expected coverage is not received, the insurer's action might be considered to violate the law.

### Attempting To Settle Under a Materially Altered Application

This is not one of the more frequently alleged unfair claims practices. However, claims people must investigate claims and verify that accurate information has been received before making coverage decisions.

For example, an adjuster advises the insured that she will receive $5,000 less for her property than the insured expects. The adjuster states that the value is based on information submitted on the insured's application. The insured states that she did not provide the alleged information. The adjuster investigates and discovers that the agent altered the application without the insured's knowledge. The insured cannot be penalized for the agent's action. If the adjuster continued to offer a settlement based on the alteration, the adjuster would be violating the law. In this example, the insurer might pursue legal action against the agent, but the insured should not be penalized for the agent's actions.

### Making Claims Payments Without Indicating the Coverage

Claims people must explain to insureds the basis under which payments are made. Most insureds do not know about limitations of liability, determination of actual cash value, application of coinsurance, and other legitimate settlement formulas. To comply with the law, adjusters must provide settlement details that the insured can understand. Also, adjusters should send detailed worksheets showing how the settlement value was determined. Insureds are entitled to know about and double-check adjusters' evaluations of their claims.

For example, an insured presents a claim for a fire loss in which the building and some contents were damaged, and the insured has to stay in a hotel for a week. The insured receives a draft from the adjuster totaling $15,000. The adjuster must state what coverages were included in the payment. In this check, the adjuster paid $10,000 for the building damage under Coverage A and $5,000 for contents under Coverage C. The adjuster advised the insured that another check would be coming for additional living expenses (staying in the hotel) under Coverage D. Although this is a simplistic example of the breakdown of a claims payment, an adjuster must explain to a policyholder how a payment was arrived at.

### Unreasonably Delaying the Investigation or Payment

Most policies contain a condition requiring the insured to submit a proof of loss before being able to collect on a covered claim. Proofs of loss exist through documentation submitted by insureds in support of their claim. A **proof of loss** is a formal submission that can contain much of the same information that has been previously submitted by an insured. Courts have established, however, that an insurer should not send proof of loss to an insured simply as a delay tactic.

For example, an adjuster who always requests a Proof of Loss form on all the claims he or she handles, simply to delay payments, is committing an unfair claims settlement practice.

### Failing To Provide a Reasonable and Accurate Explanation of Denial or Compromise

In the past, many companies issued generic denial letters to insureds or claimants. The letters did not address the particular claims. A company could hide the reason, lie to the insured, or make a mistake on the denial with no specific explanation about why a loss was not covered. This would make it difficult for the insured, claimant, or even the agent on the insured's behalf to question the specific reason for the denial.

For example, an adjuster sent a denial letter to an insured stating that the insured's claim was not covered according to policy language. The letter did not quote the specific language. This letter violates the law because the insured has nothing concrete to verify.

When an adjuster states reasons for a denial in a telephone conversation, an insured or claimant might not understand the reasons or be able to remember them. Therefore, it is a good practice to send a letter confirming a telephone conversation. The letter should be fully explanatory. Policy language must be quoted when applicable, or the legal basis for a denial or offer of a compromise must be stated in accurate, easy-to-understand terms.

### Failing To Provide Necessary Forms

Acknowledging requests for information from insureds and claimants must be done in a timely fashion. Insurers must promptly provide necessary forms to insureds and claimants to enable them to comply with policy conditions, such as providing an inventory of the stolen or damaged property and providing proof of loss.

For example, an insured calls an adjuster asking what the next step in the claim adjustment will be. The adjuster advises that a form has to be completed. If the adjuster avoids sending the form to the insured for completion, the adjuster would be considered in violation of the law.

### *Failing To Adopt Reasonable Standards for Repairs*

In some states, insurers can recommend repair shops by providing a list of approved repairers to insureds and claimants. Insurers typically choose shops that will comply with the insurers' standards and that have excellent reputations for making competent repairs. Because insureds and claimants follow the insurers' recommendations, insurers must assure that the work performed is done in a workmanlike manner.

For example, an insured who owns a Honda might feel that a Honda dealer is going to perform more competent repairs than a general body shop. The claims adjuster will probably explain that competent work can be done by the recommended body shop at a better rate than the Honda dealer charges, which is why the insurer is recommending it. The insured agrees to comply with the insurer's recommendation. If a problem arises with repairs, the insurer should step in to resolve the problem by reminding the shopowner that his shop is on the approved list and that the shop must comply with laws to provide competent service.

## *Claims Complaint Records*

Unfair Claims Settlement Practices Acts also require that each insurance company maintain accurate records of all claims complaints. Representatives from state insurance departments are permitted to review these complaints if necessary.

One purpose for keeping these records is to ensure that the insurer is complying with appropriate statutes. Additionally, the records can be reviewed to determine whether any negative patterns exist within a particular insurer's claims office. (More information on this subject appears later in this chapter under the market conduct section.)

## *Filing an Unfair Claims Action*

Procedures for filing an unfair claims action vary from state to state. If insureds or claimants are dissatisfied with how claims are or were handled, they can file complaints with insurance departments or hire attorneys to represent them against their insurance companies in unfair claims settlement actions. However, in most states, the Unfair Claims Settlement Practices Act cannot be enforced by private action.

In some states, filing frivolous unfair claims settlement practices actions against insurance companies was a trend. Claims would be filed if a claim was not settled within a few weeks. Unfortunately, many companies gave in to these suits and offered higher settlements to avoid going to court, even if the companies were sure that no unfair claims settlement practices had occurred.

Today, fewer frivolous unfair claims settlement practices actions are brought against insurance companies. Recent court decisions have allowed an insurance company to countersue a person who brings a frivolous suit against it. These court decisions have helped to significantly reduce the number of frivolous suits and have removed a barrier to file against the company.

Claims adjusters should handle claims properly and fairly. If adjusters attempt to be fair and handle claims in a timely fashion, they should not have to worry about suits involving the unfair claims settlement practices laws. Every adjuster should be familiar with the laws to know what practices are considered fair and what ones constitute bad faith.

Each state's regulations must be reviewed for adjusters who operate in more than one state. Ideally, a copy of each state's regulations should be available to each adjuster responsible for handling claims. If insurers or adjusters are found in violation of a state's unfair claims settlement practices act, they often are subject to punishment. Some states impose penalties and fines on those who violate the law. For example, Massachusetts permits double or treble damages.

## Service Standards

Statutes often include required service standards that must be met by insurers. Typical standards involve the timeliness of response requirements, the handling of salvage titles, and catastrophe response requirements. These standards provide specific guidelines to insurers that promote prompt service to consumers.

### Timeliness of Response Requirements

State statutes contain claims response requirements limited by certain time frames. These limits are imposed to protect consumers and establish reasonable guidelines for the industry to follow. The following are among the areas generally addressed:

- Time frames in which insurers must acknowledge first notices of claims
- Time frames in which status letters must be sent to insureds and claimants during ongoing investigations
- Time frames in which workers compensation claims must be accepted or rejected
- Time frames in which a claim should be paid after state forms are submitted
- The number of days in which a claim should be paid after the insurer receives a proof of loss
- Time frames in which responses to a commissioner's inquiries must be made

A Rhode Island regulation includes the following time restrictions:

- "Every insurer, upon receiving notification of a claim shall, within ten (10) days, acknowledge the receipt. . . ."
- "Every insurer, upon receipt of any inquiry from the Insurance Commissioner. . .shall, within fifteen (15) days. . .furnish. . .an adequate response. . . ."
- "An appropriate reply shall be made within ten (10) days on all other pertinent communications from a claimant. . . ."
- "Every insurer, upon receiving notification of a claim, shall promptly provide necessary claim forms. . .within ten (10) days of notification. . . ."
- "[W]ithin fifteen (15) days after receipt by the insurer of properly executed proofs of loss, the first party claimant shall be advised of the acceptance or denial of the claim. . . ."
- "If [an] investigation remains incomplete, the insurer shall...every forty-five (45) days. . .send to the claimant a letter setting forth the reasons additional time is needed. . . ."[11]

A New York regulation contains the following time limitations:

- "Every insurer, upon notification of a claim, shall, within 15 working days, acknowledge the receipt. . . ."
- "An appropriate reply shall be made within 15 business days on all other pertinent communications. Every insurer, upon receipt of any inquiry from the Insurance Department respecting a claim, shall, within 10 business days, furnish...available information. . . ."
- "Every insurer shall establish procedures to commence an investigation of any claim. . .within 15 business days of receipt of notice of claim."

- "Within 15 business days after receipt by the insurer of a properly executed proof of loss. . .[the company shall advise in writing the acceptance or denial of the claim]. . . ."[12]

Claims people must be familiar with the laws of each state in which they adjust claims. Regulations might look similar, such as Rhode Island's and New York's, but the specific time frames for response differ.

## Handling of Salvage Titles

Claims people handle salvage titles for vehicles that have been declared total losses. Insurers take possession of the titles after settling with insureds or claimants. Title laws were promulgated in an effort to protect consumers and ensure proper handling of titles. By recording the vehicle identification numbers on totaled vehicles and filing the information with the appropriate state's department of motor vehicles, potential fraud and mismanagement of paperwork can be avoided.

After being declared a total loss, vehicles are usually considered repairable or available as "parts only." Titles should reflect the difference so that the vehicle does not get into the hands of the wrong person by mistake. To ensure proper title transference, state laws provide guidelines, although each state's laws differ. New York's regulation of salvage titles includes the following provisions:

. . .

(b) In accordance with regulations of the superintendent, insurers shall, except where the insured is permitted to retain the automobile as part of the claim settlement, take possession of any salvage and the certificate of title, properly endorsed to them of private automobiles whenever a loss is determined by the insurer to be a total loss or a constructive total loss. Insurers, in disposing of the salvage, shall fully comply with the requirements of section four hundred twenty-nine of the vehicle and traffic law.

(c) Except with respect to vehicles recovered after a theft loss has been paid. . .insurers shall not, directly or indirectly transfer within or without this state any vehicle for salvage, except. . . . An insurer or its agents shall not purchase salvage vehicles. . .except from a registered vehicle dismantler or an automobile dealer.

. . .

(e) Prior to the payment of total losses, insurers shall comply with verification procedures in accordance with regulations of the superintendent.[13]

Insurers handle important papers, such as titles, every day. The possibility of losing them, improperly handling or endorsing them, or using them to the company's benefit is great. Once titles are passed on with the vehicle, the possibility of mishandling the salvage or of committing fraud exists. State regulations provide a means to control the title transference and record-keeping process to keep it legal.

## *CAT Responses*

Catastrophic losses occur across the country, and certain types of losses occur most often in a general location of the country. For example, Florida and other southern states have experienced hurricanes and their devastating effects; several Midwestern states bear the wrath of tornadoes during certain times of the year; the northeastern and northwestern parts of the country can be bombarded with blizzards; and California and similar arid locations have experienced major fires that destroy hundreds of acres of land and millions of dollars worth of property.

Adjusters across the country participate in catastrophe (CAT) planning in which special rules of operation apply. Usually, state licensing regulations are relaxed to permit adjusters in the state to assist in investigating and settling the multitude of losses. Typically, insurers develop catastrophe plans at the home-office level and send them to the branch offices for training purposes. Adjusters must be aware of the plans before any catastrophe, and, when a catastrophic loss is predicted to hit the area, the adjusters meet to discuss specific arrangements necessary to handle the increased workload as much as possible.

Some general plans that a company might develop include the following:

- Determining places to meet if the office is destroyed
- Choosing central locations across the state where policyholders can meet with adjusters (such as in agents' offices)
- Borrowing the insurer's employees from other fields of expertise to assist the insurer's property-adjusting department in any way possible
- Establishing extended work hours
- Arranging for agents to complete forms on behalf of the company
- Loosening the company requirements for obtaining estimates for repairs
- Offering draft authority to adjusters in the field
- Relaxing company procedures for taking statements, gathering proof of loss, and performing similar activities

State laws often require adjusters to file state-approved forms or check for liens with a city or town before paying claims. Requirements such as these are written in the state mandatory endorsements to insurance policies. States' departments of insurance will, however, work with insurers in relaxing certain regulations to avoid undue delays in settling the multitude of claims that occur after any catastrophe.

## Market Conduct Examination Concerns

As mentioned in Chapter 1, the typical market conduct areas reviewed by regulators are sales and advertising, underwriting, rating, and claims handling. Since claims regulation is the focus of this chapter, this section discusses market conduct examinations regarding claims handling.

Claims market conduct laws were developed to enforce licensing regulations and ensure proper claims handling practices by practitioners within the insurance industry. The state market conduct examiner reviews company claims files to determine whether any violations of the applicable state Unfair Claims Settlement Practices Act are present. Usually, an examiner reviews all aspects of an insurer at one time, including the underwriting and claims operations. Records of the review are maintained in the insurance department's office. The examiner's duties are to determine whether the insurer complied with applicable laws. If it is determined that violations exist, fines and penalties will be imposed on the insurer based on the law.

See Exhibit 5-4 for a copy of the Complaint Record Format suggested by the NAIC. The items listed in column A are the identification number of the complaint and include the license number of the agent, the staff adjuster, or other person(s) involved in the complaint—such as an independent adjuster.

**Exhibit 5-4**
Complaint Record Format

| Column A | Column B | | Column C | Column D | Column E | Column F | Column G | Column H |
|---|---|---|---|---|---|---|---|---|
| Company Identification Number<br><br>(Agent's Number)<br><br>(Staff Adjuster's Number)<br><br>(Independent Adjuster) | Function Code | Reason Code | Line Type | Company Disposition after Complaint Receipt | Date Received | Date Closed | Insurance Department Complaint | State of Origin |

Most states have either adopted this model verbatim or altered it to suit their regulatory purposes.

In column B of the NAIC's complaint form, a separate class for the claims department should be identified by a function code of the company involved. Also in Column B, a reason code would classify further complaints. Among other codes, a claim complaint could have reason code (a), which means a claims procedure; (b), which means delays; or (c), which means unsatisfactory settlements.

The NAIC's model suggests that column C of the complaint record include the line of insurance involved in the complaint, such as automobile, fire, or inland marine, among others. Column D should provide the disposition that each state's insurance department has reached. Examples of dispositions might be that corrective action was taken or that no action was necessary, among many alternatives. The last four columns are self-explanatory.[14]

Copies of certain findings, such as claims complaint record-keeping violations, are filed on record for restricted review by other state insurance departments. Many of the findings by market conduct examiners can be filed for reference by other state departments, but the records are generally not available to the public.

# Private Regulation of Claims Activities

Claims activities are regulated through state laws, but the regulation does not stop there. Insurance departments help enforce state regulation, but they are not equipped to deal with the volumes of consumers' claims complaints that are generated daily. Although many insurance departments have consumer sections available to answer consumers' questions and review claims complaints, the insurance departments are usually not expected to make decisions to resolve the complaints. So, further claims regulation is required. Many claims people consider private regulation to be the primary method to assure that claims activities are monitored and that consumers are treated in good faith.

One way that insurers promote proper claims handling practices is by providing an adequate number of trained staff. Also, insurers conduct self-audits to ensure that policies, procedures, and regulations are complied with. Self-audits help insurers find areas and practices in the company that require improvement. One method to enforce improvement is to have a policy and procedures manual incorporating the corporate mission statement. Details contained in the manual can help the claims department perform in compliance with state laws and company guidelines.

Although insurers strive to ensure that claims are handled properly and that consumers are treated in good faith, the insurers might lack the power to maintain proper claims settlement procedures. Oversight or enforcement of proper claims activities can be accomplished in many cases through other forms of "private" claims regulation, including claims suits, arbitration, and appraisal.

## Suits

Claims suits are filed against insurers and arise from disagreements between parties that typically concern contract breaches or bad faith allegations. Insurance statutes and regulations do not address disputes like these.

### Breach of Contract

Insurers have a contractual duty to defend and indemnify their insureds based on policy terms and conditions. Insurance policies are contracts with promises and conditions applicable to the insurer and the insured. A policy is a contract of adhesion and, as such, a policyholder must comply with its provisions. Because the insured is at a disadvantage when entering into a contractual agreement with an insurer (the insurer having superior knowledge of the policy language), any ambiguity in policy language is construed in favor of the insured by the courts. Claims people are aware of this principle and must adjust claims in good faith, offering the benefit of doubt to the insured when interpreting policy language.

Depending on a number of outcomes, an insured might feel compelled to hire an attorney and bring suit against an insurer for a breach of contract. The following examples show how this might occur:

- An insurer did not offer defense on a major liability claim against the insured. The insured and his attorney believe that defense should have been offered and file suit for breach of contract against the insurer.
- An insurer did not attempt to settle the liability claim against the insured within the insured's policy limits. As a result of a trial, the insured is not exposed to an excess verdict (amount awarded to the claimant in excess of the insured's policy limits).

If the insured prevails in a breach of contract action against the insurer, the insurer might be ordered to fulfill the terms of the contract, and in the case of the second example, pay the excess amount over the policy limits.

Suits resulting from alleged contract breaches occur with frequency. Allegations against insurers include any of a list of complaints:

- Not complying with conditions in the policy
- Misinterpreting the policy language
- Interpreting the policy language in favor of the insurer
- Impliedly waiving insurers' rights under the policy

Even when an insured prevails in court, the insured is typically not entitled to more than seeing that the insurer honors the contract. This means that what the insurer has to pay is only what the insurer is expected to pay under the policy provisions, and no more. This result has been considered an inadequate remedy for the insured who will not be able to recover for other damages such as attorney fees and emotional distress.

## *Bad Faith*

Over the years, courts have determined that insurance policies contain *express* contractual language and an *implied* covenant of good faith and fair dealing between the insurer and its insured; a breach of this covenant is a violation of the contract. The implied duty of good faith and fair dealing is not located in the policy language, but by breaching this duty, an insurer can be held in violation of the contractual agreement. Good faith is based on the relationship of mutual trust that should exist between the insurer and insured, beginning with the inception of the policy and continuing through the settlement of claims.

In some cases, courts have ruled that improper handling of a claim by an insurance company constitutes not only a breach of contract but also an independent *tort* (a civil wrong), the tort of *bad faith.*[15] The following list details how insurers' standard of care under the tort of bad faith has evolved:

- 1914—Brassil v. Maryland Casualty Co.[16]

  The first case to expressly identify an implied covenant of good faith and fair dealing under contract law as the basis for providing a remedy for an insured against its insurer for an excess verdict.
- 1931—Hilker v. Western Automobile Ins. Co.[17]

  In this case, the court allowed a tort cause of action against an insurance company for an excess verdict.
- 1958—Comunale v. Traders and General Ins. Co.[18]

  The court ruled that an insurance company had wrongfully refused to defend its insured, who had been sued in an underlying action. The insurer's conduct was found to be a tortious breach of an implied covenant. The company was held liable for the entire amount of the judgment, including the amount over the policy limits and other resulting damages.

- 1967—Crisci v. Security Ins. Co.[19]

  The California Supreme Court held that the insurer should be held liable for an excess judgment after it had rejected a settlement offer within the policy limits. The court recognized that the insurer's breach of its duty to settle third-party claims constituted a tort, as well as a breach of contract, and allowed recovery for mental distress. Although it did not adopt such a standard, the court in the Crisci case commented favorably on a strict liability standard for an insurer's failure to settle within policy limits. By such a standard, an insurer would automatically be liable for an excess verdict, regardless of how reasonable and careful it may have been. No court has subsequently adopted a strict liability standard, not even in California.

- 1979—Royal Globe v. Superior Court.[20]

  For the first time, a third-party claimant was given a right of direct action against the insurer. The court held that the California Unfair Claims Settlement Practices Act permitted a claimant to sue the insurer directly for the amount of an excess verdict, without the third party first getting an assignment from the insured.

- 1988—Moradi-Shalal v. Fireman's Fund Ins. Co.[21]

  In this case, the court expressly overruled the Royal Globe case. This was an important change in the direction of the law. The court ruled that the California Unfair Claims Settlement Practices Act was not intended to create a private cause of action to a third-party claimant against an insurer.[22]

By violating good faith standards, an insurer can be held responsible not only for honoring the intent of the contract (paying the claim) but also for emotional distress, attorney fees, and other damages. Legal remedies for bad faith actions apply both to first-party actions (involving the insured) and third-party actions (involving the claimant).

## Arbitration

**Arbitration** is a process that insurance companies and other parties usually use to settle disputes to avoid long, expensive court proceedings. Each party in a dispute presents its case at a hearing to a neutral person who renders a final and binding decision.

Arbitration proceedings have been used by the insurance industry since 1929, but serious discussion about using arbitration in the insurance industry originated in September 1943. Claims executives from the Association of Casualty and Surety Executives and the National Association of Mutual Casualty Companies met to consider ways and means to resolve problems arising from interinsurance company claims handling disputes. Several meetings occurred, the result of which was the Nationwide Inter-Company Arbitration program that was implemented in August 1944.[23]

Most insurance companies adhere to arbitration procedures. Some self-insurers and commercial insureds who have losses that fall within their large deductibles might also subscribe to arbitration procedures. Most of these procedures are voluntary, but some are compulsory.

Compulsory procedures are determined by the individual state departments of insurance as required by insurance statutes. For example, Massachusetts insurance law provides that underinsured and uninsured motorists cases must be arbitrated rather than settled in court.[24] The courts refuse to entertain a case that should be decided by arbitration, and the Massachusetts Division of Insurance enforces this requirement.

Initially, limited types and amounts of claims could be heard through arbitration. Currently, almost all claims, regardless of the dollar amount and lines of insurance, can be resolved by arbitration. Questions of coverage, liability, and settlement amounts can be addressed in most arbitration proceedings. Decisions are final and binding. Therefore, no costly appeal process is involved.

## Types

The types of arbitration proceedings and the number of vendors who handle arbitration proceedings are growing at an enormous pace. The reason for this growth is that disputes can now be settled out of court, benefiting both the insured and the insurer. Arbitration is a fast and economical solution to insurance disputes.

### AAA

The American Arbitration Association (AAA) was founded in 1926 as a public service, not-for-profit organization dedicated to the resolution of disputes of all kinds through the use of arbitration and other voluntary methods.

The AAA's national office is in New York City. Its source of income is from (1) administrative fees charged for services and (2) contributions from members who support its work. Membership in the AAA is open to organizations and individuals who wish to participate in voluntary dispute settlement. Among a variety of services, the AAA offers alternative systems of arbitration in addition to educational materials and publications that are available to the public.

Usually, parties who wish to use arbitration have incorporated specific language referring to arbitration in their contracts. The AAA has developed a standard arbitration clause that can easily be inserted into a commercial contract:

> Any controversy or claim arising out of or relating to this contract, or the breach thereof, shall be settled by arbitration in accordance with the rules of the American Arbitration Association, and judgment upon the award rendered by the arbitrator(s) may be entered in any court having jurisdiction thereof.[25]

Arbitration awards are generally considered legally binding and enforceable in all states. The authority to enforce the award can be found in individual state statutes; the AAA has this authority in many states. For example, in Massachusetts, the AAA can issue subpoenas.[26] In New York, regulations authorize the AAA to administer arbitration programs involving no-fault, workers compensation, and uninsured and underinsured motorists' disputes.[27]

The formal arbitration process involves submitting a dispute to one or more impartial persons for a final and binding decision. Arbitrators are usually former judges, attorneys, or claims adjusters who are familiar with insurance law and the lines of insurance under dispute. Different arbitrators participate in the process through the groups that offer arbitration services.

### AF

Arbitration Forums, Inc. (AF) began in March 1968 as a committee representing signatories to all arbitration programs. The committee was not named Arbitration Forums, Inc. until October 1986. AF's first venture into a forum for the resolution of interinsurance company disputes was the Nationwide Inter-Company Arbitration Agreement. AF has grown dramatically since then, and the AF administers the programs identified in Exhibit 5-5 for the resolution of insurance-related disputes.

The purpose and procedures for using the arbitration programs through AF are similar to those offered through other groups, such as the AAA, which was mentioned previously. In selecting arbitrators, AF looks for the formal qualifications of bar admission, professional or undergraduate degrees, practical claims experience, and so on. The minimum experience required of an arbitrator is five years. Canadian and international forums are administered by AF, along with the programs available in this country.

## Procedures

Every arbitration forum can vary to a slight degree. A typical type of intercom-

**Exhibit 5-5**
Programs Administered by Arbitration Forums, Inc.

- Nationwide Inter-Company Arbitration Agreement
- International Reciprocal Arbitration Agreement
- Special Arbitration Agreement
- Fire and Allied Lines Arbitration Agreement
- Automobile Accident Reparations Arbitration Agreement
- Uninsured Motorists Arbitration Agreement
- Workers' Compensation Inter-Insurer Arbitration Agreement
- Workers' Compensation Inter-Company Arbitration Agreement
- Workers' Compensation—Special Arbitration—Minnesota
- Medical Malpractice Inter-Insurer Arbitration Agreement
- Earth Movement Arbitration—California Special Arbitration
- Executives' Arbitration Forum
- Excess/Primary—Reinsurance Arbitration Forum
- Accident Arbitration Forum

Source: Bernard L. Hines, *Arbitration and Mediation* (1988) and Arbitration Forums, Inc., *A Guide to the Programs of Arbitration Forums, Incorporated* (1988), vol. I, pp. 8-9.

pany arbitration proceeding is described in this section for illustrative purposes.

An intercompany arbitration proceeding usually begins when a local representative of a member company files an arbitration statement with the arbitration administrator and the representative of the other member company involved in the dispute. In arbitration proceedings, the company initiating the request for arbitration is referred to as the **applicant**. The company or person against whom the claim is made is called the **respondent**.

When the intercompany arbitration statement is received by the group who will preside over the arbitration process, both parties to the process submit a signed statement and filing fee. Typically, names of possible arbitrators are submitted to the parties, who then have the right to eliminate one name from the list. Whoever remains on the list, or the first person whose name was not stricken from the list, is the arbitrator. In some cases, more than one arbitrator serves on a single claim.

Certain specific information is required for the arbitration statement. This requirement stems from the association's rules and regulations. The necessary information for intercompany arbitration usually includes the following:

- The names of the applicant and respondent companies
- The names of local representatives who are supervising the case
- The names of the applicant's and respondent company's insureds
- The claim numbers of both parties
- The types of coverage provided under the policies of each party
- The date of accident or loss
- The amount already paid by the applicant company and the applicable deductible
- The statement describing any pending litigation and its proposed disposition
- The certification that settlement efforts have been unsuccessful
- The statement of the issue involved
- A diagram of the accident or loss, if possible

The length of time in which the respondent has to file a response and the particular information required varies, depending on the arbitration processes and states involved. This is once again dictated by state statutes. An administrator will usually set a hearing date after all the required information has been forwarded. The date is usually set at least three weeks in advance.

Most hearings are informal; the information presented at them should be factual and to the point. As stated earlier in this chapter, decisions made by an arbitration panel are considered final and binding with no right of appeal.

Different arbitration forums oversee claims with varying dollar values. In one arbitration agreement, for example, claims of $100,000 or less might be filed. In another case, losses of under $25,000 might be the norm. Still other forums impose no dollar limitation on claims to be heard. In addition, those involved in some arbitration proceedings are protected by a typical "high-low" agreement that preserves the last demand and offer made.

Groups like the AAA or AF offer more services than simply providing arbitrators to resolve a dispute. These groups and many others offer variations on arbitration proceedings such as nonbinding mediation, conciliation, and alternative dispute resolution (ADR). They also provide counseling and other services to their signatories.

Arbitration hearings are considered final and binding without any right to appeal. It is expected that one side will not be pleased with the results of any hearing. If appeals were allowed, losing parties might always go forward with appeals. This would create costly delays and defeat the purpose of arbitration, which is to resolve a dispute efficiently and expeditiously.

## Appraisal

**Appraisal** is a method of resolving disputes over values in claims. This method takes less time than going to court and often assists claims settlements. Appraisal is a typical condition found in property policies.

### Policy Language

The appraisal condition found in most insurance policies applies to disputes between insurers and policyholders. Sometimes appraisal is confused with arbitration. Typically, appraisal is used when the value of a claim is disputed. Unlike arbitration, the appraisal procedure does not usually deal with coverage or liability issues.

Different states adopt their own regulations for appraisal procedures. The basic procedures for each state can usually be found on state specific policy endorsements. Individual states' regulations or policy forms address the more detailed formal procedure to be followed by both the insurer and policyholder.

The generic appraisal paragraph in the Insurance Services Office (ISO) homeowners form states:

> If [the insured] and [the insurer] fail to agree on the amount of loss, either may demand an appraisal of the loss. In this event, each party will choose a competent appraiser within 20 days after receiving a written request from the other. The two appraisers will choose an umpire. If they cannot agree upon an umpire within 15 days, you or we may request that the choice be made by a judge of a court of record in the state where the residence premises is located. The appraisers will separately set the amount of loss. If the appraisers submit a written report of an agreement to us, the amount agreed upon will be the amount of loss. If they fail to agree, they will submit their differences to the umpire. A decision agreed to by any two will set the amount of loss. Each party will: a. pay its own appraiser; and b. bear the other expenses of the appraisal and umpire equally.[28]

### State Requirements

The Massachusetts mandatory endorsement changes the above language to conform with the statutory requirements. The language on the Massachusetts ISO-issued form states:

> If [the insured] and [the insurer] fail to agree on the amount of loss, we shall, upon receipt of your written request to do so, refer this matter to a three

> member board of referees. They are selected and must act according to the procedures set by the law. Their decision will be binding. This board does not make decisions about matters of coverage or fault.[29]

The Massachusetts statute refers to the appraisal process as a reference proceeding. Arkansas, Missouri, Nebraska, Oregon, and Virginia are other states whose regulations require alteration of the language of the appraisal provision in the ISO forms. Puerto Rico simply eliminates the provision.

# Fraud Detection

Claims fraud affects everyone—both within and outside the industry. People or organizations engaged in fraudulent activities, victims of those activities, and the general public are all affected. Fraud has become so prevalent that it must be addressed in numerous ways.

## Types of Fraud

Fraud takes many forms and can be committed by consumers and insurance people. Fraudulent activities include elaborately planned operations and spur-of-the-moment actions. This section addresses fidelity/insider fraud, policy application fraud, outright fraud, and exaggeration and malingering.

### Fidelity/Insider Fraud

**Fraud from within the industry** involves adjusters and other insurance employees who are willing to take bribes or illegal income. Company employees include claims adjusters, claims supervisors, auto appraisers, appraiser supervisors, clerk typists, and claims managers. Fraudulent activities can occur inside the company with no outside involvement. Sometimes, body shop repairers, glass companies, attorneys, agents, and others will be involved with insurance company employees in fraud.

**Fidelity** is involved when someone, such as a company employee, is placed in a position of trust. Fidelity fraud often occurs when the employee willfully violates that trust. Insider fraud involves a person working on the inside (in this case, in the insurance company) who has the means to complete a fraudulent transaction.

Typically, dishonest company employees file fictitious claims and deposit the settlement checks in their bank accounts. More than one person is usually involved in the scheme, which could take a few forms, including the following examples:

- Joe, a claims adjuster, decides to add himself as another claimant on an existing claims file. Joe talks with Betty, a clerk, who agrees to issue a check to Joe and split the proceeds with him. Joe cashes the check and gives some money to Betty.
- Cindy, an auto appraiser, devises a scheme with Dave, an auto body repairman, to inflate the cost of repairs on a damaged vehicle. When the repairs are complete, the customer leaves satisfied, and the extra money not spent on repairs is split between Cindy and Dave.
- Ernie, a claims supervisor, decides to invent a claim on paper. When phony tapes, estimates, and other documentation are in the file, Ernie issues the check to himself—under a fictitious name. He has already worked out methods to cash or deposit the check under that fictitious name. This activity continues over several months.

Claims people also work with consumers in presenting fraudulent claims. Fraudulent schemes are limited only by the creativity of the individual.

## Policy Application Fraud

Insurance policy applications must be completed by anyone who purchases insurance. Application forms differ with each company. Typical information on an application includes the following items:

- The name and address of applicant
- The property to be insured
- The location and description of property
- Any prior loss experience
- Any known hazards
- Background information on the applicant
- Limits of the insurance requested
- The type of insurance requested

The most important detail is that the application be signed by the applicant. If the application contains omitted or erroneous information, the applicant might be prosecuted for fraud. However, if an honest error was made, there is no fraud. Omissions or errors must be willfully concealed and prejudicial to the insurer to be considered **policy application fraud**. Specific areas where fraud might be suspected include the following three items:

- Stating no former loss experience on the application when previous losses had occurred

- Listing operators' ages on auto policies as older than they really are to receive premium discounts or to avoid high premiums
- Omitting hazards on the premises that would increase premiums or result in rejections of coverage

In each of these instances, the insurer might be entitled to higher premiums or might have rejected the risk altogether if the correct information had been provided. Because the information was not divulged to the insurers, the insurers write the coverage and discover that more losses than expected or more severe losses than expected occurred as a result of the misrepresentations made by the policyholder on the application.

Property and liability insurance policy provisions permit insurers to void a policy if fraudulent misrepresentation has been made by the policyholder. Thus, the policy can be declared nonexistent and no coverage afforded to the former policyholder.

Insurance agents and brokers have been involved in fraudulent activities surrounding policy applications. Sometimes, agents and brokers advise the applicant to omit certain information so that the applicant will receive coverage. In addition, agents and brokers illegally sign applications instead of a policyholder, which makes it impossible for the insurer to penalize the policyholder since the policyholder did not sign the document.

### Fraudulent Claims From Consumers

Consumers commit fraud every day. Submitting fraudulent claims is a way of life for some individuals. Outright **consumer fraud** is something committed on purpose with the intent to make money through insurance settlements.

Consumer fraud includes falsifying information on a claim to recover more money than a claimant is entitled to. Even many honest individuals feel that nothing is wrong with fraudulently attempting to recover their deductibles on claims. The types of fraud leading to criminal investigation and convictions involve committing arson for profit and filing false claims. Certain sophisticated fraud rings arrange numerous and sometimes complicated fraudulent losses that can involve alleged automobile damage, injuries, and other consequential loss.

Examples of outright consumer fraud include:

- Inventing a theft loss
- Staging an automobile accident
- Alleging that injuries occurred on someone's premises

- Claiming a nonwork-related injury as a work-related injury to collect under workers compensation
- Purposely setting fire to property
- Claiming to be injured at work at the end of the summer in order to have tuition money for school
- Claims for work-related back injuries filed by pregnant women knowing that they cannot be X-rayed

### Exaggeration and Malingering

Exaggeration and malingering are fraudulent extensions of a legitimate loss. **Exaggerations** are overstatements of values or types of loss. **Malingering** is delaying recovery of an illness or injury or pretending that an illness or injury exists. Any fictitious addition to a legitimate loss constitutes fraud.

Examples of exaggeration include the following items:

- Adding nonexistent items to a valid list of stolen property
- Claiming pain and suffering on a bodily injury claim where little or no pain occurred
- Claiming the value of property as higher than the legitimate value
- Claiming pre-existing damage as part of a recent loss

Insureds and claimants who exaggerate their claims are committing fraud. It is immaterial whether the exaggeration amounts to thousands of dollars or only a few dollars.

Examples of malingering include the following items:

- Resisting returning to work, alleging an illness is still existent
- Leaving work after a brief return, alleging the same illness or injury is recurring
- Talking oneself into minor pain to justify time out of work

Although considered fraud, malingering is difficult to prove because malingering can appear similar to psychosomatic disorders. People who talk themselves into being sick are not doing so in order to miss work and commit fraud. Determining the reason someone is out from work and whether or not his or her pains are real is not a simple task. Claims people must be careful not to allege fraud where no fraudulent act has been committed.

## Antifraud Efforts

The fight against fraud—whether committed by insurers or insurance consumers—is taking place in many different arenas. Several state and federal antifraud efforts are discussed below.

## NAIC Model Act

The National Association of Insurance Commissioners has established a Model Fraud Statute that can be used by each state. The statute contains three sections.

- Section 1—Scope
- Section 2—Warning on Policy Label
- Section 3—Definition of the Statement

Section 1 of the NAIC Model Fraud Statute states that anyone who intends to injure, defraud, or deceive any insurance company is guilty of a felony and will be imprisoned for no more than five (5) years or fined no more than $5,000, or both. Examples of what constitutes fraud in this model include presenting false, incomplete, or misleading written or oral statements on claims. Also, if one conspires with another to file a fraudulent claim, both parties will be found guilty.[30]

State insurance departments can follow these guidelines for imposing penalties for incidences of fraud. States refer to the NAIC Model but often determine actual fines and penalties through their individual legislatures.

## State Antifraud Efforts

States have addressed the need to combat fraud at various levels. State antifraud efforts control and reduce incidences of fraud. State mandated antifraud plans exist in California, Delaware, Maryland, Michigan, Minnesota, New Jersey, and Pennsylvania as of August 1994. See Exhibit 5-6 for a brief outline of state antifraud requirements.

### Massachusetts

The Insurance Fraud Bureau (IFB) of Massachusetts, created in 1991, is empowered to detect, investigate, and prevent fraudulent insurance transactions for all lines of insurance. Funding to support the operations of the IFB is provided equally by the Automobile Insurers Bureau of Massachusetts and the Workers' Compensation Rating and Inspection Bureau of Massachusetts. As of August 1994, the IFB staff totaled thirty-eight full-time employees.[31]

The IFB has been successful in investigating and prosecuting fraud offenders. It has established itself as a well-used referral agency, starting with 332 referrals from insurance companies and other insurance organizations in its first year. That number increased in 1992 to 1,831 and then increased to 2,673 in the period ending January 31, 1994.

Referrals from the public increased from 93 in 1991 to 1,787 in 1994. Investigations totaled 126 in 1991, and 894 were under investigation by the Fraud Bureau as of January 1994. As of January 31, 1994, a total of 68 people had been indicted on 472 counts of crimes relating to insurance fraud, and numerous additional complaints had been filed against others.[32] Some of this information is summarized in Exhibit 5-7.

The Insurance Fraud Bureau of Massachusetts has become the model for other states primarily because it established a successful public and private partnership. Since its formation in 1990, Dan Skelly has gone from being the bureau's sole employee to being chief of a division with a $4 million budget, thirty-eight employees, and a string of successful investigations that has insurers in the state giving him even more resources to fight fraud.[33]

The Massachusetts bureau is funded solely by the insurance industry; no one in government can move the money elsewhere. Investigations and research are continually and effectively being undertaken by the Insurance Fraud Bureau of Massachusetts.

### *Texas*

Under Texas Insurance Code, the insurance fraud unit is granted the authority to investigate violations of the penal statute, including company insider fraudulent activities, unauthorized insurers' activities, and claims fraud.[34] However, only the Texas Attorney General or a District Attorney can prosecute the violators in court. The Texas Insurance Fraud Unit is not a law enforcement agency. Fourteen people and two officers staff the unit, but the officers do not have authority to arrest anyone.

According to state statutes, the Texas fraud unit cannot investigate any allegation of claims fraud until after the special unit of the insurer dealing with the alleged fraudulent claim investigates the claim. Once the insurer initiates an investigation and finds evidence of fraud, the insurance department's fraud unit can become involved.

The Texas fraud unit has been successful in combating fraud, especially in large cases of health provider fraud. The fraud unit has been working effectively with several insurers to uncover a covert fraud operation involving automobile claims.[35]

### *Other States*

Every state promotes antifraud measures. Each state handles the detection and

**Exhibit 5-6**
State Mandated Antifraud Plans

| State | Year Enacted | Lines | Submission or Notification of Plan to Ins. Dept. | Penalty for Non-Submission or Notification of Plan | Prevention of Internal Fraud |
|---|---|---|---|---|---|
| *CA | Regulation 1994 | All Lines | Submission | A maximum fine of $55,000 and/or suspension of the insurer's Certificate of Authority for not more than one year | Yes |
| MD | Law 1991 | All Lines | Notification | A fine up to $100,000 and suspension or revocation of the insurer's Certificate of Authority | Yes |
| MN | Law 1994 | All Lines | Notification | Not Addressed | Yes |
| NJ | Law 1990<br>Regulation 1992 | Motor Vehicle | Submission | 20% reduction in auto physical damage base rates | No |
| PA | Law 1990 | Motor Vehicle | Submission | A fine up to $200 per day until plan is submitted | Yes |
| | Law 1993 | Workers Comp. | Notification | | Yes |

* 1994 Senate Bill 287; Chap. 304 Sec. 24 KY Rev. Statutes.

| Prevention of Applications Fraud | Prevention of Claims Fraud | Claims Review Procedures | Submission of Annual Report | SIU[1] Unit | Reporting Required to |
|---|---|---|---|---|---|
| Yes | Yes | Yes | Yes | Yes[2] | Dept. of Ins. Fraud Division |
| Yes | Yes | Yes | Yes | No | Law Enforcement & Dept. of Ins. |
| Yes | Yes | Not Addressed | Not Addressed | No | Law Enforcement |
| Yes | Yes | Yes | Yes | Yes[3] | Insurance Fraud Division |
| Yes | Yes | Yes | Yes | No | Law Enforcement & Comprehen-sive Data Base |
| Yes | Yes | Yes | Yes | No | Law Enforce-ment (Voluntary) |

[1] No specific statute addresses a state mandated plan. However, the antifraud plan is mandated under the SIU regulation, §2698.40 ct. seq. CA Code of Regulations.
[2] Sec. 2698.40 ct. seq. CA Code of Regulations.
[3] NJ Administrative Code 11:16-4.
Note: Kentucky has enacted a provision requiring an SIU, but is not presently requiring an antifraud plan.

Reprinted with permission from National Insurance Crime Bureau, August 1994.

**Exhibit 5-7**
Massachusetts Insurance Fraud Bureau Statistics

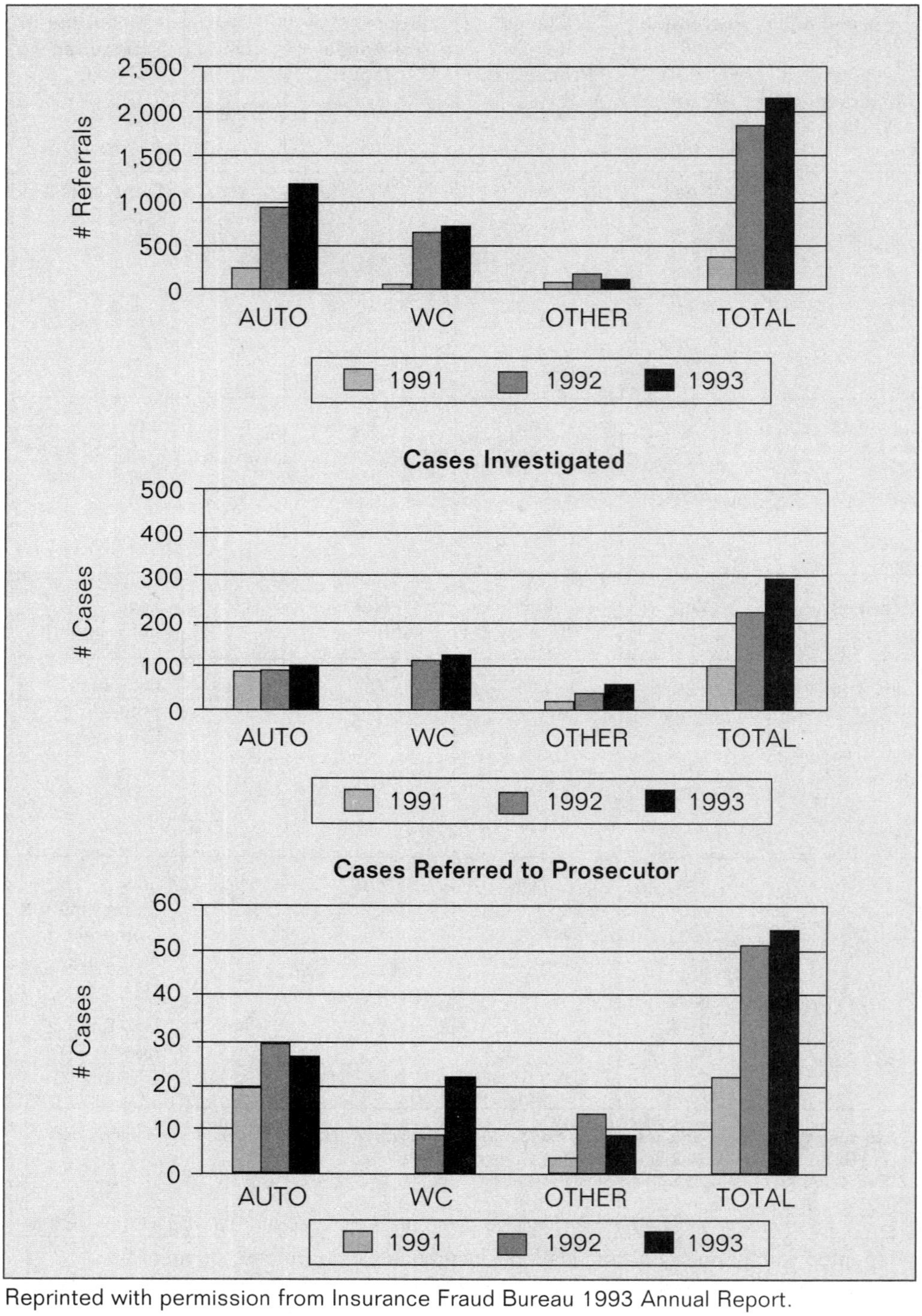


Reprinted with permission from Insurance Fraud Bureau 1993 Annual Report.

prosecution of fraud differently. The following paraphrased news headlines illustrate activities across the country involving fraud:

- Michigan's proposed antifraud legislation is pro-consumer[36]
- Three agents in Arizona sued for misrepresentation[37]
- Five Connecticut agencies accused of diverting premiums[38]
- California approves department's fraud detection standards[39]
- Oregon's SAIF antifraud effort recovers millions[40]
- Maryland makes insurance fraud a felony[41]
- Rhode Island fines [an insurer] for deceptive sales[42]
- Oklahoma accuses five in scam involving [an insurer][43]
- Alabama jury slams [an insurer] for its agent's fraud[44]
- Florida charges eighty-seven agents with fraud[45]
- Kansas strengthens antifraud law[46]
- Maine worker gets jail term for workers compensation fraud[47]
- Three jailed in Louisiana fraud[48]

Many state insurance departments and other organizations are attempting to combat fraud more strenuously. Fines and penalties for committing fraud are becoming more serious. The message is being sent that fraud affects everyone and will not be tolerated.

## SIU Requirements

Special investigative units (SIUs) typically operate in insurance companies, with units located in each branch office of a company. The first company SIUs were established around the mid-1970s. SIUs can also be found in state department of insurance offices and serve as experts in investigating fraud and the staff often comprises persons who worked in law enforcement and special investigative areas.

The All-Industry Research Advisory Council (AIRAC) was formed by the property-casualty insurance industry to provide the public and the industry with timely, reliable research information relevant to public policy issues affecting risk and insurance. AIRAC has since changed its name to the Insurance Research Council. The Insurance Research Council publishes material on SIU use by insurers for fraud investigations.[49]

The International Association of Special Investigation Units (IASIU) is working with the National Insurance Crime Bureau[50] to create model guidelines for fraud plans. Two types of laws are being considered by states: those mandating fraud plans, and those specifying the creation and use of an SIU.

The fraud plan mandate entails educating the consumer, the agent, and others about fraud, adding an investigative element to it.[51]

State regulations of special investigative units vary from requiring some basic accountability to detailed descriptions of staffing numbers and their expected expertise.

Exhibit 5-6 shows which states regulate SIU units as of the end of 1994. Other states have introduced bills in the legislature to promote similar regulations. New Jersey's regulation appears to be a model for some of these bills.

The following is the purpose of New Jersey's Fraud Prevention Act:

> to confront aggressively the problem of insurance fraud in New Jersey by facilitating the detection of insurance fraud, eliminating the occurrence of such fraud through the development of fraud prevention programs, requiring the restitution of fraudulently obtained insurance benefits, and reducing the amount of premium dollars used to pay fraudulent claims.[52]

## Racketeer Influenced and Corrupt Organizations Act

The Racketeer Influenced and Corrupt Organizations Act (RICO) was passed in 1970. Its initial purpose was to create a right of action by government rather than by private parties. RICO was designed to combat racketeering and organized crime by imposing harsh criminal penalties on those involved in racketeering enterprises. However, before being passed into law, the RICO bill was redrafted to include right of action by private plaintiffs.

RICO outlaws four kinds of business activities:

1. Using income derived from a pattern of racketeering activity to acquire or operate an enterprise engaged in interstate commerce
2. Acquiring or maintaining any interest in or control of an enterprise engaged in interstate commerce through a pattern of racketeering activity
3. Conducting or participating in the affairs of an enterprise engaged in interstate commerce through a pattern of racketeering activity
4. Conspiring to do any of the acts set forth in items 1 through 3 above[53]

Racketeering activity includes mail fraud and wire fraud. The National Council on Compensation Insurance (NCCI) often uses RICO in combating corporate workers compensation fraud. RICO is one of a handful of federal laws with both civil and criminal provisions. That is, perpetrators of wrong can be indicted under the criminal provisions of RICO and can be sued by injured individuals under the civil provisions of the law.

RICO is now being used with increasing frequency in an attempt to impose civil liability against professionals such as attorneys and accountants. As a result, professional malpractice claims handlers are seeing a greater number of RICO counts being brought against their insureds. This increases the potential exposure in professional malpractice actions. Under RICO, liable defendants face penalties such as mandatory multiple damages and attorneys fees.[54]

# Effects of Claims Regulation on Consumers

As described throughout this chapter, regulations regarding claims activities are formulated with the interests of the consumer in mind. For years, consumers were often at a disadvantage in the claims adjustment process because claims people did not have to explain their positions as readily as they do today. This is not to say that all insurers operated in bad faith, but if adjusters chose to do so, their activities might never have been scrutinized.

## Consumer Assistance

Insurance consumers have the right to know what is happening with their claims. They should be informed about the status of their claims and kept involved throughout the claims adjustment process.

Many of the claims regulations protect the insurance consumer and guide insurance professionals to act fairly. Regulations set standards for the insurance industry to follow. These laws and statutes can differ from state to state, but the message is generally the same: do what is right and keep consumers informed.

Consumers are protected by these regulations, whether or not they are aware of particular laws within the insurance industry. However, consumers do need to be aware of certain laws to pursue specific legal actions against an insurer. For example, if an Unfair Claims Settlement Practices action can be filed against an insurer, a consumer needs to know the law to cite the specific violations. Consumers will receive assistance from attorneys in pursuing bad faith actions against insurers.

The government and the insurance industry have published numerous booklets and pamphlets to educate consumers about their rights and about insurance in general. Today's consumers are more knowledgeable about insurance matters than ever before. If claims are not handled properly, today's consumers are apt to file complaints against companies and adjusters.

Many state regulations specify that when insurers mail certain letters to consumers, such as denials or compromise offers, the company employee must include information about the consumer's rights. Included in this information might be an invitation to contact the state's insurance department if the consumer has a complaint or disagrees with the insurance company's decision. The following is an example of New York's statutory language:

> Should you wish to take this matter up with the New York State Insurance Department, you may write to or visit the Consumer Services Bureau, New York State Insurance Department, at either 160 West Broadway, New York, New York 10013; Agency Building One, Governor Nelson A. Rockefeller Empire State Plaza, Albany, New York 12257; or 220 Delaware Avenue, Suite 229 Buffalo, New York 14202.[55]

This recourse is provided for the consumer's assistance and protection. Sometimes consumers disagree with an insurer's decision, but do not know either that they can question the decision or where to go when questioning it. This disclosure helps answer consumers' questions.

Insurance agents are becoming more knowledgeable about claims laws and often share this knowledge with consumers. State insurance departments process claims complaints and ensure that insurers provide appropriate responses to claimants. Consumers do not always win a disputed claim, but they have the opportunity to complain against insurance practitioners and receive an answer from those practitioners. For example, receiving a better explanation from an insurer for its action might help the consumer understand why a loss was not covered. Although the disputed claim was not paid, the consumer at least understands the reason for the denial.

## Negative Effects of Fraudulent Claims

Many fraud statutes are established to catch consumers in fraudulent acts and punish them accordingly. The NAIC's Model Insurance Fraud Statute, described earlier, addresses consumer fraud. The scope of the NAIC Model contains serious implications for consumers who present fraudulent claims.

While each state has employees at its department of insurance who investigate incidents of fraud against insurers, insurance companies have SIUs that review claims suspected of involving fraudulent activities. Company claims adjusters usually refer the claims to this unit if there are enough questions to warrant further investigation.

Today, insurers are more willing than they used to be to pursue actions against consumers who present fraudulent claims. The public must know that fraud will not be tolerated. To protect their companies and their assets, insurers pursue those who present fraudulent claims. Additionally, insurers want to protect the majority of insurance consumers who do not engage in fraudulent activities, but who can be indirectly and adversely affected by those activities through increases in insurance premiums.

# Summary

The purpose for claims regulation is to protect consumers while ensuring good faith dealings through insurers. States regulate claims through licensing adjusters and monitoring claims transactions. Unfair Claims Settlement Practices Acts have been adopted by most states to monitor specific claims activities. Service standards imposed by statutes also ensure that claims are handled in a proper and timely manner. Each state's department of insurance monitors the activities of insurers through market conduct examinations. Many states follow the NAIC guidelines.

Claims activities are also regulated privately through internal company monitoring, the legal system, and special insurance proceedings such as arbitration and appraisal. Suits brought by a breach of contract and allegations of bad faith have been addressed by many courts. Decisions rendered by the courts differ from state to state with one state allowing private causes of action against an insurer and another state prohibiting them.

Fraud from within and outside the insurance industry is a specific area addressed by state, industry, and joint state and industry efforts. Fidelity/insider fraud occurs within companies. Policy application fraud occurs through industry and consumer actions. Outright consumer fraud and malingering are the primary areas addressed by antifraud efforts. Special investigative units are formed in companies voluntarily or through state statutes.

Insurance consumers benefit from state and private claims regulations aimed at promoting fair business practices and reducing fraud. Consumers who commit fraud, however, are more likely to be caught because of the increasing antifraud efforts of various state and group activities.

# Chapter Notes

1. New York Regulation 10, Public Adjusters, Para. 25.3.
2. New York Regulation 10, Public Adjusters, Para. 25.3.
3. New York Regulation 10, Public Adjusters, Para. 25.3.
4. Alaska, Arizona, Arkansas, California, Colorado, Connecticut, Delaware, Florida, Georgia, Hawaii, Idaho, Kentucky, Maine, Michigan, Minnesota, Mis-

sissippi, Montana, Nevada, New Hampshire, New Mexico, New York, North Carolina, Oklahoma, Oregon, Rhode Island, South Carolina, Texas, Utah, Vermont, Washington, West Virginia, and Wyoming. Also, Puerto Rico requires licensing.

5. Florida, Georgia, Mississippi, New Hampshire, North Carolina, Texas, Wyoming.
6. *NAIC Model Laws, Regulations and Guidelines*, vol. IV, Unfair Trade Practices Act, p. 880-1.
7. *NAIC Model Laws, Regulations and Guidelines*, vol. IV, pp. 880-6 to 880-7.
8. Maine Insurance Code, Chapter 24-A, subsection 2436-A titled Unfair Claims Practices.
9. State of New York Insurance Department Circular Letter No. 7 (1993), July 15, 1993.
10. *NAIC Model Laws, Regulations and Guidelines*, vol. IV, Unfair Claims Settlement Practices Act, pp. 900-2 to 900-3.
11. Rhode Island Insurance Code, Regulation LXXIII (73).
12. New York Insurance Code, Regulation 64—Unfair Claims Settlement Practices and Claim Cost Control Measures.
13. New York Regulations, Subsection 3412, automobile physical damage insurance covering private passenger automobiles; salvage; total losses; thefts; duties of insurers.
14. *NAIC Model Laws, Regulations and Guidelines*, vol. IV, pp. 884-3 to 884-6.
15. James J. Markham, Kevin M. Quinley, and Layne S. Thompson, *The Claims Environment* (Malvern, PA: The Insurance Institute of America, 1993), p. 237.
16. Brassil v. Maryland Casualty Co., 210 N.Y. 235, 104 N.E. 622 (1914).
17. Hilker v. Western Automobile Ins. Co., 204 Wis. 1, 235 N.W. 413 (1931).
18. Comunale v. Traders and General Ins. Co., 50 Cal. 2d 654, 328 P. 2d 198 (1958).
19. Crisci v. Security Insurance Co., 66 Cal. 2d 425, 53 Cal. Rptr. 13 (1967).
20. Royal Globe Insurance Co., 23 Cal. 3d 880, 153 Cal. Rptr. 842 (1979).
21. Moradi-Shalal v. Fireman's Fund Insurance Co., 46 Cal. 3d 287, 250 Cal. Rptr. 116 (1988).
22. Markham, Quinley, and Thompson, pp. 238, 239.
23. Bernard L. Hines, *Arbitration and Mediation* (Washington, DC: Colortone Press, 1988), pp. 3-5.
24. Massachusetts Insurance Law, Chapter 175.
25. American Arbitration Association, *Facts About the American Arbitration Association* (October 1989), panel 5.
26. Massachusetts Insurance Law, Chapter 251.
27. New York Insurance Code, regulations 35D and 68.
28. Insurance Services Offices, Inc. (ISO) form H0 00 03 04 91, p. 11 of 18.
29. Insurance Services Offices, Inc. (ISO) form H0 01 20 04 91, p. 2 of 4.
30. *NAIC Model Laws, Regulations and Guidelines*, vol. IV, Model Insurance Fraud Statute, vol. IV, pp. 680-681.

31. Insurance Fraud Bureau of Massachusetts, 1993 Annual Report.
32. *The Standard*, January 25, 1994, p. 15.
33. *Auto Insurance Report*, (Laguna Niguel, CA: Risk Communications, June 13, 1994), pp. 1, 2.
34. Texas Insurance Code, Section 110D.
35. Texas Insurance Fraud Unit information received from the Texas Department of Insurance, Austin, Texas, 1994.
36. *Taylor's Insurance Digest*, June 4, 1994, p. 77.
37. *National Underwriter* (Life-Health ed.), June 4, 1994, p. 3.
38. *Insurance Times*, May 31, 1994, p. 1.
39. "OAL Approves DOI's Fraud Detection Standards," *Smart's Insurance Bulletin*, May 20, 1994, p. 3.
40. Louise Kertesz, "Oregon's SAIF Anti-fraud Effort Recovers Millions," *Business Insurance*, May 23, 1994, p. 15.
41. "Maryland Legislature Passes Bill to Make Insurance Fraud a Felony, Expands Definition," *Insurance Advocate*, April 23, 1994, p. 15.
42. Penny Williams, "Hancock Fined for Misleading Agency Sales Practices in RI," *Insurance Times*, April 19, 1994, p. 5.
43. Douglas McLeod, "State Seeks to Recover Funds," *Business Insurance*, May 16, 1994, p. 2.
44. Robert G. Knowles, "Alabama Jury Slams Pru for $25M Over Agent's 'Fraud'," *National Underwriter* (Life-Health ed.), April 18, 1994, p. 37.
45. "Florida Charges 87 Agents of Metropolitan with Fraud," *BestWeek*, March 14, 1994, p. 6.
46. "Kansas Strengthens Insurance Fraud Law," *Taylor's Insurance Digest*, March 12, 1994, p. 34.
47. Penny Williams, "Maine Worker Gets Jail for Workers Compensation Fraud," *Insurance Times*, November 16, 1993, p. 3.
48. "Three Sent to Jail for Louisiana Fraud," *National Underwriter* (Property-Casualty ed.), September 13, 1993, p. 6.
49. All-Industry Research Advisory Council, *Special Investigative Units: Surveys on Insurance Company Use of SIUs For Fraud Investigations*, 1984.
50. Bill Thorness, "The New SIU Team," *Claims Magazine* (September 1994), p. 53.
51. The National Insurance Crime Bureau is a group comprised of property-liability insurers and self-insured companies that is fighting insurance crime and vehicle theft.
52. New Jersey Fraud Prevention Act, 17:33A-2.
53. "RICO: Can a *Good* Law Still Have Some *Bad* Side Effects?," *Journal of American Insurance*, Second Quarter, 1985, p. 1.
54. Morrison, Mahoney, and Miller, *The Standard*, October 23, 1992, p. 8.
55. *New York Insurance Regulations*, (Chatsworth CA: NILS Publishing Company, July 1993), p. 880.256.

# Chapter 6

# Solvency Regulation

At the core of each insurance transaction is a guarantee of financial performance conditioned on some future loss event. More than anything else, viability of the insurance mechanism depends on insurers' abilities to fulfill contractual obligations as claims are made under the policy for insured losses. A major part of insurance regulation is devoted to monitoring and maintaining insurer solvency. This chapter explores the techniques used to accomplish that objective. First, the meaning of solvency and the significance of policyholders' surplus are discussed. Second, the uniform financial reporting system used for property-liability insurers is introduced and differences between statutory accounting principles (SAP) and generally accepted accounting principles (GAAP) are identified. Third, specific systems for monitoring and analyzing insurer performance are described and the financial examination process is summarized. The chapter closes with discussion of two recent additions to solvency regulation: the risk-based capital model for property-liability insurers and the accreditation of state insurance departments.

## Why the Concern About Solvency?

Many argue that bankruptcy, or insolvency, is a natural phenomenon that eliminates inefficient producers from the market and increases the market share for those remaining producers competing to provide the same product for less. Why should we be concerned about solvency when it comes to property-liability insurers? The market price of insurance would decrease, would it not, if this natural phenomenon were allowed to occur? Perhaps it would in the short run. In the long run, however, the scenario would be quite different.

In most businesses, goods or services are delivered at the point of sale for a price that covers known production costs and a reasonable margin for profit. In the insurance business, however, the product is a contractual guaranty of future financial performance (at some unknown time) contingent on the occurrence of an insured event resulting in loss (for some unknown amount) but sold for a specific (known) premium amount. Compared to those of other businesses, insurance transactions involve a considerable amount of risk. As the likelihood of insurer insolvency increases, the risks retained by the insured and others also increase.[1]

Opportunities for insurer mismanagement abound because of the large short-term gains that can be realized from underwriting. The nature of insurance transactions creates large cash inflows when coverage is first written. However, as policies mature and losses develop, insurers can experience tremendous drains on cash and other resources. Even the most conscientious insurer management can misjudge the exposure when pricing a product or when estimating an unpaid claims liability. Left unchecked, unscrupulous management can fraudulently siphon off company resources and cash flows before liabilities for claims develop.

Insurers have a fiduciary responsibility to their policyholders and society at large. Not only must insureds be able to recover insured loss amounts from their insurers; they must be able to trust the insurer to operate responsibly on a long-term basis. Consumers' general inability to evaluate the financial condition and long-term viability of insurers makes regulatory intervention a necessity in the public interest.

## The Meaning of Solvency

Several terms have been used to describe a company's inability to meet its financial obligations. Generally, *technical insolvency* refers to a company's inability to pay its bills when they become due. Technical insolvency is quite different from the term bankruptcy as used in business. **Bankruptcy** means that a company's liabilities exceed the market value of its assets.[2]

For an insurance company, **solvency** is used to describe its ability to meet financial obligations as they become due, even those resulting from insured losses that might be claimed at a time several years in the future. Most often, insolvency is used in the same context as the term bankruptcy, indicating that an insurer's total liabilities exceed its total assets. Unfortunately, that does not accurately describe solvency as viewed by insurance regulators.

Statutes in every state require that insurers maintain capital above some minimum level. An insurer violating those requirements would be considered **technically insolvent**, even though the insurer's admitted assets exceed its total liabilities, and even though the insurer is able to pay its current bills. Statutory accounting principles prohibit certain assets from being included on the balance sheet and prescribe conservative valuation rules for others. Recognizing those limitations, assets shown on an insurer's balance sheet are called **admitted assets**.

In addition to the requirement that admitted assets exceed total liabilities, insurance regulators require that those assets be sufficiently liquid to ensure their immediate availability when needed to satisfy financial obligations. **Liquid** means that an asset is in the form of cash or is readily convertible to cash with minimal loss in value. Asset liquidity helps ensure that even those obligations due to claims, for which considerable uncertainty exists regarding the eventual time and amount of payment, can be satisfied from existing assets.

Statutory accounting principles, discussed in a later section, directly focus on liquidity and the amount by which an insurer's assets exceed its liabilities. For noninsurance businesses, that excess amount (assets minus liabilities) is referred to as the firm's **net worth** or **owners' equity**. For insurers, recognizing their fiduciary responsibility to insureds, the excess value of admitted assets over liabilities is called **policyholders' surplus**. Directly or indirectly, nearly all of solvency regulation is dedicated to ensuring that policyholders' surplus is adequate so that cash resources are available to pay the insurers' financial obligations as they become due.

## Roles of Policyholders' Surplus

The strength and long-term viability of any insurer is determined by its policyholders' surplus. Representing the statutory equivalent of net worth for an insurer, policyholders' surplus provides financial capacity to support growth and underwriting activities and is a financial buffer against unforeseen loss events, catastrophes, reserving errors, and price inadequacy.

### Financial Capacity

Financial capacity is critical to the survival of any business. Generally, **financial capacity** can be defined as a firm's ability to fund *additional* operations from *existing* resources. For noninsurance entities, financial capacity is determined by the firm's net worth. An insurer's financial capacity is determined by the amount of its policyholders' surplus.

#### Growth

Whether an insurer or a noninsurer, a firm's financial capacity provides internal funding sources supporting business expansion or new project investments. Financial capacity can also provide security for assuming additional liabilities should the firm elect to use external capital resources such as fixed debt or bank financing.

Insurers, like other businesses, occasionally need additional capital resources to finance expansion into new territories. Costs of new facilities, office furniture, and fixtures must be funded from either internal or external resources. The greater a firm's financial capacity, the more readily it can respond to changing consumer demands for its goods and services. The most typical form of growth for an insurer is the growth in underwriting sales volume.

### *Underwriting*

The sale of insurance generally requires advance premium payment from the insured in exchange for the insurer's promise of future performance over the policy term. The actual premium revenue received is not earned until service under the contract is performed. As a result, the insurer must maintain a liability representative of the full amount of service yet to be performed. That liability represents amounts that the insurer anticipates having to pay for operating expenses and future losses under the contract or, if the contract were canceled before expiration of the term, the amount of unused premium that would be owed to the insured.

Up to this point, the sale of insurance products appears to be accounted for like the sale of any other service-related product. What is unique about insurance transactions, however, is that statutory accounting requires that acquisition expenses be recognized at the time of sale instead of being *capitalized* (proportioned) over the life of the contract as they would be under generally accepted accounting principles (GAAP). Under statutory accounting principles (SAP), an insurer realizes an operating loss on each policy the day it is sold.

For example, assume that the XYZ Insurance Company must maintain a minimum policyholders' surplus amount of $1 million. On the last day of 19X1, XYZ writes 1,000 one-year fire insurance policies at a premium of $100 each. Acquisition expenses for agents' commissions and underwriting costs total $30 per policy. Exhibit 6-1, part (a), provides the 19X1 before-transaction financial statements for XYZ, and the 19X1 and 19X2 SAP-based after-transaction financial statements. Part (b) of Exhibit 6-1 shows the same financial statements reported on a GAAP basis.

As can be seen in part (a) of Exhibit 6-1, the policies must run to expiration before net income (from underwriting gain) is fully recognized. The initial costs for policy acquisition (a $30,000 expense) must be supported by free policyholders' surplus. In the case of XYZ Insurance Company, that policyholders' surplus is *not* free surplus because it is dedicated to fulfilling the minimum capitalization requirement of the insurer's state of domicile. Obviously, an insurer that expands underwriting sales volume must have not only adequate surplus to meet required capitalization levels but also sufficient surplus to cover the acquisition costs of any new business written.

Part (b) of Exhibit 6-1 represents the same transaction for XYZ Insurance Company reported on a GAAP basis. Comparison of the after-sale SAP-based and GAAP-based balance sheets for year-end 19X1 demonstrates a fundamental purpose of statutory accounting, *conservative valuation of policyholders' surplus*. Statutory accounting principles and the primary differences between SAP and GAAP are discussed in a later section.

## Margin for Risk and Uncertainty

For any business, care should be taken to ensure that the entire net worth amount is not considered an available resource for growth or new business activity. Consideration must be given to the company's business exposure and market risk and its use of financial leverage. Those considerations are particularly important for property-liability insurers because of the unique characteristics of the insurance business.

Unlike a manufacturer that can determine with relative certainty the production costs for a certain volume of sales, insurers cannot determine in advance what their actual costs will be. At best, the insurer can only estimate what its ultimate exposure will be, based on past experience. If ultimate costs exceed those estimates, the realized deficiency must come from available resources represented by policyholders' surplus.

The very nature of insurance products requires that insurers maintain a sufficient amount of free policyholders' surplus to provide a margin for risk and uncertainty. That margin should also be isolated from any adverse effects of financial leverage, explaining the general reluctance of insurers to use fixed debt as a source of funding. Like other businesses, insurers are exposed to business risk and market risk. As will be explained, even though they typically avoid using fixed debt for financing, insurers are also exposed to financial risk.

### Risk Usual to All Business

All businesses experience risk in their operations. Employing the most sophisticated of forecasting techniques cannot guaranty what the future holds in terms of revenues and expenses. From an investor's perspective, risk related to the individual business is often referred to as **unique risk**. Unique risk can

Risk=is unique

**Exhibit 6-1**
Comparison of SAP-Based and GAAP-Based Financial Statements

**(a)**
**SAP-Based Statements for XYZ Insurance Company**

| **Balance Sheet as of December 31, 19X1** | | | | **Income Statement for year 19X1** | |
|---|---|---|---|---|---|
| Cash | $1,000,000 | Unearned premiums | $ 0 | Premiums earned | $ 0 |
| | | | | Underwriting expenses | 0 |
| | | Policyholders' surplus | 1,000,000 | | |
| Total assets | $1,000,000 | Total liab. & surplus | $1,000,000 | Net income (loss) | $ 0 |
| **as of December 31, 19X1** | | | | **for year 19X1** | |
| Cash | $1,070,000 | Unearned premiums | $ 100,000 | Premiums earned | $ 0 |
| | | | | Underwriting expenses | 30,000 |
| | | Policyholders' surplus | 970,000 | | |
| Total assets | $1,070,000 | Total liab. & surplus | $1,070,000 | Net income (loss) | $ (30,000) |
| **as of December 31, 19X2** | | | | **for year 19X2** | |
| Cash | $1,070,000 | Unearned premiums | $ 0 | Premiums earned | $100,000 |
| | | | | Underwriting expenses | 0 |
| | | Policyholders' surplus | 1,070,000 | | |
| Total assets | $1,070,000 | Total liab. & surplus | $1,070,000 | Net income (loss) | $100,000 |

**(b)**
**GAAP-Based Statements for XYZ Insurance Company**

| Balance Sheet as of December 31, 19X1 | | | | Income Statement for year 19X1 | |
|---|---|---|---|---|---|
| Cash | $1,000,000 | | | Premiums earned | $ 0 |
| | | | | Underwriting expenses | 0 |
| | | Policyholders' surplus | $1,000,000 | | |
| Total assets | $1,000,000 | Total liab. & surplus | $1,000,000 | Net income (loss) | $ 0 |
| **as of December 31, 19X1** | | | | **for year 19X1** | |
| Cash | $1,070,000 | Unearned premiums | $ 100,000 | Premiums earned | $ 0 |
| Prepaid UW expense | 30,000 | | | Underwriting expenses | 0 |
| | | Policyholders' surplus | 1,000,000 | | |
| Total assets | $1,100,000 | Total liab. & surplus | $1,100,000 | Net income (loss) | $ 0 |
| **as of December 31, 19X2** | | | | **for year 19X2** | |
| Cash | $1,070,000 | Unearned premiums | $ 0 | Premiums earned | $100,000 |
| | | | | Underwriting expenses | 30,000 |
| | | Policyholders' surplus | 1,070,000 | | |
| Total assets | $1,070,000 | Total liab. & surplus | $1,070,000 | Net income (loss) | $ 70,000 |

further be divided into business risk and financial risk. **Business risk** refers to a firm's inability to maintain a competitive position and stable growth in earnings.[3] Variability in revenues or costs, as well as management inefficiency, contributes to business risk. **Financial risk** refers to a firm's inability to cover fixed debt obligations as they become due.[4] During periods of operating loss, a firm's failure to maintain sufficient net worth can impair its ability to cover fixed debt obligations. Although insurers rarely issue fixed debt instruments, they can still be affected by financial risk. Insurers lever themselves by using policyholder-supplied funds to finance operations. During periods of adverse underwriting experience, an insurer can suffer the downside effect of financial risk, particularly when reserve levels for losses are also inadequate.

### *Risk Unique to Insurance*

In addition to those risks identified for other businesses, insurers are exposed to risks unique to the business of insurance. Risks that are unique to the insurance business or that take on a different connotation when applied to insurance are (1) price inadequacy, (2) reserve error, and (3) underwriting risk.

***Price Inadequacy*** Like other businesses, insurers can experience high variability in revenues and expenses. In most instances, however, insurers also face the risk of **price inadequacy**. As with most products, insurance markets are competitive. Competitive influences can cause insurers to sell coverage at or below cost to gain market share. Unfortunately, the true cost of the product is not determinable until some time after the policy has expired. In many states, insurance rates must be approved before use, often introducing delays before necessary price adjustments can be implemented. Seasonal variations in loss development can result from changing weather conditions in such lines as automobile physical damage. Additional risk can result from an insurer's lack of experience when assessing the loss exposures it underwrites.

***Reserve Error*** Insurers are also exposed to the risk of **reserve error**. Since loss and loss adjustment expense reserves are *estimates* of the amounts needed to pay incurred losses, reserving errors occur. Errors can result from inadequately assessing reported losses, misestimation of incurred but not reported (IBNR) losses, or changing economic conditions that inflate future loss costs. Additionally, reserving errors can result from deliberate insurer misstatement to bolster surplus position.

***Underwriting Risk*** An insurer also faces the risk that the exposures underwritten will change during the policy term or that multiple risks will be affected by a common occurrence. **Underwriting risk** can occur when the insured does not fully disclose information concerning the exposure being insured or when unusual events such as catastrophes simultaneously affect multiple exposures.

## Insolvency Is More Than Just Bankruptcy

As identified in earlier discussion, bankruptcy is often considered to be the ultimate cost borne by organizations that operate inefficiently. Organizations that cannot compete are forced from the market, releasing their market shares to the remaining competitors. Consumers actually benefit from most bankruptcies instead of being disadvantaged by them. If inefficient firms become bankrupt, it helps assure a more competitive price and better product quality than when those firms continue as market participants. Although long-term market benefits might similarly be derived from insurer insolvency, the short-term consequences can be severe in terms of consumer cost and market dislocation.

## Costs to Insureds and Insurers

For most lines of insurance, the costs of insurer insolvency are borne by all market participants. Those insured by the insolvent company are directly affected. They often lose the premiums paid for coverage not yet provided or receive only a partial and much delayed settlement on claims already reported. Although state guaranty funds offer protection to insureds for many lines of coverage, those funds frequently settle a claim at reduced or minimum coverage limits. Affected indirectly, however, are all market participants. Costs incurred for settlements paid through guaranty funds are assessed against the remaining *solvent* insurers in the market. Those assessments against solvent insurers are ultimately borne by all insureds through increased premium rates.

## Regulatory Activities To Ensure Solvency

A major portion of insurance regulators' activities concerns maintaining insurer solvency. Previous discussion has identified the importance of solvency and the benefits to insurers of maintaining sufficient amounts of free policyholders' surplus. Subsequent discussion will focus on major areas of regulatory activity that, in combination, provide a coordinated system that safeguards the security provided by insurance transactions and protects the interests of both insurers and insureds. Exhibit 6-2 provides an organizational chart describing the financial regulation units for a typical state insurance department.

Regulatory activities directed toward maintaining insurer solvency can generally be classified into one of four categories: (1) maintaining a uniform system

**Exhibit 6-2**
Illustrative Organizational Chart of Insurance Department Financial Regulation Units

**Insurance Commissioner**

***Examinations:***

Financial

- Routine
- Special
- Targeted

Market Conduct

***Monitoring and Surveillance (Financial Analysis):***

- Collection and analysis of financial information
- "Desk audits" of selected financial data
- Review of nonfinancial information regarding insurance companies that is routinely collected by other departments
- Classification of insurance companies and identification of troubled insurance companies
- Review of special insurance company transactions
- Coordination of efforts and communications with other department functions

***Regulatory Actions:***

- Determining regulatory courses of action regarding troubled insurance companies
- Evaluating and monitoring corrective plans for troubled insurance companies
- Communicating the results of regulatory actions

Chart created based on information contained in *Troubled Insurance Company Handbook* (Kansas City, MO: NAIC, June 1989), pp. 2-4 and used with permission of the NAIC.

of financial reporting, (2) monitoring insurer solvency, (3) monitoring capital adequacy through risk-based capital, and (4) accreditation of state insurance departments. Major sections that follow will explore each of those four categories individually.

# Maintaining a Uniform System of Financial Reporting

At the heart of regulators' efforts to maintain insurer solvency is a uniform system of financial reporting and accounting procedures. The rules and procedures governing insurer financial reporting for regulatory purposes are referred to as **statutory accounting principles (SAP)**. Uniform application of those principles ensures comparability of financial statements among insurers. SAP also provides a reporting format designed to assist regulators in identifying financially troubled insurers.

The primary purpose of an accounting system is to provide users with decision-making information. The financial accounting system used by insurers is designed for one principal user group, insurance regulators. Since a primary role of insurance regulators is determining whether a company reporting the accounting information is financially sound, specific accounting principles have been adopted that focus on liquidity and conservative surplus valuation.

## Financial Reporting Requirements

Property-liability insurers must file certain financial reports with state insurance regulators and the National Association of Insurance Commissioners (NAIC). Those reports provide the financial information necessary for regulators to monitor insurer performance and surplus position and to determine whether adverse financial trends are developing. Three financial reports required of property-liability insurers by regulators are the *Annual Statement*, including the *Insurance Expense Exhibit*, and the *Quarterly Statement*.

### The Annual Statement

Each insurer must prepare a comprehensive statement reporting its financial position and operating results on an annual basis. That statement must be filed with the insurance regulatory authority in each state in which the insurer is authorized to conduct business and with the NAIC. The Annual Statement has a format prescribed by the NAIC. That format is called the Annual Statement, sometimes referred to as the Convention Blank. The Annual Statement reports the company's financial position as of December 31 and must be filed on or before March 1 of the following year. Preparation of the

Annual Statement is governed by uniform accounting instructions contained in the NAIC publication *Annual Statement Instructions for Property and Casualty* and line instructions contained in the blank itself.

The Annual Statement includes the statutory balance sheet, the statement of income, summary of the capital and surplus account, and the statement of cash flow. Major exhibits and schedules included in the Annual Statement are the Underwriting and Investment Exhibit, lettered investment schedules, several parts to a schedule summarizing reinsurance transactions (Schedule F), and several parts to a schedule summarizing losses and unpaid loss development (Schedule P). Those supporting schedules and exhibits provide an in-depth disclosure of financial information. As supplements to the Annual Statement, insurers must file an annual audit report, prepared by an independent CPA, and a statement of actuarial opinion, signed by a qualified actuary, rendering an opinion about the insurer's loss and loss adjustment expense reserves.

### Insurance Expense Exhibit

As a supplement to the Annual Statement, property-liability insurers must file the NAIC's Insurance Expense Exhibit. This exhibit provides a statement of operating gain or loss before federal income taxes by each line of insurance. The disaggregated reporting of premiums and expenses by line of insurance can be used in ratemaking to determine appropriate expense levels by line and by function within each line. The Insurance Expense Exhibit must be filed on or before April 1 of the year following the calendar year it covers.

### The Quarterly Statement

Much more abbreviated than the Annual Statement, the Quarterly Statement includes the statutory balance sheet, statement of income, summary of the capital and surplus account, cash flow statement, the reconciliation of ledger assets, and a few supporting schedules.[5] Quarterly Statements must be filed on or before the forty-fifth day following the end of the quarter reported. Quarterly Statements are filed only for the first three quarters. Because the Quarterly Statements report financial information for the year's operations through the close of the quarter, the fourth quarter's statement content would be redundant to that of the Annual Statement.

## Statutory Insurance Accounting

Although many of the financial statements contained in the NAIC Annual Statement resemble summary financial statements of noninsurance companies, the information they provide can differ because the statements are prepared using different accounting principles. Financial statements for most noninsurance businesses are prepared in accordance with GAAP. Applying uniform procedures makes it possible to compare financial statements of different organizations. To comply with the reporting requirements of state insurance regulators and their unique information needs to monitor insurer solvency, financial statements for insurers are prepared in accordance with SAP. GAAP and SAP principles differ in the areas of valuation, continuity, and realization.

## Valuation Principles

Valuation rules of statutory accounting have been designed to satisfy two criteria:

1. Valuation should result in a *conservative statement of policyholders' surplus.*
2. Valuation should, as much as is reasonably possible, *prevent sharp fluctuations in policyholders' surplus.*

The first criterion is accomplished by conservative valuation of assets and liabilities. In the context of the basic accounting equation, the combined effect of minimizing asset valuation and maximizing liability valuation results in a conservative statement of policyholders' surplus. The basic accounting equation is stated as follows:

Assets = Liabilities + Policyholders' surplus

By transforming the basic accounting equation, the policyholders' surplus variable is moved to the left-hand side of the equation.

Policyholders' surplus = Assets – Liabilities

This form of the equation can be used to demonstrate the effect on policyholders' surplus valuation of minimizing asset valuation and maximizing liability valuation. Minimizing asset valuation is accomplished by using the lowest value of assets derived by applying alternate valuation methods. Conversely, maximizing liability valuation is accomplished by using the highest value of liabilities derived by applying alternate valuation methods.

For example, assume that an insurer reports $100 in assets and $70 in liabilities. Using the transformed equation, policyholders' surplus for the insurer would be $30, as shown in (a). Next, assume that minimizing asset valuation results in a conservative asset value of $90, and that maximizing liability valuation results in a conservative liability valuation of $80. Policyholders' surplus would then be more conservatively stated at an amount of $10, as shown in (b).

Policyholders' surplus = Assets – Liabilities

| | | | | | | |
|---|---|---|---|---|---|---|
| (a) | $30 | = | $100 | – | $70 |
| (b) | $10 | = | $90 | – | $80 |

Property-liability insurers own assets that fall into one of two categories, admitted assets or nonadmitted assets. Only one category, *admitted assets*, is permitted to be listed on the insurer's statutory balance sheet. By excluding nonadmitted assets, effectively assigning them a value of zero, an insurer's total reported assets are conservatively valued. **Admitted assets** have the following characteristics:

- They are allowed to be reported by state insurance statutes.
- They are highly liquid, meaning that they can be readily converted to cash without a significant loss of value.

**Nonadmitted assets** are those assets that are (1) not allowed to be reported by state insurance statutes or (2) relatively illiquid. Examples of admitted assets are cash, investments in stocks and bonds, and agents' balances that are not over ninety days outstanding. Examples of nonadmitted assets are computer software (other than operating system software) and agents' balances that are more than ninety days outstanding.

Examples of conservative liability valuation can be seen in the valuation of reserves for unpaid losses and in the application of minimum reserve requirements imposed by regulators for certain liability lines of insurance. Under statutory accounting, loss reserve estimates for most lines of insurance are reported at their *nondiscounted* future value, which ignores the time value of money. If the potential for investment return were recognized, loss reserves could be stated at their present value, obtained by applying a discount rate to the reserves' estimated future value. For example, if an insurer estimates that a litigated claim will ultimately cost $318,000 to settle and that the judgment is not expected to be delivered for twelve months, statutory accounting requires that the loss reserve be reported at $318,000. If the insurer were permitted to report the reserve at its discounted present value and were able to obtain a 6 percent return on its investments, the loss reserve would be reported at $300,000 ($318,000 ÷ 1.06). Also, if for certain lines of insurance the insurer reports loss reserves at a value of less than that required by regulators, the insurer must report the difference between the required amount and its statement reserve (estimated reserve amount) as an additional liability item titled *Excess of statutory over statement reserves*.

## Continuity Principles

The **continuity principle** is one of the basic principles of GAAP. The principle assumes that the business is a *going concern*, meaning that it should be viewed as though its operations will be long-term in nature and that ownership interests can be transferred without liquidating the business. A *liquidation perspective* is generally used to view property-liability insurers, however, because the overriding concern of regulators is that the owned financial resources of the insurer be adequate and readily available to satisfy insured claims or refund unearned premiums if insurance contracts are canceled. There are, however, some rules under SAP that reflect the going concern assumption. For example, reporting bonds at amortized value instead of market value implicitly assumes that those bonds will be held until maturity.

## Realization Principles

**Realization** refers to a gain or loss from an economic transaction. In its usual form, an economic transaction involves the sale of goods or service for cash. Even for such a basic transaction, inconsistency can arise from the way the transaction is recorded. Should the cash received be recorded at the time the order is placed, at the time the goods are shipped or service begins, or at the time the customer receives the goods or the entire service has been provided? The process is complicated further when we try to match with the cash received those expenses incurred to produce the goods or services or when credit is introduced into the transaction.

As indicated earlier in this chapter, GAAP requires that (1) revenues be recognized as earned and (2) associated costs incurred to generate those revenues be matched to the same accounting period in which the revenues are recognized (reported as earned). The first requirement is referred to as the **revenue recognition principle**, and the second requirement is referred to as the **matching principle.**

Also as indicated earlier in this chapter, SAP is consistent with GAAP in that revenue is recognized as it is earned. The insurance product, being a contract representing a guaranty of future performance, is a service product. Revenues are recognized gradually over time as the contract and remaining service obligations expire. An inconsistency between GAAP and SAP, however, occurs in the recognition of acquisition expenses related to the sale of insurance. As shown in Exhibit 6-1, SAP recognizes acquisition expenses immediately as they are incurred. GAAP capitalizes those expenses by establishing an asset for prepaid expenses and amortizing those expenses over time as the associated revenues are recognized. GAAP employs the matching principle; SAP does not.

This discussion does not provide an exhaustive list of the differences between SAP-based financial statements and those prepared according to GAAP.

Those differences identified, however, constitute the principal areas in which regulatory emphasis on solvency and surplus adequacy has its greatest effect.

# Monitoring Insurer Performance and Solvency

A significant part of regulatory activity is devoted to monitoring the performance of those insurers conducting business within insurance regulators' respective states. Regulators are concerned not only about those insurers licensed or otherwise authorized to conduct business. They are also concerned about unauthorized insurers that sell insurance directly to consumers and that participate in reinsurance agreements with authorized insurers. The topics of insurance regulation related to market conduct, insurer and agent licensing, are discussed in other parts of this text. The discussion that follows addresses regulators' activity dedicated to monitoring insurers' operating performance and financial condition.

As described in an earlier discussion, a uniform system of financial reporting is an essential prerequisite for effectively monitoring and evaluating insurer performance and financial solidity. If insurers were not required to universally conform to a standardized reporting format, regulators and other users of accounting information would not be able to compare one company's performance to that of another company or to an industry norm. Therefore, an essential part of monitoring insurer performance is to check for compliance with SAP as required by the NAIC. Ensuring compliance is a major purpose of any financial examination or audit of a property-liability insurer.

Beyond determining that insurers are in compliance with SAP, the need exists to accumulate a tremendous volume of accounting information as quickly as possible following the close of an accounting period. Traditional methods of accumulating hard-copy financial statements at offices of the NAIC and individual state regulators as the exclusive source of data for examination and review have given way to current high-technology-oriented data retrieval and analysis systems. Hard-copy Annual and Quarterly Statements are still required for archival purposes. Today, however, the vast majority of insurers file their statement data on computer diskettes that facilitate rapid entry to the NAIC database. The following discussion focuses on specific elements of the regulatory information system and on how those elements are used to monitor insurer operations and to maintain insurer solvency.

## Insurance Regulatory Information System (IRIS)

The Insurance Regulatory Information System (IRIS) began as the Early

Warning System in the early 1970s. At first, it consisted of only a few financial ratios that could be applied to data from insurer financial statements. An analytical system under continual change, the original system has been expanded over the past two-and-one-half decades to include a companion solvency information system, the Financial Analysis and Solvency Tracking (FAST) system. Originally developed by a committee of state insurance regulators, the IRIS system was designed to assist state insurance departments in monitoring the financial condition of insurers operating in their respective states.[6] In its current form, the IRIS system consists of two phases: (1) the statistical phase and (2) the analytical phase.

## Statistical Phase

The statistical phase is a mechanized process of calculating a series of ratios from accounting information contained in insurers' statutory Annual Statements filed with the NAIC. Today, nearly 90 percent of companies file their Annual Statements on computer diskettes.[7] Results from the ratio calculations are made available to state regulators over the NAIC's computer network and to examiner teams and the Financial Analysis Working Group (FAWG) for purposes of prioritizing insurers for financial examinations. The IRIS system has two sets of financial ratios: (1) the IRIS ratios, consisting of a basic set of twelve financial ratios each for property-liability insurers and life-health insurers and (2) a series of ratios developed for the FAST system against which weights can be applied to provide point values based on the ratio results.[8] Points can be aggregated by various algorithms to help regulators prioritize their solvency surveillance activities.

### IRIS Ratios

Twelve IRIS ratios are used to analyze property-liability insurers' financial condition. Based on the analysis of companies that have become insolvent or have experienced financial difficulties in recent years, a "usual range" of results has been established.[9] The usual range is periodically modified to reflect changes in industry performance or market conditions. The NAIC warns users of IRIS ratio results that "[f]alling outside the usual range is not considered a failing result."[10] The IRIS ratios are designed to evaluate four dimensions of an insurer's financial condition:

1. Overall financial condition
2. Profitability
3. Liquidity
4. Reserves

Twelve ratios for property-liability insurers are provided in Exhibit 6-3.

**Exhibit 6-3**
IRIS Tests for Property-Liability Insurers

| IRIS RATIOS 4323 |
|---|
| OVERALL FINANCIAL CONDITION RATIOS |
| Gross Premium to Surplus |
| Net Premium to Surplus |
| Change in Net Writings |
| Surplus Aid to Surplus |
| PROFITABILITY RATIOS |
| Two-Year Overall Operating Ratio |
| Investment Yield |
| Change in Surplus |
| LIQUIDITY RATIOS |
| Liabilities to Liquid Assets |
| Agents' Balances to Surplus |
| RESERVE RATIOS |
| One-Year Reserve Development to Surplus |
| Two-Year Reserve Development to Surplus |
| Estimated Current Reserve Deficiency to Surplus |

Source: NAIC, *Using the NAIC Insurance Regulatory Information System*, Property and Liability Edition (Kansas City, MO: NAIC, 1993), p. 30.

Although the NAIC provides usual ranges for each of the twelve IRIS ratios, examples using two of the ratios should illustrate how those usual ranges might be used to analyze an insurer's financial position. Two of the IRIS ratios that often result in unusual values when an insurer abruptly changes its rate structure, underwriting policy, or reserving practice are (1) the *change in net writings* ratio and (2) the *change in surplus* ratio. The usual range for a change in net premiums written is between –33 percent and +33 percent. The usual range for a change in policyholders' surplus is between –10 percent and +50 percent.

An unusual value for the change in net writings ratio indicates that a company has either made a radical change in its rate structure or that it has experienced a tremendous growth or decline in written business compared to the norm established by all property-liability insurers. Abnormal growth in writings, without an accompanying increase in policyholders' surplus to support that growth, might indicate that the insurer is expanding too rapidly or that the insurer is not reserving adequately for incurred losses.

An unusual value for the change in surplus ratio might indicate that the insurer has experienced an unusual drain on surplus from unexpected claims or a catastrophe (causing surplus to decrease), or that the insurer has decreased its unpaid loss reserves (causing surplus to increase). In either case, when changes in policyholders' surplus appear to be abnormal when compared to the industry norm, a serious problem might exist that, if not corrected, could threaten the insurer's solvency.

Each insurer receives a report tabulating its IRIS ratio results and key financial figures from the Annual Statement. That report provides the insurer an opportunity to review the results and report any errors to the NAIC. The IRIS results are also sent to insurance regulators in the insurer's state of domicile and are entered in the NAIC's networked computer system, where the results can be accessed by all state insurance regulators.

### FAST Ratios 9

Integrating the Financial Analysis and Solvency Tracking system into the IRIS system increased the number of analytical tools available to regulators and examiners. The FAST ratios, consisting of several of the IRIS ratios with others designed to measure relationships not captured by the IRIS ratios, provide a total score for an insurer based on the number of points assigned according to set parameters for each ratio.[11] Higher scores indicate a higher risk of future insolvency. The FAST ratios focus on the following dimensions of an insurer's financial condition:

- Profitability
- Asset quality
- Investment yield
- Affiliate investments
- Reserves
- Reinsurance
- Liquidity
- Cash flows
- Leverage[12]

## Analytical Phase

The purpose of the analytical phase of the IRIS system is to identify those insurers requiring immediate regulatory attention.[13] An experienced team of financial examiners meets annually at the NAIC offices to review (1) information developed in the statistical phase, (2) Annual Statements for the current and prior periods as needed, and (3) reports generated by regulators or examiners. Externally produced information might also be used in the analytical phase. It is common for examiners also to use Securities and Exchange Commission (SEC) filings, ratings from independent rating organizations, or information from trade periodicals. Outcomes of the preliminary review and analysis are used to make recommendations to the individual states to assist regulators in prioritizing the review of their domiciliary companies within constraints of available departmental resources. Companies that are assigned a *high priority* status are identified for monitoring by the NAIC's Examination Oversight Task Force to ensure that the insurer is reviewed by its domiciliary state.[14] If no action is taken at the state level, the task force has the authority to conduct its own review.

### Financial Analysis Working Group (FAWG)

Along with the addition of the FAST system to IRIS, a new analytical process was added to provide peer review of domiciliary regulation of *nationally significant* insurers.[15] Part of the NAIC's Financial Analysis Division (FAD), the Financial Analysis Working Group (FAWG) provides additional assurance that insurers displaying indications of financial difficulty, particularly those of national significance, will not fall through the cracks and escape the examination process. A property-liability insurer is considered *nationally significant* if it writes business in seventeen or more states and has gross premium writings (direct writings plus assumed business) in excess of $30 million.[16] Exhibit 6-4 describes the review procedure of the Financial Analysis Working Group.

### Examiner Team Process

Each year, a team of experienced examiners meets at the NAIC offices to review results of the IRIS ratios and selected insurers' Annual Statements. IRIS results falling outside of the usual range for four or more ratios are only one of fifteen criteria used to identify insurers requiring further review.[17] In typical years, only about 15 percent of the companies evaluated using IRIS ratios are expected to fall outside the usual range for four or more ratios.[18]

### State Regulators' Bench Audits

Each insurer domiciled or authorized to conduct business in a state is required to file an NAIC Annual Statement with the insurance regulatory authority of that state. Examiners at the state level conduct bench audits of those statements, reviewing them for accuracy and compliance with statutory accounting requirements and performing a detailed financial analysis of the information they report. State examiners place particular emphasis on conducting ratio

**Exhibit 6-4**
Financial Analysis Working Group Procedures

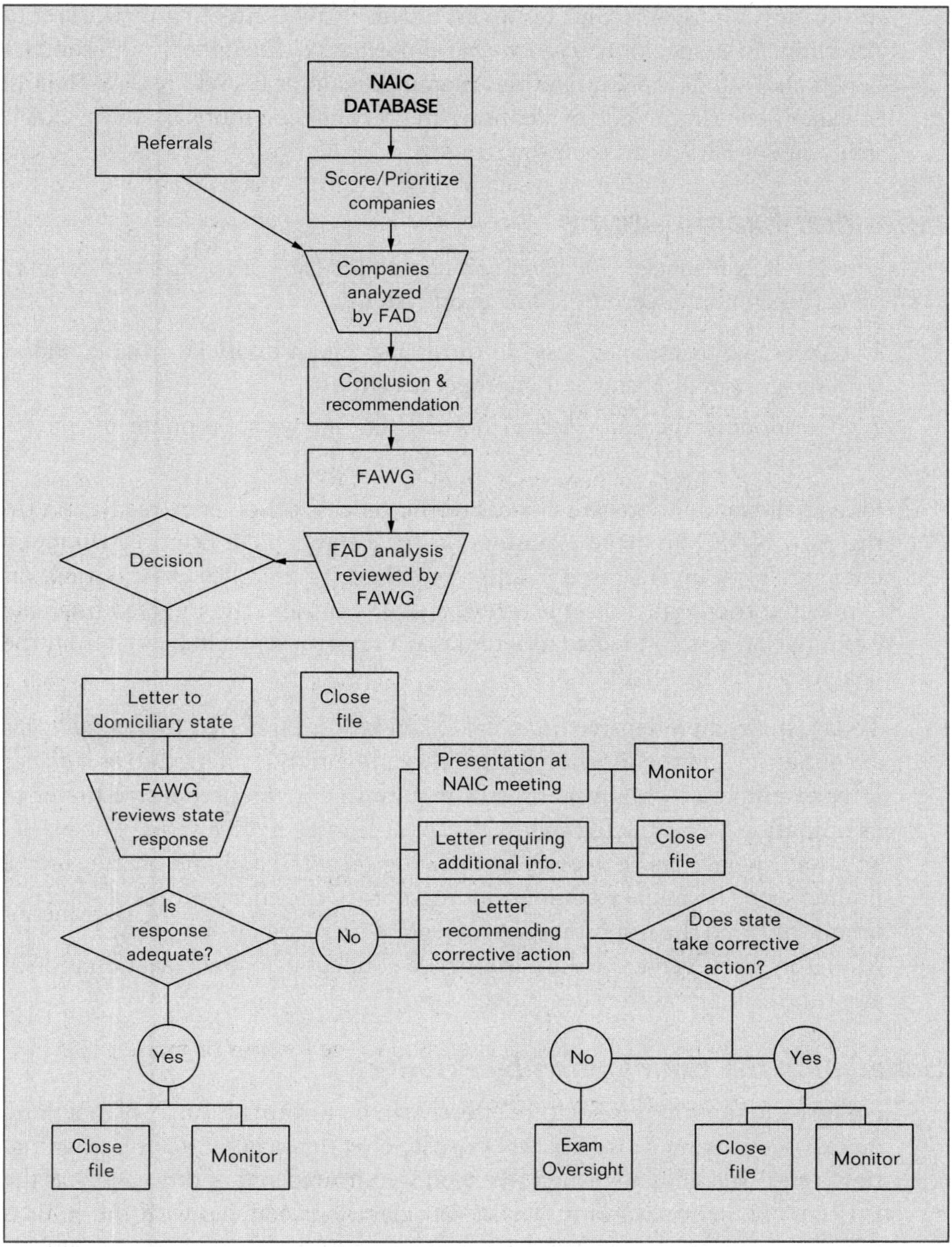


Reprinted with permission from NAIC, *Financial Analysis and Solvency Surveillance*, 1994, p. 5.

analyses to identify unusual relationships among financial variables that might indicate a troubled company. Alone, results of financial tests do not identify insolvency. Unusual results, however, might justify contacting the insurer to determine the specific cause of the abnormality. Examiners can conduct bench audits independently of the examiner team or FAWG review process, or examiners can include evaluations and recommendations from the examiner team or FAWG in their own review.

## Financial Examinations

The NAIC's *Financial Condition Examiners Handbook* identifies two primary objectives for an effective examination system:

1. Detecting as early as possible those insurers in financial trouble and/or engaging in unlawful and improper activities
2. Developing the information needed for timely, appropriate regulatory action[19]

Financial examinations are critical to the process of solvency regulation. In the past, NAIC financial examinations of insurers have been of two types: comprehensive and targeted.[20] The comprehensive financial examination was conducted triennially, or at least every five years, and the targeted financial examination was conducted as a result of a priority status indicated from the analytical phase of IRIS.

Today, the comprehensive financial examination is referred to as a *full scope* examination and the targeted financial examination is referred to as a *limited scope* examination. Many states still require that a comprehensive financial examination be conducted triennially, or at least every five years. The NAIC and state regulators, however, are placing greater emphasis on the use of limited scope financial examinations to improve the effectiveness of solvency monitoring and the responsiveness of regulatory action, when needed.[21] State regulators, however, have the authority to conduct a financial examination at any time or interval they deem necessary.[22]

### Scheduling the Examination by Priority

For an examination process to be effective in monitoring insurer solvency and quickly identifying those insurers experiencing financial difficulty, examinations must be conducted when the need is indicated and as thoroughly as the existing conditions warrant. Those considerations coupled with the limited resources of most state insurance departments make prioritization of examination efforts necessary. As described in earlier discussion, regulators receive priority recommendations from the examination team and the FAWG, which are developed during the analytical phase of IRIS. Many factors are considered when assigning one of five examination priorities. Those factors identified in the NAIC's *Troubled Insurance Company Handbook* as "financial conditions indicating a potential troubled insurance company situation" are summarized below:

1. Adverse findings in financial condition and market conduct examination reports might indicate a need for regulatory intervention.
2. IRIS ratio results might indicate a need for further examination.
3. Ratios of key financial variables can indicate unprofitable operations, which, if not corrected, could impair capital and surplus.
4. Ratios of financial leverage might indicate undercapitalization.
5. Abnormally good financial results for a particular line of business might indicate questionable reliability of financial information.
6. An asset portfolio, when viewed relative to current economic conditions, appearing inadequate, illiquid, and poorly diversified—should raise questions about a firm's ability to pay outstanding obligations when due.
7. Future illiquidity might be indicated when maturities of assets and liabilities appear to be mismatched.
8. Ability or willingness of the company's reinsurers to meet obligations under reinsurance contracts might appear to be questionable.
9. Ability of the reinsurance program to protect insurer's remaining surplus might appear questionable.
10. An affiliate, subsidiary, or significant reinsurer might be insolvent, financially impaired, or delinquent in payment of its obligations.
11. An insurer might have contingent liabilities, pledges, or outstanding guarantees that, individually or collectively, could affect the insurer's solvency.
12. An operating loss in the most recent reporting period that represents a significant portion of an insurer's remaining surplus requires further assessment of surplus adequacy.
13. An agent or a "controlling person" of the insurer might be delinquent in transmitting or paying net premiums due the company.
14. An insurer's receivables might show an unusual increase in age.
15. An insurer might have a history of adverse loss reserve development, indicating deliberate or chronic underreserving.[23]

Based on the examiner team's assessment of an insurer's financial condition, one of five priority classifications is assigned: (1) first priority, (2) second priority, (3) third priority, (4) no priority or average priority, or (5) no synopsis or summary report required. State regulators are advised by the NAIC to schedule their analysis of domiciled insurers according to the priorities established by the examiner team.

A conceptual model that can be used by state insurance regulators independently of priority referrals from the NAIC examiner team is presented in the NAIC's *Troubled Insurance Company Handbook*. That model also produces five priority classifications that roughly correspond to those assigned by the NAIC examiner team. Exhibit 6-5 provides a flow chart summarizing the model's evaluation process for determining examination priorities. As used in the exhibit, a Troubled Insurance Company is defined in the following way:

> . . .an insurance company that has not maintained a financial position, or whose operations are moving toward a financial position, that would indicate that its policyholders, claimants, and other creditors are subject to greater-than-normal financial risk, including the possibility that the company may not maintain the applicable statutory minimum capital and/or surplus requirements.[24]

## Planning and Conducting the Examination

The financial examination, at whatever level of detail it is conducted, should place utmost emphasis on those areas that could most critically affect the insurer's solvency. Prioritization of the examiners' efforts will help the chief examiner ensure that the examiner team meets its objectives. The chief examiner should clearly establish the responsibilities of each examiner and schedule their activities so that the insurer's transaction cycles assessed as being high risk are reviewed first. The risk assessment takes into account environmental factors, analytical reviews, and the adequacy of controls and work performed by actuaries and independent CPAs.[25]

To avoid duplication of effort in conducting financial examinations, the NAIC encourages the use of association examinations if the examination team is made up of examiners representing the different zones in which an insurer operates. The country is divided into four zones: Northeastern, Southeastern, Midwestern, and Western. Often referred to as *zone examinations*, **association examinations** are used when insurers are licensed in more than three states in one zone or are licensed in more than one zone.[26] Exhibit 6-6 identifies which states and territories are included in each of the four association examination zones.

When an insurer is scheduled for an association examination, the domiciliary regulator invites the participation of an examiner from the other zones in

**Exhibit 6-5**
Establishing Priorities for Financial Examinations

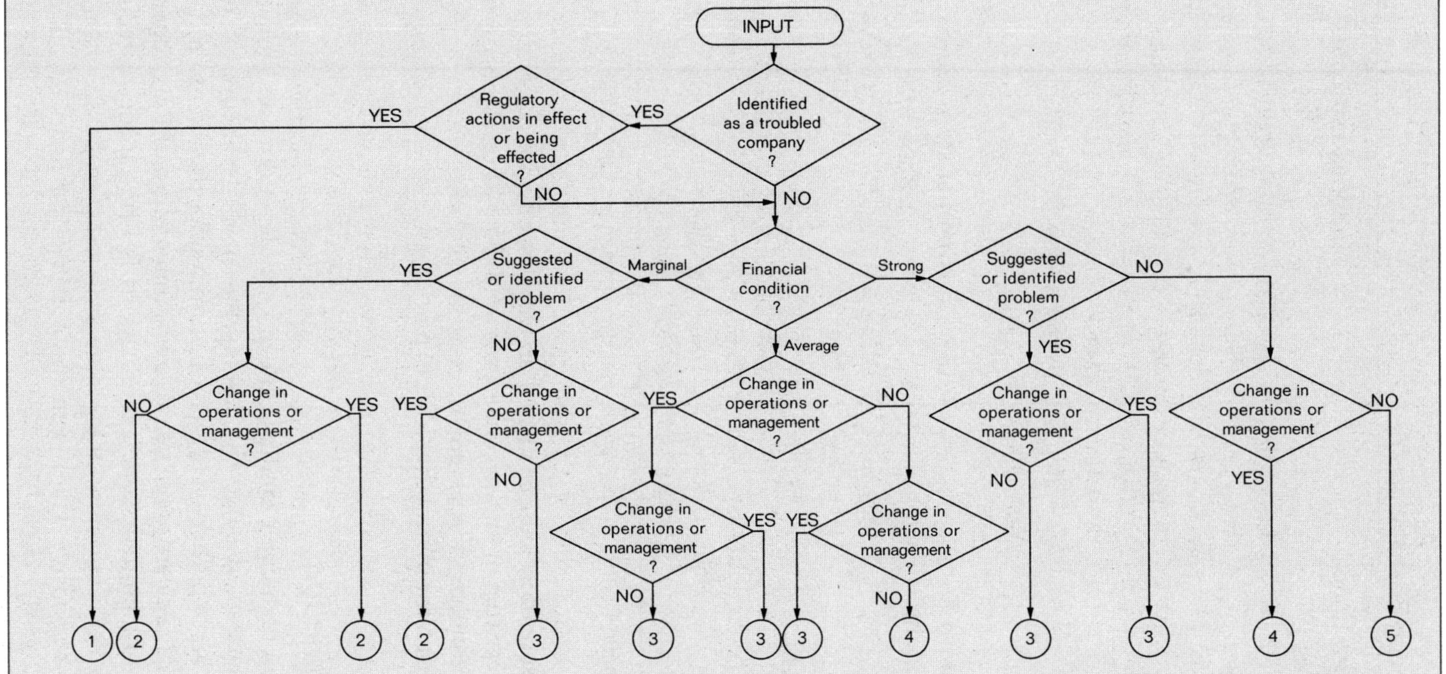


1. The insurance company has been identified as a troubled insurance company, and regulatory actions are in effect or being effected.
2. The insurance company has been perceived or identified as a troubled insurance company, and additional monitoring and investigation efforts are required to determine whether regulatory actions are necessary.
3. The insurance company displays the characteristics indicating the potential to become a troubled insurance company.
4. The insurance company is average priority.
5. The insurance company is a low priority.

Chart created based on information contained in *Troubled Insurance Company Handbook* (Kansas City, MO: NAIC, June 1989), pp. 1-2 and used with permission of the NAIC.

**Exhibit 6-6**
States by Association Examination Zones

| Western Zone Zone IV | | Northeastern Zone Zone I | |
|---|---|---|---|
| Alaska | Montana | Connecticut | New Jersey |
| American Samoa | Nevada | Delaware | New York |
| Arizona | New Mexico | District of Columbia | Pennsylvania |
| California | Oregon | Maine | Rhode Island |
| Colorado | Texas | Maryland | Vermont |
| Guam | Utah | Massachusetts | Virgin Islands |
| Hawaii | Washington | New Hampshire | |
| Idaho | Wyoming | | |
| **Midwestern Zone Zone III** | | **Southeastern Zone Zone II** | |
| Iowa | Missouri | Alabama | Mississippi |
| Illinois | Nebraska | Arkansas | North Carolina |
| Indiana | North Dakota | Florida | Puerto Rico |
| Kansas | Ohio | Georgia | South Carolina |
| Michigan | Oklahoma | Kentucky | Tennessee |
| Minnesota | South Dakota | Louisiana | Virginia |
| Wisconsin | | West Virginia | |

Source: NAIC, *Financial Condition Examiners Handbook* (Kansas City, MO: NAIC 1994), pp. 1-5.

which the insurer does business based on established criteria.[27] If an insurer's annual direct written premium equals or exceeds $5 million in a zone, or if less than $5 million has 30 percent of its total writings within a zone, the domiciliary regulator invites that zone to participate in the association examination.[28]

## *Scope of Examination*

The scope of a financial examination can vary, depending on the length of time that has elapsed since the last examination, the scope of the last examination, and whether events have occurred since the last examination to cause regulators' concern about the insurer's financial condition or operations. Increasing use of limited scope examinations is being made to reduce the length of time between financial examinations and to make the examination process more responsive when even the potential for financial difficulty is identified.

### *Full Scope Examinations*

Comprehensive or **full scope examinations** are very broad and encompass a thorough review of the insurer's records and financial position. Association examinations are full scope examinations. The following are examples of those insurer areas reviewed in a full scope examination:

- Management and control
- Plan of operation
- Corporate records
- Accounts and records
- Financial statements
- Business in force
- Loss experience
- Reserves
- Quality of assets
- Reinsurance

In the past, financial examinations have concentrated on verification of the insurer's financial condition and ensuring compliance with SAP and financial reporting requirements imposed by the NAIC.[29] More recently, however, examiners have placed greater emphasis on risk-based analysis to identify potential problems stemming from the insurer's unique business practices and asset and liability mix that could effect solvency either now or at some time in the future.[30]

### *Limited Scope Examinations*

**Limited scope examinations** can be scheduled between regularly scheduled association examinations. Limited scope examinations occur when the regulator needs to validate information or to review an insurer's operations in response to requests by other regulators or in response to unusual complaints by insurers or insureds. The *Financial Condition Examiners Handbook* identifies ten circumstances that will generally prompt a limited scope examination:

1. Unusual values identified through IRIS
2. Internal department analysis of NAIC Annual or Quarterly Statements
3. Follow-up from a prior examination report
4. Request from another insurance department
5. Need for information necessary to examine another insurer
6. Unusual complaint volume
7. Transactions disclosed under the Holding Company Act
8. Preliminary investigations

9. Limited purpose examinations required by statute
10. Examination planning and risk assessment analysis[31]

### Special Association Examinations

When circumstances justify direct intervention by the NAIC, a *special association examination* can be called by the Financial Condition (EX4) Subcommittee. The **special association examination** is conducted by personnel selected from state insurance departments by the EX4 subcommittee, and the examination reports are addressed directly to that subcommittee.[32] There are generally three situations that can cause the subcommittee to call a special association examination:

1. Written reports from the zone examiners indicate that the examination conducted by the company's state of domicile is inadequate.
2. The domiciliary state is reluctant to schedule an examination when IRIS results or other information indicate the need to do so.
3. A state in which a company is licensed requests a special association examination.[33]

# Monitoring Capital Adequacy Through Risk-Based Capital

During the past decade, the increased frequency of insurer insolvency and the intense criticism of state insurance regulation by federal legislators have been catalysts in the reform of traditional solvency regulation. Previous discussion indicated that financial examiners are paying increased attention to internal and external risk factors that can affect an insurer's financial position and current or future solvency. Solvency surveillance that consists only of determining whether an insurer is technically solvent and is maintaining state-required capitalization levels is no longer adequate in today's business environment. Because each insurer's operations are unique, considerable variation exists among insurers' asset structures, underwriting portfolios, and reserving practices. It would be unreasonable to expect that capital and surplus needs do not also vary among insurers.

## Fixed Capitalization Requirements

Historically, **fixed capital requirements** have been specified in state insurance statutes to ensure that applicants seeking licenses to conduct insurance business within the state's jurisdiction have sufficient capital to support underwriting activity. Unfortunately, the capitalization requirements for insurers that many states have today are what they were several decades ago. Not only have the statutory minimums remained static over several years—the statutes rarely made any provision for adjustments to capitalization requirements to reflect an insurer's changing operations, growth, or underwriting emphasis. The task of monitoring insurer activity and ensuring that adequate capitalization is maintained was delegated to the state insurance regulator.

## Inconsistency Among States

Considerable differences exist among minimum insurer capitalization requirements. Those differences are primarily attributable to three factors: (1) the company's legal form, (2) the lines of insurance the company intends to underwrite, and (3) the state in which the company is seeking a license. State insurance statutes often impose different capitalization requirements for different forms of business ownership. Capital requirements might differ between stock and mutual insurers or between reciprocals and Lloyds associations. Requirements might also differ for an insurer writing fire insurance exclusively or for one writing both fire and inland marine insurance. Significant differences also exist among individual state capitalization requirements for the same business ownership form and for the same lines of insurance. For example, a stock insurer intending to write fire insurance exclusively would be required to have initial capital of $150,000 in the state of Pennsylvania but must have $2 million in the state of Illinois.[34]

## Capitalization Rarely Adequate for Exposure

Introductory sections of this chapter discussed various forms of business risk. The effect of business risk on insurers can be much more severe than on other business entities because the insurance business involves assumption of risk. Effects of market and financial risk on insurers are compounded by the additional risks they assume by underwriting exposures to loss. Those exposures to loss, that is, property and liability affected by other businesses' management of their own operations, are also affected by market and financial risk. Fixed capitalization requirements do not recognize those risks inherent in the business of insurance, except that different lines of insurance might present different risk characteristics and capital needs.

As discussed earlier, capital and surplus are needed to support growth and to provide a buffer against risk and uncertainty. A new company, one entering the market with only cash and capital on its balance sheet, is not exposed to the compound effects of market, financial, and underwriting risks. Minimum fixed capital requirements should be adequate for such a firm. As the firm grows and assumes increasing amounts of risk through its underwriting activity and reinsurance transactions, the firm must also maintain increasing amounts of capital and surplus. It is the capital and surplus that provide the financial security for an insurance transaction. The insurer is providing a promise that it will be able to pay insured losses as they become due.

## Risk-Based Capital Requirements

Addressing the problems inherent in traditional fixed capitalization requirements, the NAIC has recently developed an alternate approach to determining capitalization levels, which sets requirements according to a *risk-based* standard. The **risk-based capital (RBC) model** develops an insurer capitalization requirement based on the risk characteristics inherent to that insurer's unique operations. The model addresses four major categories of risk:

1. Off-balance sheet risk
2. Asset risk
3. Credit risk
4. Underwriting risk[35]

A minimum desirable capitalization level, called the **authorized control level**, is developed for each insurer by following a procedure composed of three steps:

1. Applying established risk-factor weights to individual financial statement items (for example, .30 x defaulted bonds, .05 x collateral loans, or .10 x real estate)[36]
2. Aggregating the risk-adjusted statement items by major risk categories (off-balance sheet risk, asset risk, credit risk, and underwriting risk)
3. Combining the major risk categories in accordance with the RBC formula

Exhibit 6-7 shows the components of the risk-based capital formula proposed for implementation with the 1994 Annual Statement and how that formula combines the major risk categories. **Asset risk** represents the risks associated with market volatility that can affect the value of an insurer's invested assets and the security of those investments. In the RBC formula, asset risk is composed of a *fixed income investment risk* (R1) segment and an *equity investment risk* (R2) segment. **Credit risk** (R3) is related to the collectibility of the insurer's receivables, including reinsurance recoverables and agents' balances due the insurer. **Underwriting risk** consists of a component for *net written premium risk* (R5) which represents those risks associated with price inadequacy, when the loss exposure of assumed risks is deliberately (because of competitive pressure) or unintentionally mispriced. Underwriting risk also includes a *net loss reserve and loss adjustment expense risk* (R4) component recognizing those risks associated with reserving errors. **Off-balance sheet risk** (R0) includes risk associated with abnormal premium and reserve growth,

**Exhibit 6-7**
Risk-Based Capital Formula for Property-Liability Insurers

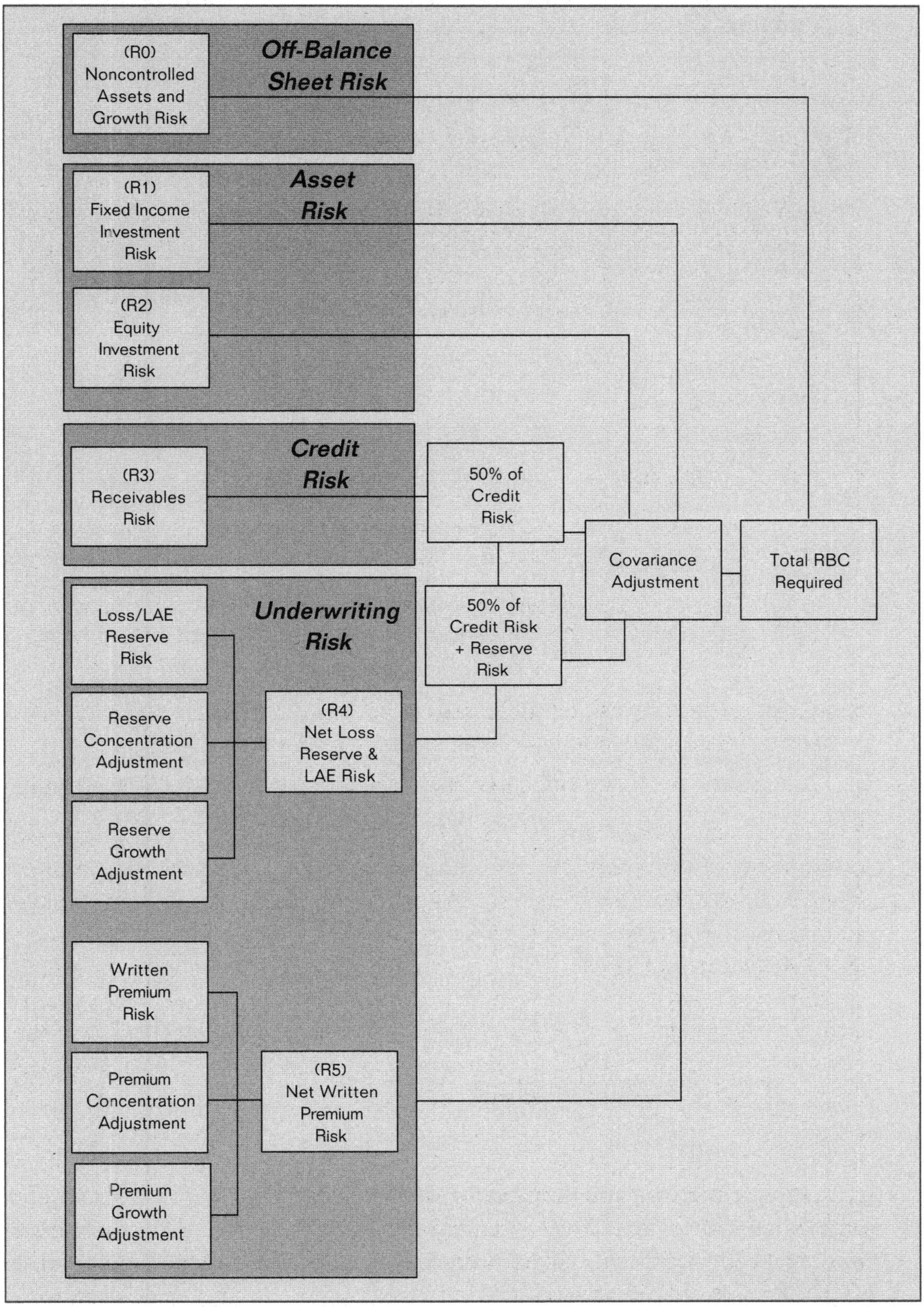


Adapted from illustration in "NAIC's RBC: A Virtual Reality," *Best's Review*, Property-Casualty (February 1994), p. 92. Used with permission from the NAIC and A.M. Best Company.

investments in affiliates, and financial guarantees made on behalf of affiliates.[37] The major risk categories are combined in accordance with the following formula to determine the total risk-based capital requirement.

$$RBC = RO + \sqrt{(R1)^2 + (R2)^2 + (.5 \times R3)^2 + [(.5 \times R3) + R4]^2 + (R5)^2}$$

In addition to the model for computing a required capitalization amount, the NAIC drafted the *Risk-Based Capital (RBC) for Insurers Model Act* that ". . .establishes specific duties for both the insurer and the regulators based upon the figures generated by the RBC formulas."[38] Four different RBC levels have been developed, each designating specific requirements of insurers and regulators. Exhibit 6-8 describes those four different RBC levels and how they are determined.

**Exhibit 6-8**
Risk-Based Capital Levels

| RBC Level | Percent of Authorized Control Level RBC | Action Required |
|---|---|---|
| Company Action Level | 200 percent | Insurer files comprehensive plan |
| Regulatory Action Level | 150 percent | Regulator performs exam as necessary; Insurer files comprehensive plan |
| Authorized Control Level | 100 percent | Regulator may seize control |
| Mandatory Control Level | 70 percent | Regulator required to place insurer under regulatory control |

An important characteristic that distinguishes the NAIC RBC Model Act from other minimum capitalization techniques is that the model establishes specific responsibilities both for regulators and for insurers. Fixed capitalization requirements only establish the minimum capitalization level that the insurer must establish and maintain. Again, the authorized control level RBC is considered the absolute minimum that an insurer should maintain, given the insurer's risk profile.

If an insurer's actual capitalization level falls to a level below 70 percent of the authorized control level, the insurance regulator *is required* to place the insurer under regulatory control.[39] If an insurer's capitalization level falls between the mandatory control level and the authorized control level, the regulator can place the insurer under regulatory control but is not required to do so. Actual capitalization between the regulatory action level and the authorized control level requires that the regulator perform an examination or analysis as deemed necessary. The insurer is also required to file a comprehensive financial plan with the state insurance regulator. Actual insurer capitalization between the company action level and the regulatory action level requires that the insurer submit a comprehensive financial plan to the regulator containing proposals to correct the company's financial problems.[40]

Several benefits are provided by the RBC capitalization model and the Risk-Based Capital for Insurers Model Act. First, the system will provide consistency among the states regarding insurer capitalization requirements. Second, capitalization requirements will reflect an estimation of the actual risks to which an insurer is exposed rather than apply a fixed capitalization level regardless of the insurer's specific operations. Third, not only does the system develop a capitalization requirement; it also establishes specific requirements of both regulators and insurers if required capitalization levels are not maintained.

# Accreditation of State Insurance Departments

Another response of the NAIC to the increasing frequency of insurer insolvency and the severe criticism by federal legislators of the effectiveness of state insurance regulation was to develop a formal certification program for state insurance departments. Preceded by the NAIC's Financial Regulation Standards in June 1989, the NAIC's accreditation program subsumed those standards and was adopted in June 1990. As of December 1994, forty-four states were accredited.

## Objectives of the Program

The purposes of the accreditation program are to (1) provide consistency of solvency regulation among the states and (2) improve the standards of solvency regulation and financial examinations conducted in all states. Individual state insurance departments meeting the NAIC standards are to be publicly acknowledged, and ". . .beginning in January 1994, accredited states will not accept reports of zone examinations from unaccredited states. . . ."[41] The NAIC has consistently encouraged uniformity in state insurance regulation through the model legislation it develops.

## Requirements for Accreditation

The Financial Regulation Standards require that a substantial list of legislative and administrative prerequisites be in place for an effective solvency regulatory program.[42] Those prerequisites establish a framework for state solvency regulation in three areas: (1) laws and regulations, (2) regulatory practices and procedures, and (3) organizational and personnel practices.[43]

### Laws and Regulations

Minimum standards for laws and regulations that should be in place for a state insurance department to be accredited are as follows:

1. Regulators should have the authority to examine insurers whenever regulators deem it necessary.
2. State law should specify a minimum capital and surplus requirement (RBC Model Act required beginning January 1, 1996).
3. All insurers reporting to the department should file the appropriate NAIC Annual Statement blank.
4. State law should contain the Model Regulation to Define Standards and Commissioner's Authority for Companies Deemed to be in a Hazardous Financial Condition.
5. Securities owned by insurance companies should be valued according to standards promulgated by NAIC's Securities Valuation Office.
6. State law should contain the Model Holding Company Systems Act or a similar act.
7. State law should specify that the maximum net amount of risk to be retained by a property-liability insurer for an individual risk be no larger than 10 percent of the insurer's capital and surplus.
8. State statute should require a diversified investment portfolio for all domestic insurers regarding both type and issue and should include a requirement for liquidity.
9. State statute should describe those assets that can be admitted, authorized, or allowed as assets in the statutory financial statement of insurers.
10. State statute should prescribe minimum standards for establishing liabilities and reserves of insurers (The Standard Valuation Law and Actuarial Opinion and Memorandum Regulation are required beginning January 1, 1996).
11. State law should contain the Model Law on Credit for Reinsurance, the Credit for Reinsurance Model Regulation. (This model law is required beginning January 1, 1996.)

12. State statute or regulation should contain a requirement for annual audits of domestic insurers by independent CPAs.
13. State statute or regulation should require an opinion on reserves and loss and loss adjustment expense reserves by a qualified actuary or specialist.
14. State law should establish a receivership scheme for the administration, by the insurance commissioner, of insurers found to be insolvent as specified in the Insurers Rehabilitation and Liquidation Model Act.
15. State law should provide for a statutory mechanism to ensure the payment of policyholder obligations when an insurer is deemed insolvent. (This is required as of January 1, 1996.)
16. State statute should contain a provision requiring participation in the NAIC's IRIS.
17. State law should contain a provision similar to the NAIC's Model Risk Retention Act for the regulation of risk retention and purchasing groups.
18. State statute should contain the Model Law for Business Transacted with Producer Controlled Property/Casualty Insurer Act or a similar provision.
19. State law should contain a provision similar to the Managing General Agents Act.
20. State law should contain a provision similar to the Reinsurance Intermediary Model Act.
21. State statute or regulation should mandate diskette filings for Annual and Quarterly Statements.
22. State law should contain the Disclosure of Material Transactions Model Act or an act substantially similar. (This is required beginning January 1, 1996.)[44]

## *Regulatory Practices and Procedures*

The regulatory practices and procedures requirements address issues regarding financial analysis, financial examinations, communication with states, and the reporting of regulatory actions.[45] Requirements specified for financial analysis stipulate minimum qualifications for the number and proficiency of financial analysts, the administration of internal financial analysis procedure, and the prioritization of analyses by a scheme similar to that used in the NAIC's IRIS system.

Financial examinations require adequate resources to be conducted effectively. The accreditation standards specify that insurance departments "...should have the resources necessary to examine all domestic companies on a periodic basis that is commensurate with the financial strengths and position of the insurer."[46] Additionally, examination staff should consist of competent specialists with training and/or experience, and financial examination procedures should follow those specified in the NAIC's *Examiners Handbook*.

When insurance departments report findings or address other communications to state regulators, they should follow those procedures specified in the NAIC's *Troubled Insurance Company Handbook*. Regulatory actions taken by the insurance department must be reported to the NAIC's Regulatory Information Retrieval System (RIRS), investigative information must be reported to the NAIC's Special Activities Database (SAD), and summary information on complaints must be reported to the NAIC's Complaints Database Systems (CDS). Participation in the NAIC databases will be required beginning January 1, 1996.[47]

### Organizational and Personnel Practices

Organizational and personnel practices requirements encourage professional development of insurance department staff through job-related college courses, professional programs, or other programs funded by the insurance department. All financial regulation and surveillance activities should be the responsibility of one individual who reports to the commissioner or to the commissioner's designee.

Insurance department staff members who are regularly involved with financial regulation and surveillance should be periodically reviewed to ensure that their performance is satisfactory and that their delegated responsibilities are being discharged with dispatch.[48] The insurance department should establish minimum educational and experience requirements, provide a competitive pay structure, and ensure that funding is available to assure that financial surveillance and regulation staff are able to attend periodic meetings and training sessions of the NAIC and any meetings related to review, coordination, and implementation of regulatory action for troubled insurers.

## Summary

Solvency regulation is possibly the most important regulatory activity performed by insurance regulators. That area of insurance regulation concentrates on performing periodic and frequent reviews of insurers' financial condition to identify those insurers at the brink of financial difficulty and, as troubled insurers are identified, on taking immediate action to correct the situation.

This chapter began by discussing risk and its effects on business in general and on insurers specifically. A major focus of solvency regulation is to monitor insurers' policyholders' surplus to ensure its adequacy and liquidity. Policyholders' surplus is generally the same to an insurer as net worth is to a noninsurance company. Policyholders' surplus, the excess of admitted assets over liabilities, provides financial capacity, which allows the insurer to grow and to expand underwriting and provides a financial buffer against risk and uncertainty.

The process of solvency regulation involves monitoring insurer performance by reviewing and analyzing the financial statements filed with state regulators and the NAIC. To ensure consistency in reporting and conservative surplus valuation, insurers must comply with statutory accounting requirements. Solvency regulation also includes periodically conducting on-site financial examinations that provide an in-depth review of an insurer's performance and validates its compliance with statutory accounting requirements. Recently added to the process of solvency regulation are the Risk-Based Capital (RBC) requirements, to ensure capital adequacy based on an insurer's actual exposure from its unique operation, and the accreditation of state regulators, to ensure that solvency regulation is conducted consistently and effectively among all states.

# Chapter Notes

1. Robert W. Klein, "Solvency Monitoring of Insurance Companies: Regulators' Role and Future Direction" in Edward I. Altman and Irwin T. Vanderhoof, eds., *The Financial Dynamics of the Insurance Industry* (New York: Irwin, 1995), p. 54.
2. Stanley B. Block and Geoffrey A. Hirt, *Foundations of Financial Management*, 6th ed. (Homewood, IL: Irwin, 1992), p. 494.
3. Block and Hirt, p. 265.
4. Block and Hirt, p. 265.
5. William D. Ward, "NAIC Statement Reporting," chapter in *Property-Casualty Insurance Accounting*, 6th ed. (Durham, NC: Insurance Accounting and Systems Association, Inc., 1994), p. 2-13.
6. National Association of Insurance Commissioners, *Using the NAIC Insurance Regulatory Information System* (Kansas City, MO: NAIC, 1993), p. 1.
7. Klein, p. 65.
8. Klein, p. 81.
9. NAIC, *Using the NAIC Regulatory Information System*, p. 2
10. NAIC, *Using the NAIC Regulatory Information System*, p. 2
11. National Association of Insurance Commissioners, "Financial Analysis and Solvency Surveillance," a supplementary publication to *Services to NAIC Members* (Kansas City, MO: NAIC, 1994), p. 1.

12. Elizabeth Malone and Jim Rose, "NAIC: Regulatory Systems Perspectives, Solvency Surveillance Tools" (presentation at the A.M. Best Users' Conference, September 1, 1992).
13. NAIC, *Using the NAIC Insurance Regulatory Information System*, p. 3.
14. Klein, p. 67.
15. Klein, p. 80.
16. Klein, p. 80.
17. Klein, p. 77.
18. NAIC, *Using the NAIC Insurance Regulatory Information System*, p. 2.
19. National Association of Insurance Commissioners, *Financial Condition Examiners Handbook* (Kansas City, MO: NAIC, 1994), p. 1-1.
20. NAIC, *Financial Condition Examiners Handbook*, p. 1-2.
21. Klein, p. 85.
22. Klein, p. 85.
23. National Association of Insurance Commissioners, *Troubled Insurance Company Handbook* (Kansas City, MO: NAIC, June 1989), pp. 2-7 to 2-8.
24. NAIC, *Troubled Insurance Company Handbook*, p. 1-2.
25. NAIC, *Financial Condition Examiners Handbook*, p. 1-2.
26. NAIC, *Financial Condition Examiners Handbook*, p. 1-4.
27. Klein, p. 86.
28. NAIC, *Financial Condition Examiners Handbook*, p. 1-5.
29. Klein, p. 86.
30. Klein, p. 85.
31. NAIC, *Financial Condition Examiners Handbook*, p. 1-7.
32. NAIC, *Financial Condition Examiners Handbook*, p. 1-8.
33. NAIC, *Financial Condition Examiners Handbook*, p. 1-8.
34. *Illinois Insurance Code* § 13 [§ 625], p. 15; and *Pennsylvania Insurance Laws* §40-5-106, p. 55 (Chatsworth, CA: NILS Publishing Company, 1989). Purdon's Statutes Thus: 40 P.S. §382.
35. NAIC, *Risk-Based Capital Requirements for Insurers: A New Solvency Tool for Consumer Protection*, (Kansas City, MO: NAIC, 1994), p. 5.
36. Douglas A. Hartz and David John Masini, "Financial Strength," *Property-Casualty Insurance Accounting* (Durham, NC: IASA, 1994), pp. 16-17.
37. NAIC, *Risk-Based Capital Requirements for Insurers: A New Solvency Tool for Consumer Protection*, (Kansas City, MO: NAIC, 1994), p. 6.
38. NAIC, *Risk-Based Capital Requirements for Insurers: A New Solvency Tool for Consumer Protection*, p. 2.
39. NAIC, *Risk-Based Capital Requirements for Insurers: A New Solvency Tool for Consumer Protection*, p. 9.
40. NAIC, *Risk-Based Capital Requirements for Insurers: A New Solvency Tool for Consumer Protection*, p. 9.

41. NAIC, *Financial Regulations Standards and Accreditation Program*, p. 1.
42. Klein, p. 68.
43. Klein, p. 68.
44. NAIC, *Financial Regulations Standards and Accreditation Program*, pp. 6-10.
45. NAIC, *Financial Regulations Standards and Accreditation Program*, pp. 11-13.
46. NAIC, *Financial Regulations Standards and Accreditation Program*, p. 11.
47. NAIC, *Financial Regulations Standards and Accreditation Program*, p. 13.
48. NAIC, *Financial Regulations Standards and Accreditation Program*, p. 14.

# Chapter 7

# Regulation of Agents and Brokers

Agents and brokers are a principal contact for most consumers who have insurance questions. Consumers frequently place a high level of trust in their agents and brokers. The duties and responsibilities of agents and brokers are regulated because consumers rely upon the expertise of these insurance professionals.

The laws affecting agents and brokers are promulgated at the state level and vary from state to state. One state will stringently regulate every aspect of the agents' or brokers' duties, while another state's regulations will seem lax in comparison. Proposals have been made to regulate the licensing of agents and brokers federally, but no law has taken effect as of the end of 1994.

The judicial system also plays an important part in determining the duties of agents and brokers. Often, court decisions are made that (1) reaffirm regulations established by the state insurance departments and (2) create new obligations for agents and brokers.

This chapter includes definitions and descriptions of insurance agents and brokers; regulatory information affecting agents' and brokers' duties and obligations to consumers, insurance companies, and other groups; licensing requirements and continuing education laws; the Unfair Trade Practices Laws; and agents' and brokers' fiduciary responsibilities. Reference to specific property and liability state statutes and regulations is included for illustrative purposes.

# Agents and Brokers

The terms agent and broker are often used interchangeably. However, as discussed below, depending on the state, the terms can mean different things.

## Agent

The National Association of Insurance Commissioners (NAIC) offers a generic definition of an agent in its Agents and Brokers Licensing Model Act. The definition describes an **insurance agent** as the following:

> . . .an individual, partnership, or corporation appointed by an insurer to solicit applications for a policy of insurance or to negotiate a policy of insurance on its behalf.[1]

In other words, an insurance *agent* is one who represents an insurance company in the sale of insurance to consumers. Agents can sell auto, property, liability, umbrella, inland marine, and other lines of insurance. An agent has a duty to (1) sell only the lines of insurance in which he or she is knowledgeable and (2) fully advise the consumer of the coverages being purchased.

An agent is empowered by an insurance company by contract to act on behalf of the company in many transactions with the policyholder. Contracts between agents and companies are addressed in upcoming paragraphs.

Many agents operate as independent agents. The **independent agent** operates an independent business and is able to place accounts with several insurers through contractual agreements. The independent agent owns his or her book of business, that is, all of the client accounts. If an insurer cancels its contract with an agent, the agent has the right to move his or her accounts to another insurer.

An **exclusive agent** contractually works for one insurer and places business primarily through that insurer and any of its affiliates. This agent usually obtains business for the insurer with the insurer owning the book of business. An exclusive agent might also be called a *direct writing agent* or *captive agent*, although direct writing agent is sometimes used to refer to sales people who are employees of an insurance company.

An insurance agent is authorized by law to conduct certain transactions with the policyholder. An agent, for example, can describe and recommend insurance that a consumer needs or wants. In addition, the agent can collect premiums, explain the purchased coverage, update coverage information, and talk to the consumer about coverage issues. All of these transactions are based on trust, with the consumer assuming that the agent or broker knows what he or she is selling. An agent also has a fiduciary responsibility to the insurer and consumer that will be described further in this chapter. It is the transaction of providing insurance to consumers that subjects the agent to so much regulation.

## Broker

The NAIC offers a generic definition of a broker in its Agents and Brokers Licensing Model Act. The definition describes an **insurance broker** as follows:

> . . .any individual, partnership or corporation who, for compensation, not being a licensed agent for the company in which a policy of insurance is placed, acts or aids in any manner in negotiating contracts for insurance or placing risks or effecting insurance for a party other than himself or itself.[2]

In other words, an insurance *broker* is one who directly represents a policyholder in obtaining coverage from an insurance company. A broker does not typically enter into contracts with insurance companies. Brokers place some business with standard, state-licensed insurers, but they often place insurance through less standard markets, such as with surplus or nonadmitted insurers.

The term "broker" is not used in every state to describe someone who actually conducts business as a broker. This can become confusing when someone wants to obtain a brokers license for more than one state at the same time.

For example, Florida requires agents and **customer service representatives (CSRs)** to be licensed. The definition of a CSR includes one who greets and services customers, answers insurance coverage questions, and communicates with other insurance professionals. In many agencies, the job description of a CSR includes selling insurance. Florida's description of agents' and CSRs' duties includes brokers' duties. Thus, in Florida, brokers need a license to transact business.

Rhode Island changed its law in 1994 to license various individuals who fall into the category of **producer**. A producer is described in the Rhode Island licensing handbook as a person who does the following:

- Solicits, negotiates, effects, procures, delivers, renews, continues, or binds insurance policies in Rhode Island
- Offers insurance advice, counsel, opinion or service in Rhode Island[3]

Thus, a broker would fall somewhere into the description of a producer in Rhode Island to satisfy the legal requirements of the state.

Several courts have made the determination that brokers are viewed as representing the policyholder. Following are two of these cases:

1. Rich Maid Kitchens, Inc. v. Pennsylvania Lumbermens Mut. Ins. Co., in which the insured relied on the broker to obtain his insurance from whichever insurance company the broker thought best; therefore the broker was held to be the agent of the insured.[4]
2. Owens v. Aetna Life & Casualty Co., in which it was determined that "[a] broker acts for the insured for the purpose of making the application and procuring an insurance policy."[5]

However, while the broker is collecting insurance premiums or delivering the policy, courts have determined that he or she is acting on behalf of the insurer. Two such cases are Fredman v. Consolidated Fire & Marine Ins. Co.,[6] and Marsh & McLellan, Inc. v. City of Los Angeles.[7]

Several courts have recognized that a broker acts in a dual capacity as an agent for the insured and insurer, but at different times. In Diplomat Homes, Inc. v. Commercial Standard Insurance Co., the court stated:

> We are aware that the general rule in regard to agents is that the same person can not act as agent for both the company and insured. However, this rule is subject to some exceptions. . . . [The broker] may be the agent for insured, although as to the procuring of the insurance he also represents the company. Whether in a particular case or particular matter one acts as agent for the company or for [the] insured depends upon the intention of the parties. . . .[8]

In Teleco Oilfield Services, Inc. v. Skandia, the court states:

> At first the broker is the agent of the insured, and then the agent of the insurer. Connecticut has codified this common law rule that, after the issuance of the policy, a broker acts as the insurer's agent in collecting premiums. . . . Similarly, in the instant case, M & M Hartford and M & M Scandinavia (the broker) worked to obtain the policy for the plaintiff (the insured), but M & M Scandinavia also collected the premiums for the defendants (the insurer).[9]

## Employees Within an Agency

An agency may consist of just one person, or it can employ hundreds of people. People who work for an agency might have responsibilities for answering the telephone, inputting computer data, answering insurance questions, selling insurance, or managing various departments. Employees of one agency might possess different job titles from those of another yet perform similar duties for their agency.

For example, an agency salesperson can be called a *salesperson*, *solicitor*, or *producer*. Other titles for the sales position also exist and sometimes are left up to the imagination of the agency owner. Regardless of their title, though, **agency salespersons** are responsible for contacting prospective clients, analyzing the client's insurance needs, providing quotes and insurance information, making recommendations on coverage, and following up with service in a variety of forms. In addition, agency salespersons are usually the persons who collect the insurance premiums and deliver the policies to the clients. Therefore, *people who sell insurance are the predominant targets of licensing laws in most states.*

CSRs, defined earlier, often have different job responsibilities that depend on the agency with which they are employed. Some CSRs are responsible for completing basic paperwork and answering simple questions for policyholders. Other CSRs are expected to have substantial technical insurance knowledge, and they can sell insurance as well as provide specialized services to clients. In the latter instance, the CSRs in many states would be required to be licensed.

Some state regulations indicate that it is acceptable for an unlicensed CSR to sell insurance if a licensed agent is on the premises. In this case, should the licensed individual leave the agency premises, the CSR should not sell insurance until the licensed individual returns. If the CSR makes a sale while the licensed person is away, the CSR could be fined for impersonation. **Impersonation** means that the CSR is holding himself or herself out as a licensed agent. Impersonating an agent is a violation of insurance statutes.

Other state laws, such as Rhode Island's, require any individual, regardless of his or her title, to obtain a license if he or she is to sell insurance. Under the heading "Who Needs A License" in the Rhode Island Insurance Licensing Examination Candidate Handbook, is the following material:

> Anyone who does any of the things that a producer does, including full-time fraternal benefit society representatives; Anyone who says that he or she is a producer or does or says things that would cause a member of the public to think that he or she is a producer. . . .[10]

Certain state laws require that individual retirees maintain their licenses if they continue to receive insurance commissions. These retirees might no longer sell insurance, but they are still required to maintain their license and comply with applicable regulations, such as taking approved continuing education courses. The State of Maine, for example, observes this practice.

Other employees within an agency can include insurance brokers. Additionally, agents might act as brokers in some transactions. Brokerage firms can be set up similarly to the way agencies are. Employees and job descriptions in brokerage firms vary as they do within agencies.

# Agent and Broker Licensing

Agents and brokers must certify their knowledge of their products before they are eligible to sell them in a particular state. The process whereby states verify agents and brokers professional expertise is licensing.

## Purpose of Licensing Requirements

Agents, brokers, solicitors, producers, customer service representatives and similar insurance persons are required to be licensed because of the nature of their business. Individually or as an entire agency, they possess a tremendous amount of responsibility toward the public, and, as a result, their conduct is regulated.

Agents or brokers can be licensed in many different lines of insurance. Some agents and brokers obtain licenses for several lines of insurance, while others might hold a license for only one line, such as workers compensation. Examples of lines of insurance that are subject to licensing requirements are fire and allied lines, comprehensive personal and general liability coverage, burglary and theft insurance, homeowners and farmowners insurance, and workers compensation. In some states, such as Florida and Massachusetts, licenses are issued in a few broad categories such as life, accident and health, and property and casualty.

Some states license a partnership or corporation as an insurance agent or broker. The following is the NAIC description of this requirement as listed in the Licensing Model Act:

> A partnership or corporation may be licensed as an insurance agent, insurance broker, surplus lines insurance broker or limited insurance representative. Every member of the partnership and every officer, director, stockholder and employee of the corporation personally engaged in this state in soliciting or negotiating policies of insurance shall be registered with the Commissioner as to its license, and each such member, officer, director, stockholder or employee shall also qualify as an individual licensee. An additional license fee shall be paid as to each individual registered as to the organization's license; provided, however, that this section shall not apply to a management association, partnership, or corporation, whose operations do not entail the solicitation of insurance from the public.[11]

## Administration of Licensing Requirements

Individual state statutes indicate how licensing of an agent or broker will take place. Presently, this is done through each state's department of insurance.

Much of the regulation and administration of the requirements is addressed by the NAIC in the Licensing Model Act. Some functions, such as prelicensing registration and examination procedures, can be administered by local or national testing services that work closely with each state's department of insurance.

Most states have an agents and brokers licensing department within the insurance department. This department is responsible for answering questions from applicants across the country and processing vast amounts of paperwork related to the licensing requirements. Department employees will accept and review the applications, process the payments, review the information to confirm that the applicant qualifies for licensure as dictated by the state statute, and so on.

The departments of insurance in all states have some form of investigative unit that follows up on complaints surrounding violations of the law committed by agents or brokers. In its administrative function, an insurance department can investigate, review, and make a determination on each case as to whether an insurance statute was violated and what further action should be taken.

## Application Procedures

All states have licensing procedures that usually indicate that applications must be on a form approved by the state Commissioner. Most applications are included in some type of licensing bulletin issued by each state. Often, these bulletins will be printed by outside organizations responsible for administering the licensing examinations, but the language contained in the bulletin is written by an insurance department member and subject to the department's approval. Applicants must file applications whether they are residents or nonresidents of a state.

An initial application might be required if the applicant completes general information to initiate the filing process. Another application might be completed at the time the applicant can demonstrate that he or she has successfully passed the appropriate state examination.

Typical information contained on an application includes the name, address, and age of the applicant. A photograph of the applicant is requested in certain states. Some description of the applicant's insurance experience and insurance education may be contained within an application. In addition, the applicant needs to send a check for the license fee and a certificate of completion indicating that an appropriate prelicensing program was completed in accordance with the law.

Each state's statute indicates who is eligible to become an agent or broker. Most states require the individual who is seeking either a resident or nonresident license to be at least eighteen years of age as suggested by the NAIC model act.

The applicant is usually asked to provide information relating to any prior convictions or pleadings to any misdemeanor or felony. Many states, including Texas, require that nonresident licenses include a Certificate of Good Standing issued by the state in which the nonresident resides and practices.[12]

Under Part I in Rhode Island's Producer License Application, shown in Exhibit 7-1, the applicant can check *individual* or *firm* for the license type desired. The lines of authority provide a choice of three categories: property and casualty, life and health, and limited travel.

Part III of Rhode Island's application requires information on the applicant's background, including whether other licenses are held or whether the applicant has violated insurance regulations of other states. In addition, Section H requires completion if the applicant intends to broker business. The description of brokering states, "You are brokering business if you place business through a company with which you do not have an agent's contract or by which you are not employed. . . ."[13]

Once the application is received and reviewed by a state's insurance department, the next step will take place. In many states, the next step is to issue the license. However, in Texas, only a temporary license will be issued. In some instances, the insurance department will deny the applicant a license. This occurs if the applicant has committed certain violations of the law described later in this chapter.

## License Fees

License fees vary from state to state. Certain required fees consist of an initial licensing fee for either residents or nonresidents, an exam fee, an appointment fee, an annual renewal fee, and an annual renewal of appointment fee for agents. In almost all cases, the revenue from fees exceeds the costs of licensing and supervising agents and brokers. The excess represents income to the state's general fund.

The following two state examples illustrate specific requirements. As of the summer of 1994, Rhode Island's applicant fees were $50 plus a $5 continuing education fee due at the time of the application and paid annually thereafter.[14] License fees in Texas include a $50 fee to become licensed as a local recording agent (LRA), a $20 fee to be a solicitor for an LRA, and a $30 fee to become licensed as a managing general agent (MGA).[15]

**Exhibit 7-1**
Rhode Island's Producer License Application

**STATE OF RHODE ISLAND AND PROVIDENCE PLANTATIONS**
DEPARTMENT OF BUSINESS REGULATION
INSURANCE DIVISION
**RI-001**—*Oct-93*–SUBMIT AFTER PASSING EXAM, IF REQUIRED.

233 RICHMOND STREET
SUITE 233
PROVIDENCE, RI 02903-4233
(401) 277-2223

**PRODUCER LICENSE APPLICATION**
INDIVIDUALS AND FIRMS

**PART I. LICENSE INFORMATION** ☐ NEW ☐ REINSTATEMENT ☐ AMENDMENT

A. LICENSE TYPE (check one):
☐ INDIVIDUAL ☐ FIRM

B. RESIDENT STATUS (check one):
☐ RESIDENT ☐ NONRESIDENT

C. LINES OF AUTHORITY (check all lines for which you are applying):
☐ PROPERTY & CASUALTY ☐ LIFE & HEALTH ☐ LIMITED TRAVEL

**PART II. IDENTIFICATION**

A. Social Security or Federal ID Number______________ B. Date of Birth: ______________
(INDIVIDUALS ONLY) MONTH DAY YEAR

C. Full Legal Name of Individual or Firm ________________________________
(FOR INDIVIDUALS) LAST NAME FIRST NAME MI JR., SR.

D. Residence Address ________________________________
STREET CITY STATE ZIP

Business Address ________________________________
STREET CITY STATE ZIP

E. Home Phone (____)_____ – _________ Business Phone (____)_____ – _________

F. Are you a citizen of the United States? ☐ YES ☐ NO *If NO, attach a copy of visa.*

**PART III. BACKGROUND INFORMATION**

A. Do you hold or have you ever held an insurance license in another state?

☐ YES ☐ NO *If YES, and the license is still in force, attach a certification letter (no more than 90 days old) from your home state. If the license is not in force, attach a letter of clearance (no more than 90 days old) from the last state where you held a resident license.*

B. Has any disciplinary action, including but not limited to refusal, suspension or revocation of a license or certificate, ever been commenced against you or any business with which you have been directly connected by any regulatory agency in any state?

☐ YES ☐ NO *If YES, provide full explanation on a separate sheet of paper.*

C. Have you ever been convicted of or pled *nolo contendere* (no contest) to any misdemeanor or felony or currently have pending misdemeanor or felony charges against you? (Misdemeanor does not include traffic violations.)

☐ YES ☐ NO *If YES, give date, name and address of court, basis of charge, outcome and whether you received an executive pardon. Also, attach certified copies of the information or indictment and the final adjudication.*

D. Are you an officer, director or employee of a lending institution (bank, savings and loan or other such institution which accepts deposits and lends money) or of a bank holding company or an affiliate of one of the above?

☐ YES ☐ NO *If YES, give name and address of institution.*

***Please turn this sheet over and answer the remaining questions.***
***BE SURE TO SIGN THE CERTIFICATION.–IF YOU ARE A NON-RESIDENT, SIGN THE APPOINTMENT.***

*Continued on next page*

E. If address has changed in the last 12 months, list former residence address(es) for past year.

________________________________________________________

F. Applicants who are required to take pre-licensing education and/or pass an examination must attach a Certificate of Completion for pre-licensing education and/or an exam grade report. Which of the following is attached?

☐ CERTIFICATE OF COMPLETION ☐ GRADE REPORT

G. INDIVIDUALS ONLY: If you transact business under a trade name(s) [d/b/a], state the trade name(s).

________________________________________________________

H. Do you intend to broker business? [You are brokering business if you place business through a company with which you do not have an agent's contract or by which you are not employed, except that placing business through the following will not be considered to be brokering: the Fair Access to Insurance Requirements Plan, the Automobile Assigned Risk Plan, the Beacon Mutual Insurance Company, the Rhode Island Medical Malpractice Joint Underwriting Association, and the National Flood Insurance Plan or a surplus lines broker licensed in RI.]

☐ YES ☐ NO

TOTAL PREMIUMS: $ ________

*If YES, state total premiums that you brokered in the past calendar year. Enclose with this application a bond equal to 5% of total premiums, but not less than $2,500 nor more than $25,000. [§27-2.3-21]*

☐ Bond is enclosed.

I. FIRMS ONLY: 1. State name and title of the licensed officer within your firm responsible for compliance with insurance laws [§27-2.3-5(b)(4)]

________________________________________________________

NAME TITLE

2. Attach a list stating **<u>all</u> officers', directors' or partners'** names and social security numbers and stating, for each, "licensed" or "not licensed".

**PART IV. APPLICANT'S CERTIFICATION**

I, the undersigned, declare under penalty of refusal, suspension or revocation of the license that the statements made in this application are true, correct and complete to the best of my knowledge and belief.

________________________________________

SIGNATURE OF APPLICANT

(Firm applications must be signed by the person named in Part III, F.)

Signed and sworn to before me this ______ day of ____________ 19___

My commission expires ____________________ . ________________________

MONTH DAY YEAR NOTARY

**PART V. APPOINTMENT OF DIRECTOR—non-residents only**

In consideration of the issue to me of a license to act as an insurance producer in the State of Rhode Island, I stipulate and agree that in any action or special proceeding brought against me in the State of Rhode Island for or on account of any act or transaction done or performed by me in connection with such license, any document or process may be served on the Director of Business Regulation with the same legal effect and force as though served upon me personally, and such service will give jurisdiction to the same extent as if I were a resident of Rhode Island.

________________________________________

SIGNATURE OF NON-RESIDENT APPLICANT

(Firm applications must be signed by the person named in Part III, F.)

**PART VI. FEES** NEW: $50.00 license fee + $5.00 continuing education fee = **$55.00 TOTAL FEE**

REINSTATEMENT: **$105.00 TOTAL FEE** AMENDMENT: **$50.00 TOTAL FEE**

Make checks payable to: General Treasurer, State of Rhode Island. **NO REFUNDS** if you overpay.

**Veterans <u>are not exempt</u> from license fee.**

Did you sign the ✓ CERTIFICATION and (if a non-resident) ✓ APPOINTMENT, include a ✓ CHECK for the fee, attach all ✓ DOCUMENTATION and ✓ EXPLANATIONS requested, and include your ✓ BOND, if you plan to broker?

## Prelicensing Programs

Many states' statutes indicate which programs are eligible for approval as prelicensing training sessions. Some states have detailed statutes describing exactly what needs to be included in the training programs. Other states simply provide basic standards that any education provider has to follow when developing a training program. That program can then be expanded beyond those standards in any manner that is deemed appropriate.

For example, one state might publish a prerequisite for what is to be included in the approved training materials such as an explanation of the basic homeowners forms and definitions of certain specific perils. The author has to include this information in order to have the program approved, but the author can add information in the text about unusual perils and additional categories of property coverage that is not required by state law.

Prelicensing education outlines are often included in each state's information bulletins sent to license applicants. The outlines indicate what information is likely to appear on the exam and, therefore, what should be studied. The approved educational materials for each state should contain at least this information. For example, the Massachusetts Insurance Licensing Examination Candidate Workbook indicates subjects to be studied under a Property Content Outline and a Casualty Content Outline. One section of the Property Outline is located in Exhibit 7-2. A portion of the Massachusetts Casualty Outline section is located in Exhibit 7-3.

In addition to attending a mandatory prelicensing seminar, most state statutes indicate that the license applicant must obtain a certificate of completion of the approved course. Usually, this certificate is required to be handed over to a designated individual at the time the exam is taken. In other states, the certificate will need to be submitted with the completed application for the license.

Several state regulations describe circumstances under which a prelicensing program does not need to be taken. This is usually based on the applicant's existing knowledge of insurance. Pennsylvania, for example, does not require completion of a prelicensing program before an examination. (See the section on prelicensing exemptions and exceptions, which appears later in this chapter.)

Whether prelicensing programs are designed for a classroom or for self-study, they will occasionally be reviewed and audited. Typically, the auditing process is conducted by designated employees of a state's insurance department to confirm that adequate and accurate information is provided in each program. The state law section is the most important portion of a program that the insurance departments review. Because laws change often and vary by state, the books must be properly updated so that the applicants study current information that is likely to appear on the state exam. For example, the mandatory auto liability limits are increased every so often in many states, so the workbooks should reflect the correct limits.

**Exhibit 7-2**
Excerpt From the Massachusetts Insurance Licensing Examination Candidate Workbook Property Outline

I. Types of policies (22 questions)
   A. Personal lines
      1. Dwelling and contents
      2. Personal liability
      3. Homeowners
   B. Commercial lines
      1. Commercial property
         a. Commercial building and personal property form
         b. Causes of loss forms
         c. Business income coverage form
         d. Extra expense coverage form
      2. Business owners
      3. Boiler and machinery
   C. Inland Marine
      1. Personal floaters
      2. Commercial floaters
   D. Others
      1. Flood
      2. Watercraft
         a. Homeowners
         b. Boatowners
         c. Yacht

## Prelicensing Vendors

Vendors who provide insurance education programs come in all shapes and sizes. A vendor is one who offers a service to those who want or require it. Because insurance education is mandated by most states, vendors who offer insurance training programs are in abundance throughout the country. One individual might write and sponsor seminars, a small group might jointly offer seminars or materials to licensees, large agents' associations provide services through their education departments, and colleges offer insurance education training.

**Exhibit 7-3**
Excerpt From the Massachusetts Insurance Licensing Examination Candidate Workbook Casualty Outline

II. Insurance terms and related concepts (16 questions)
  A. Risk
  B. Hazard
  C. Indemnity
  D. Insurable interest
  E. Actual cash value
  F. Negligence
  G. Liability
  H. Accident
  I. Occurrence
  J. Burglary
  K. Robbery
  L. Theft
  M. Mysterious disappearance
  N. Binders
  O. Warranties
  P. Representations
  Q. Concealment
  R. Bodily injury liability
  S. Property damage liability
  T. Personal injury liability
  U. Limits of liability
  V. Deductibles
  W. Insured contract

*State of Massachusetts Insurance Licensing Examination Candidate Handbook*, March 1992.

Most education vendors develop their own prelicensing training materials. They can have staff educators on hand to conduct the seminars, or they might hire outside specialists to assist in the training.

Generally, vendors have to be approved by a state before offering seminars in that state. For example, Texas must approve the vendor as well as the prelicensing material to be offered. Other vendors are not required to be approved as vendors, but their programs must be individually approved. For example, in Massachusetts, the Insurance Library is a vendor that offers insurance education to its members and nonmembers. The Massachusetts Division of Insurance approves the seminars that the Insurance Library offers, such as Property and Casualty Pre-Licensing. Ohio's laws indicate that the individual instructor for prelicensing programs must be approved by the state department.

Self-study programs for prelicensing examinations often are provided by the same vendors who conduct seminars. Some vendors, such as Rough Notes, use the same workbooks for either method of study. Other vendors, such as Pictorial, offer a prelicensing workbook for self-study, which differs from the book used in seminars.

## Licensing Examinations

The NAIC Agents and Brokers Licensing Model Act provides certain criteria for examinations. Among the criteria are the following:

> (a) After completion and filing of the application with the Commissioner, except as provided in Section 6 of this Chapter, the Commissioner shall subject each applicant for license as an insurance agent, insurance broker, surplus lines insurance broker, consultant or limited insurance representative to a written examination as to his competence to act as such licensee which he must personally take and pass to the satisfaction of the Commissioner.
>
> . . .
>
> (d) All the lines of insurance which the applicant proposes to transact under the license applied for shall have a separate examination.
>
> . . .
>
> (f) The Commissioner shall give, conduct and grade all examinations in a fair and impartial manner and without discrimination as between individuals examined.[16]

Examinations are held at approved sites in the state in which the individual wishes to obtain a license. Some states offer exam locations both within and outside the state to provide applicants with easier access to exam facilities. Examinations are offered frequently in most states; some states even provide the opportunity for daily exams.

The exam questions and content are broken down differently in each state, but the test usually consists of one or more sections surrounding coverage issues and one or more sections addressing the state laws applicable to insurance. For example, the coverage area might include questions about the coinsurance formula, the definition of burglary, and the loss settlement clause. The law section might ask questions about the minimum liability limits required under automobile policies, the state approved average weekly wage for workers compensation payments, and the duties of the commissioner. The questions are tied to the particular field of insurance for which the examinee is sitting and are specific to that state's laws.

Some states approve a national service company to author and grade the examinations, but the state reviews the material for approval before it is used on any test. The review usually is performed first by practitioners within the state and then by members of the insurance department. After the exam is graded, a notice is sent to the applicant advising whether or not he or she has passed the exam. If the applicant did not pass all of the exam, he or she will have to (1) retake the exam in its entirety or (2) take the test again in just the failed areas, as the state law requires. If the entire exam was passed, then the applicant can attach the form to his or her application as required by the state(s) in which he or she is seeking a license. Some states license the individual on the spot.

## *Prelicensing Exemptions and Exceptions*

Certain individuals are considered to be exempt from having to take prelicensing education programs as dictated by state regulations. For example, in Texas, individuals who have achieved the Chartered Property Casualty Underwriter (CPCU) or the Certified Insurance Counselor (CIC) designation are exempt from taking mandatory education programs. In addition, persons who have received a bachelor's degree with a major in insurance from a four-year college or university or who have held a Licensed Recording Agent's (LRA) license since October 1, 1971, are not required to fulfill the education requirements. In its Agents and Brokers Licensing Model Act, the NAIC describes similar exceptions.

Certain individuals will be considered exempt from having to take the written licensing examination. These people include any applicant for a license in the same line in which he or she was licensed within the state at some time during the preceding twelve months. For example, Texas has several exemptions from testing depending on the license that the applicant wishes to obtain. To obtain an LRA license, the applicant will be exempt from testing if he or she was previously licensed as an LRA. But, if the person qualifies for this exemption, he or she must complete the Texas application jointly with his or her sponsoring insurance company. Similar exemptions apply to an applicant for the license of solicitor for an LRA.

Some states will exempt nonresidents who have passed licensing exams in their own states from taking the technical insurance portion of the licensing exam, but the applicant in the new state would have to sit for the state law portion of the exam because each state's laws and regulations are unique. Other states may only apply this procedure to persons who have moved and who now reside in the state in which they wish to obtain a license. Many variations in licensing examination practices apply, which is why licensing candidates must check the current law of each state in which they wish to obtain a license.

The NAIC also suggests in their Agents and Brokers Licensing Model Act that those who have attained the CPCU designation be only required to take the portion of the exam that pertains to rules, regulations, and state laws. Many states have adopted this NAIC requirement, and some states have waived even that part of the exam for CPCU designees.

## Continuing Education

After an applicant has (1) successfully passed the examination and been approved and duly licensed or (2) been licensed with a waiver of the examination, he or she might be subject to continuing education requirements to maintain his or her license. Forty-two states[17] and Puerto Rico require continuing education for all licensed agents and brokers. Many states' continuing education laws specifically address producers rather than use the title agent or broker. New York passed a law requiring continuing education to be effective in 1994 but was still defining the requirements as of the end of 1994. Alaska; Washington, D.C.; and Pennsylvania are also in the process of developing continuing education laws at the time of this writing.

The purpose for mandating continuing education is to keep agents and brokers informed on important insurance updates and coverage changes. These updates and changes affect consumers, and consumers rely on the agents' or brokers' expertise in order to make decisions about their insurance purchase. If agents and brokers were not subject to continuing education, they might become complacent with their knowledge and discover too late that what they know has become outdated. As a result, consumers would not be properly advised about insurance issues.

### Continuing Education Programs

In the NAIC Model Regulation Service—Agents Continuing Education Regulation, certain courses are suggested as meeting the Commissioner's standard for continuing educational requirements. Also listed are a certain number of classroom hours for which they are equivalent. A partial list of courses follows:

. . .

(3) Any part of the Insurance Institute of America's program in general insurance - 25 hours.

(4) Any part of the American Institute for Property and Liability Underwriter's Chartered Property Casualty Underwriter (CPCU) professional designation program - 30 hours.

(5) Any part of the Certified Insurance Counselor program - 25 hours.

(6) Any insurance-related course approved by the Commissioner taught by an accredited college or university per credit hour granted - 15 hours.

(7) Any course. . .developed and/or sponsored by any authorized insurer, recognized agents' association or insurance trade association or any independent program of instruction, shall, subject to the approval of the Commissioner, qualify for the equivalency of the number of classroom hours assigned thereto by the Commissioner.

(8) Any correspondence course approved by the Commissioner. . . .[18]

Most state continuing education laws list the types of programs that are eligible for credits in a format similar to the NAIC Model Act's language. Typically, programs that offer *product* material are approved. Programs that include subjects such as automobile coverage, commercial property coverage, and workers compensation coverage are considered as offering product material and are therefore approved for credits. The focus on product is to deliver to insurance practitioners technical information that is essential for maintaining a level of expertise that will continue to benefit consumers. For obvious reasons, the subject of ethics is required, or at least approved, in some states for continuing education credits for agents and brokers. For example, California requires ethics training for prelicensing; Oklahoma and Texas require ethics training for continuing education; and Maine, Massachusetts, and New Hampshire approve ethics programs for continuing education credits.

By statute, programs usually ineligible for continuing education credits include marketing, sales, management, and similar courses. Although these courses will benefit agents and brokers in their daily operations, and can indirectly assist the consumer, they are not generally considered product material.

In complying with the NAIC Model Act, most states require a specified number of hours worth of education to be completed each licensing period. The laws often do not stipulate how those hours are to be spent, such as reading, teaching, self-studying, or studying in a classroom. However, a few laws state that a certain number of hours must be spent in the classroom and the rest of the hours may be completed through self-study programs.

Examples of the number of hours required under state laws and the compliance period include the following:

- Arkansas requires sixteen hours of continuing education biennially.
- Idaho requires forty hours biennially.
- Iowa requires ten hours annually.
- Nevada requires thirty hours every three years.
- West Virginia requires twenty-four hours biennially.

Several states, such as Massachusetts, permit excess hours to be accumulated during the licensing period. The excess hours can be carried over to the next licensing period. The NAIC suggests this procedure in its Model Act.

Unlike most other states, Texas's education requirements seem to fall between prelicensing and continuing education requirements. Prelicensing study does not have to be met *before* taking the exam. The requirements must be met *after* successfully passing the exam and after receiving a *temporary license* in the area in which the individual wishes to be licensed. During the next year, the licensee must take an eighty-hour course that must be held in a classroom. If the licensee complies with this requirement, he or she will receive a permanent license. After that point, the license holder must take thirty hours of approved education every two years. This education can be in the form of self-study or classroom attendance. If the licensee has multiple agent license types, he or she can mix and match the education. If the education requirements are not met by those who are subject to the law, their license(s) can be revoked.[19]

## Continuing Education Vendors

As mentioned in the section on prelicensing vendors and self-study programs, some states approve the vendors, others approve the programs, and still others approve the individual instructors. Each state's requirements applicable to vendor approval are generally the same for prelicensing and continuing education purposes.

Ohio has developed continuing education requirements under which each individual instructor of a course must be approved. The vendor who hires the individuals must approve the instructors, based on certain qualifications, such as having several years' experience in the subject that would be taught, or at least carrying certain approved insurance designations such as CPCU, CLU, and CIC. The vendor provides the information on an approved form to the state department of insurance. This means that if one course could be taught by five individuals, five separate reviews and approvals would have to be made by the vendor in Ohio.

### Continuing Education Exemptions and Exceptions

Some exceptions to the continuing education laws exist that usually take the form of *grandfathering*. In Massachusetts, for example, anyone who had a license before April 5, 1983, is grandfathered (exempt) from the continuing education law. These individuals do not have to attend seminars unless they obtain an additional license in another insurance line or fail to renew their license for a certain length of time. Texas has updated its statutes to allow grandfathering of individuals who have maintained twenty years of licensure and who provide a written request for exemption to the state insurance department. Other states also have grandfathering laws that differ from these examples; however, not every state permits grandfathering people from the law.

## License Renewal

Agent licenses typically must be renewed every two or three years as determined by the individual state's statute. For example, Florida agent and CSR licenses are renewable every two years, as are agent licenses in Kansas, Missouri, and New Hampshire. Delaware, Georgia, and Illinois agents renew their licenses every year. Nevada renews its licenses every three years. The licenses in Rhode Island are renewed every three years at the beginning of the quarter within which the licensee's birthday falls. Massachusetts renews its brokers licenses every thirty-six months.

In states requiring continuing education, the agent or other licensed individual usually completes a renewal form sent by the state department of insurance. The renewal form requires evidence of the individual's compliance with the continuing education statute. The state insurance department often wants a copy of state forms issued at the end of each training session or on satisfactory completion of an exam in a self-study program. The renewal form also requires the appropriate renewal fee(s) to be included as indicated by the statute(s).

## License Termination

The NAIC Model Regulation Act provides detailed information pertaining to the denial, nonrenewal, or termination of agent and broker licenses. Some causes under which the commissioner can suspend, revoke, or refuse to continue or renew a license include the following activities of a licensee:

(a) Any materially untrue statement in the license application;

(b) Any cause for which issuance of the license could have been refused had it then existed and been known to the Commissioner at the time of issuance;

(c) Violation of. . .any insurance laws. . .;

(d) Obtaining or attempting to obtain any such license through misrepresentation or fraud;

. . .

(h) . . .[G]uilty of any unfair trade practice or fraud defined in this Code;

. . .

(l) . . .[C]heating on an examination for an insurance license.[20]

Each state's regulations dictate when an agent's or broker's license can be suspended, revoked, or nonrenewed. Many states use language similar to that found in the NAIC Model Act.

Rhode Island's law permits the revocation of producers' licenses for a variety of reasons primarily aimed at more effectively protecting consumers. For example, the Rhode Island insurance department can revoke or suspend a license or impose a fine on a producer who has done any of the following:

- Been found to have violated the insurance laws of another state
- Had a license revoked in another state
- Misappropriated money in the course of conducting an insurance business
- Cheated on an insurance license examination
- Forged a name on an insurance application or accepted business from an unlicensed person
- [Had] a felony conviction
- [Violated] the Rhode Island unfair trade practice or fraud laws
- [Paid] directly or indirectly. . .any commission, service fee, brokerage or other valuable consideration to an unlicensed person for services that require a producer's license[21]

Violation of Rhode Island's licensing requirement is a misdemeanor. (A misdemeanor is typically considered to be a crime less serious than a felony.) The maximum misdemeanor penalty is a $1,000 fine and a year in prison.

Generally, if a licensed agent or broker is discovered to have violated certain laws, his or her license will be suspended or revoked. Massachusetts will impose a fine or further penalties affecting an agent's or broker's license if he or she has committed a misrepresentation, larceny, rebating, unfair and deceptive practices, or other illegal activities.

In the Florida case of Devor v. Dep't of Ins., the agent's license to sell insurance was revoked because of misconduct. The Florida Department of Insurance filed a ten-count administrative complaint against the insurance agent, alleging that he had directed his agency to sell accidental death and dismemberment policies to clients who thought they were only purchasing personal injury protection. Penalties were initially imposed as license revocation. However, if a $2,000 fine were paid, license suspension would be only for two years and remission of the revocation after two years if no further violations occurred. The Department of Insurance later increased the penalty to unconditional revocation of all licensing. The Florida District Court of Appeal agreed with the action taken by the Department of Insurance.[22]

In the Missouri case, Ballew v. Ainsworth, an insurance license applicant brought suit against the state director of insurance, challenging the director's refusal to issue him an insurance license. The director's refusal was based on the applicant's apparent lack of trustworthiness. The applicant had been involved in a number of burglaries while licensed as an agent and, accordingly, had lost his license. The director's decision was upheld by an administrative hearing commission and the court. The court made the following statement:

> [The applicant] practiced or aided or abetted in the practice of fraud, forgery, deception, collusion, or conspiracy in connection with [an] insurance transaction, which were statutory grounds for terminating his license.[23]

# Fiduciary Responsibilities

Agents and brokers have fiduciary responsibilities towards the insurance consumer and, especially in the case of agents, to the insurance company. **Fiduciary responsibility** exists when a person is entrusted with some power or property of another. With respect to insurance agents and brokers, the insurance contract and premiums serve as property of another, that of the consumer or the insurance company, depending upon the exact point in the transaction. Agents are in a position of trust with insurance companies since they act on the companies' behalf in accordance with their respective contracts.

The *Massachusetts Insurance Law Digest* describes fiduciary responsibilities as follows:

> An insurance agent or broker who acts in negotiating or renewing or continuing a policy of insurance or an annuity or pure endowment contract and who receives any money or substitute for money as a premium for a policy or contract from the insured or holder is deemed to hold the premium in trust for the company. If he fails to pay the same over to the company after written demand [is] made upon him, less his commission and any deductions to which by the written consent of the company he may be entitled, the failure is prima facie evidence that he has used or applied the premium for a purpose other than paying the same over to the company, and upon conviction he is guilty of larceny.[24]

Another example of fiduciary responsibility can be seen in the Florida court case Natelson v. Dep't of Ins. in which an insurance agent pled guilty to a charge of conspiracy to distribute marijuana. As a result, his license was revoked. The agent appealed the Department of Insurance's decision, and the court found that the agent demonstrated a lack of fitness and trustworthiness necessary to engage in the business of insurance. In denying the appeal, the court made a further statement:

> Insurance is a business greatly affected by the public trust, and the holder of an agent's license stands in a fiduciary relationship to both the client and the insurance company.[25]

## Agency-Company Relationship

Contractual language typically dictates what type of relationship the agency and company will experience. The agent is considered an agent of the company and is often called the eyes and ears of the company. As described earlier, there is a fiduciary relationship between the agent and company.

Agents and brokers often become members of insurance associations and groups to enhance their relationship with companies and the industry as a whole and to improve their knowledge of state regulatory changes. The larger associations have governmental and legal experts available to assist and advise members of the ever-changing insurance regulatory climate.

An insurance broker often does not enter into contracts with insurance companies. A broker is traditionally considered to be the representative of the policyholder. There are exceptions as described under the heading of Broker in this chapter. A broker will gather the same type of information on each customer as the agent does. However, in most cases if a dispute arises as a result of some insurance activity, an agent would be considered the agent of the insurance company; a broker would be considered the agent of the policyholder.

Overall, agents and insurers work side by side in their efforts to provide insurance to consumers and service their clients appropriately.

Insurance agents enter into contracts with insurers they will represent. Agency contracts differ with each insurer. Some contracts provide the agent with a wide array of responsibilities and obligations towards the company. Other companies restrict the agent's duties to a limited number of services.

Agency contracts usually identify the parties who enter into the contract along with the expiration or renewal date and basic expectations of the insurer. Commissions and an agent's binding authority will be addressed, with commissions and the collection of premiums being the main portion of most contracts that is subject to some state regulation. Insurers have to comply with state guidelines and limits when drafting their contracts, but insurers can use their discretion as to what a certain agent will receive within the bounds of the law. In other words, agency contracts issued by insurers can differ slightly from one another.

Some agency contracts include a clause that protects agents against a liability action from the insurer named in the contract. Other agency contracts do not protect agents in errors and omissions situations. In this case, an insurer could sue its agents for errors that caused some type of financial burden for the insurer.

For example, when an agent neglects to provide coverage on one piece of property for an insured, the insurer might pursue a claim against the agent. Suppose that the insured was provided coverage for a building and business contents, but that the agent omitted providing coverage for the outside sign that advertises the business. When the insured has a loss to that sign, the insurer's position might be that the insured should reasonably have expected to have coverage and, therefore, the insurer might offer payment to the insured. This can be done despite the fact that coverage really did not exist at the time of loss.

The insurer in this example might have lost the opportunity to collect premiums from the insured for that sign coverage. Even if the insurer does collect back-premium for the sign coverage, he or she might not have wanted to cover the risk if information about the sign was provided at the time of application for coverage. If this is the case, the insurer is considered *prejudiced* by the agent's actions and the insurer can pursue a claim against the agent for the error.

Several court cases address the contractual agreements between agents and insurers. The Georgia case, Preferred Risk Ins. Co. v. Boykin, involved a contract between an independent agent and an insurer. The insurer agreed to comply with certain terms in the contract if it decided to terminate the agreement. The agent filed suit after termination was made because the insurer violated the contractual language. The Georgia court found the insurer at fault for breaching the agency contract.[26] Another case arising in Puerto Rico involved an agent who brought suit against a Florida insurer, alleging that the insurer breached its General Agent's Agreement. The agent stated that the contract was terminated without cause. In this instance, the U.S. Court of Appeals, First Circuit, held in favor of the insurer, finding that the agent's agreement was null and void because of the agency's lack of a general agent's license.[27]

## Agent-Client Relationship

Agents consider their clients, or policyholders, to be their customers. As mentioned earlier in this chapter, agents are considered to be representatives of insurers that have appointed them throughout the insurance transaction and particularly at the time of an insurance dispute. However, this does not mean that agents do not have obligations to policyholders. Agents often feel confused because of the conflict in feelings about their duties to policyholders and insurers.

As suggested by NAIC, the duties of an agent are described in the following paragraph:

> Every agent or limited insurance representative who solicits or negotiates an application for insurance of any kind shall, in any controversy between the insured or his beneficiary and the insurer be regarded as representing the insurer and not the insured or his beneficiary. This provision shall not affect the apparent authority of an agent.[28]

Agents are obligated through certain sections of state statutes to represent insurers and provide insurers with all material information about policyholders as it becomes known to them. These requirements and regulations may be located within the unfair claims settlement practices laws, the unfair trade practices acts, or in other areas of the law that vary from state to state. Most states also hold that knowledge of the agent about something is considered to be knowledge by the insurance company because of the contractual ties of each party.

For example, suppose an agent overhears a conversation between a policyholder and another person. The agent hears the policyholder state that he was involved in his arson claim. The agent must report that information to the insurer at once. Any factual information heard or seen by an agent must be conveyed to the insurer as soon as it is received, so the insurer can act accordingly. However, employees of the insurance company will not take direct and immediate action against the insured based on what was stated by the agent. The insurance company employee would simply acknowledge the information and most likely conduct an investigation to determine whether the information is factual and worth pursuing.

Insurance brokers, on the other hand, are considered to represent policyholders throughout most of their insurance transactions. Some state laws indicate that brokers totally represent policyholders and not insurance companies. Many other states recognize that brokers represent insurance companies during the time in which they collect premiums and deliver insurance policies to clients.

Both agents and brokers owe a duty to be honest and forthright to policyholders, claimants, and other individuals involved in insurance transactions. If asked whom they represent, both the agent and broker would probably answer "the policyholder." Because agents and brokers sell insurance, advise policyholders about their insurance needs, and continuously ask questions and update coverage, the agent-client relationship must be taken very seriously. This relationship is also the catalyst for most regulation directed toward agents and brokers today.

Courts have determined that a broker, as an insurance professional, can be held liable for failure to serve a client with reasonable professional skill. See Consolidated Sun Ray, Inc. v. Lea, where the broker failed to obtain loss of use and occupancy coverage for a client who successfully prevailed in the suit against the broker.[29] In Hardt v. Brink, the broker was found negligent in failing to advise the insured to secure particular liability coverage.[30]

The following two cases included questions about new statutory language in South Carolina that allegedly affected agency agreements. In G-H Ins. Agency, Inc. v. Continental Ins. Co., the agent filed suit against the insurer for terminating the agency contract.[31] The same action was filed in Morgan v. Kemper Ins. Cos. Both cases were based on the same premise:

> [A]fter the contracts were made, the South Carolina legislature passed a comprehensive statute regulating the sale of automobile insurance in that state. Included in that statute was a section which provided that no automobile insurer could cancel representation by an agent primarily because of the volume of automobile insurance placed with it by the agent.[32]

Certain state statutes address contractual agreements between agents and insurers from the point of revocation. States generally do not regulate what must be contained within an insurer's contract; rather, the statutes are promulgated to protect the rights of the agent upon modification or termination of a contract by the insurer. Rhode Island's laws contain subsection 27-3-45, which is titled Revocation of Agency. This section includes extensive language surrounding the conditions on which an insurer can legally cancel an agent's contract. The insurer must indicate all changes in writing to the agent at least 180 days before the proposed effective date of the change or cancellation. If there is a dispute surrounding the changes or cancellation, a reference proceeding can be used. The law continues:

> The referees shall not order continuance or renewal of any policies if they find that the reason for the cancellation or expiration of the agency agreement by the company was legitimately based upon one of the following grounds:
>
> (a) The agent was convicted of a dishonest act related to his or her occupation as an insurance agent;
>
> (b) The agent's license to engage as an insurance broker was revoked;
>
> (c) The company surrendered its license to do business in the state.[33]

## Errors and Omissions Insurance

A few states are attempting to mandate that all producers carry errors and omissions insurance. For example, Rhode Island imposed this requirement as of January 1, 1995. The reason for the action is primarily for the protection of consumers.[34] The bill also created Rhode Island General Law, which says:

> All holders of insurance producers licenses by the insurance division of the State of Rhode Island department of business regulation shall as a condition of retaining such license carry and maintain errors and omissions insurance covering all business activities contemplated.[35]

Agents and brokers are eligible for obtaining errors and omissions insurance. This insurance protects insurance practitioners against various claims involving errors or omissions regarding insurance transactions. Insurance consumers, in the form of policyholders or claimants, are the typical people who sue agents and brokers for their errors or omissions surrounding coverage.

Usually, claims are alleged against agents and brokers after insurance claims have produced an adverse effect for policyholders, claimants, or insurers. For example, a policyholder might be upset because the agent did not recommend flood coverage that could have protected the policyholder more comprehensively in the event of a flood loss. When a flood occurred, the policyholder's claim was denied because of inadequate coverage. Another example occurs when third-party claimant Mary sues her insurance agent, Joe, after discovering that the person with whom she had an accident did not carry adequate liability limits to compensate her for her loss. As a further example, an insurer might decide to sue an agent for errors or omissions if the agent bound coverage for which he or she had no authority and the insurer had to pay a claim.

## Insurance Premiums and Commissions

Agents or brokers who collect premiums from insureds are considered liable for their payment to the insurer. This relates to the fiduciary responsibilities of agents and brokers. The following case, Copeland Ins. Agency v. Home Ins. Co., explains the reasoning:

> A Florida agent was president of an incorporated agency. He signed an agency agreement with an insurer which provided that the agency would collect premiums it solicited for the insurer and send the required sums to the insurer. The agency collected $75,000 in premiums but never paid this sum to the insurer. The insurer filed a lawsuit against the agent for the agency's failure to make payment and account for premiums it collected. A Florida circuit court ruled in favor of the insurer, and the agent appealed to the Florida District Court of Appeal. Florida statutes provide that an insurance agent is held fully liable and accountable for the wrongful acts and misconduct of people under his or her direct supervision and control when they are acting on behalf of an incorporated agency. . . .[T]he agent alleged that the statute did not apply because the premiums were not wrongfully taken by him personally. . . . The. . .court noted that an intent to misappropriate premiums is not a necessary element to prove a violation of Florida agency statutes. . . .The circuit court's ruling was affirmed.[36]

A Louisiana case affirmed its state statute, which provides that payment of a premium to an agent or broker shall be deemed to be payment to the insurer.[37]

The subject of commissions also enters into state regulatory requirements on occasion. Agents and brokers are entitled to commissions based on their insurance sales. A **commission** is a share of the premium paid to the producer for providing business to the insurer. The amount of commissions to be awarded to agents or brokers varies from state to state and from company to company. How commissions are distributed and what percentages will be awarded are not generally subject to state statutes. However, some state regulations place a cap on the amount of commissions to be provided to agents and brokers. Through contracts with insurers, agents will forfeit collecting commissions if they violate certain laws or commit acts of fraud against the insurer.

# Unfair Trade Practices

The NAIC set the purpose of the Unfair Trade Practices Act:

> The purpose of the Unfair Trade Practices Act is to regulate trade practices in the business of insurance in accordance with the intent of Congress as expressed in the Act of Congress of March 9, 1945 (Public Law 15, 79th Congress), by defining, or providing for the determination of, all such practices in this state that constitute unfair methods of competition or unfair or deceptive acts or practices and by prohibiting the trade practices so defined or determined.[38]

With respect to agents and brokers, unfair trade practices can include the following items listed below as excerpted from the NAIC Unfair Trade Practices Act.

Subsection A in the act is titled *Misrepresentations and False Advertising of Insurance Policies*. It deals with the following:

> Making, issuing, circulating, or causing to be made, issued or circulated, any estimate, illustration, circular or statement, sales presentation, omission or comparison that:
>
> (1) Misrepresents the benefits, advantages, conditions or terms of any policy; or
>
> (2) Misrepresents the dividends or share of the surplus to be received on any policy; or. . .
>
> (4) Is misleading or is a misrepresentation as to the financial condition of any insurer. . .
>
> (5) Uses any name or title of any policy or class of policies misrepresenting the true nature thereof; or
>
> (6) Is a misrepresentation, including any intentional misquote of premium rate, for the purpose of inducing or tending to induce the purchase, lapse, forfeiture, exchange, conversion or surrender of any policy; or. . . .[39]

These excerpts identify the acts of misrepresentation, twisting, and rebating as described further in this chapter. Fines, penalties, suspension of a license, the ultimate revocation of a license, or similar consequences can beset an agent or broker who is engaged in the above-mentioned activities.

Additional excerpted titles of sections appearing in the NAIC Unfair Trade Practices Act include "False Information and Advertising Generally"; "Defamation"; and "Boycott, Coercion and Intimidation."

Further sections of Subsection E, titled False Statements and Entries of the

NAIC Unfair Trade Practices Act include the following clauses that define what is meant by **false statement** or **entry**:

> (1) Knowingly filing with any supervisory or other public official, or knowingly making, publishing, disseminating, circulating or delivering to any person, or placing before the public, or knowingly causing directly or indirectly, to be made, published, disseminated, circulated, delivered to any person, or placed before the public, any false material statement of fact as to the financial condition of an insurer.
>
> (2) Knowingly making any false entry of a material fact in any book, report or statement of any insurer or knowingly omitting to make a true entry of any material fact pertaining to the business of such insurer in any book, report or statement of such insurer, or knowingly making any false material statement to any insurance department official.[40]

Under item (1), an agent or broker could be found in violation of the NAIC Unfair Trade Practices Act for advising a prospective customer that the insurer with which the customer is to be placed has an "A" rating indicating that the insurer is financially stable when, in fact, the insurer's financial condition has been steadily declining. One of an agent's or broker's responsibilities is to monitor the financial status of insurers through any number of means, including trade newspapers and Best's publications, and to advise customers accordingly.

Subsection G of the NAIC Unfair Trade Practices Act is titled Unfair Discrimination. Several entries that appear under this section apply to agents and brokers, including the following excerpt:

> (3) Making or permitting any unfair discrimination between individuals or risks of the same class and of essentially the same hazard by refusing to insure, refusing to renew, cancelling or limiting the amount of insurance coverage on a property or casualty risk solely because of the geographic location of the risk, unless such action is the result of the application of sound underwriting and actuarial principles related to actual or reasonably anticipated loss experience.[41]

This section pertains more to insurance companies since it relates to underwriting standards and practices. However, agents can become involved with insurers in this practice. As an example, when a company redlines a neighborhood, it means that the neighborhood is illegally marked for insurance ineligibility by the company. An article that appeared in the *National Underwriter* magazine describes one incident that involved an insurer and its agents:

> The Missouri insurance department has filed a statement of charges against [an insurer] alleging the insurer has for the past 17 years redlined

> the entire city of St. Louis and policyholders in other urban areas of the state. One of the most damaging pieces of evidence against the company could be its own underwriting manual, which insurance department examiners say clearly prohibits [the company] agents from selling homeowners policies in St. Louis.[42]

As a result, agents and brokers should be aware of the laws and regulations regarding discrimination. Complicity with insurers in discrimination actions would place agents in a situation of violating the laws along with the insurers.

## Misrepresentation

The NAIC Unfair Trade Practices Act describes generic actions involving misrepresentation as mentioned earlier in this section. Various forms of **misrepresentation** qualify as violating agents' and brokers' licensing laws in most states.

An agent or broker could directly misrepresent facts to an insurer, which would cause an insurer some harm. For example, an agent might omit information about prior losses that he knows a client had in an effort to secure more desirable coverage at reasonable rates for the client. Had the insurer known about the prior losses, the underwriter might have rejected the application or at least charged a higher premium because of the increased hazard.

The term *misrepresentation* might be seen more often in insurance policies in a section titled something like *misrepresentation* or *fraud.* Here, the policy language implies that the policy will be canceled or declared void if the insured misrepresents pertinent facts relating to the insurance involved. If the agent was the originator of that untrue information and the policyholder did not sign the application, then the policy would not be canceled or voided because the policyholder was not to blame. The agent, however, would be penalized by the insurer in a number of ways, such as by canceling the agency contract, notifying the insurance department of the agent's activities, and filing an errors and omissions claim against the agent to recover the amount paid under the insurance policy that was obtained by misrepresenting the facts.

Some forms of misrepresentation involve something detrimental to policyholders. An agent might misstate certain policy information to a client and lead the client to make a poor insurance decision. For example, an agent could tell a prospective client that he will have coverage for all types of loss that occur to his house. The agent might have said this in an attempt to get the client's homeowners business. The agent was aware that the policy contains certain exclusions and that the client would not be covered for all types of losses. This is a direct and factual misrepresentation against the policyholder.

If an agent acts in this fashion, and if the insurance department becomes aware of this action, the agent's license would most likely be suspended and eventually permanently revoked.

An agent might misrepresent himself in a transaction and advise a client about subjects in which he is not really an expert. For example, an agent might make the mistake of telling a prospective client that the commercial property Causes of Loss—Special Form provides coverage for all types of disasters that can happen to a client's business property. It might turn out that this agent is a life and health agent and knows nothing about property coverage. The agent might not purposely have lied to the client about the coverage; he might honestly believe that everything is covered. This agent should not have been selling property insurance to a prospective client because he knows that he cannot knowledgeably address specifics about the coverage. This would be considered misrepresentation and would also subject the agent to suspension or permanent revocation of his license—even in the life and health side of the business.

The courts in various states have ruled on allegations of misrepresentation against agents and brokers. In Hope v. Allstate Ins. Co., the Texas Court of Appeals ruled that a couple should be awarded treble (triple) damages as a result of misrepresentations made by their insurance agent. The agent advised the couple that they had coverage when the application had not yet been approved by the insurer. Upon a loss, the insurer denied liability since it had not yet approved the coverage. Texas statutes at the time of the loss provided that treble damages be awarded to a party who wins a lawsuit for damages caused by misrepresentation or other "unfair and deceptive acts or practices in the business of insurance."[43]

In the Florida case Peninsular Life Ins. Co. v. Wade, the District Court of Appeals found that the insurer's agent held himself out as an expert on certain policies and misinformed the insured as to the meaning of the limitation provision. The agent was found guilty of misrepresentation.[44]

## Rebating

**Rebating** is described as the act of giving or offering some benefit to a customer other than those described in the policy in an effort to induce a customer to purchase insurance. Rebating is considered a violation of the law in all states except Florida and California.

A common example of rebating is an agent's offering a prospective client a portion of his commission if the client will purchase insurance from his office. Although an agent is entitled to the commission from the sale of the insurance product, the agent is not permitted to offer any portion of that money to a prospect in an effort to swing that prospect into the agent's favor.

In Maine, the question of rebating has even been addressed through agency advertising. Some agents in the state advertised that they provided free quotes to prospective clients. Although this was true, *every agent was providing free quotes*. Because clients were going to those who advertised free quotes without knowing that every agency operated that way, the Maine insurance department issued notice to agents to stop this practice. The state felt that these claims were a form of rebating because it was an offer to clients that would unfairly benefit those few agents who included the comment in their advertisement.

The NAIC describes rebating in detail in its Unfair Trade Practices Act under Section H. Rebates. This type of activity seems to apply more often in life, accident, and health insurance, which is the primary subject of the NAIC language.[45]

## Twisting

**Twisting** is described as an act in which the agent or broker convinces the customer to cancel one policy in order to purchase another policy that is detrimental to the customer. It is considered misrepresentation and also is a violation of the law.

Twisting is a term associated more often with life, accident, and health insurance. For example, Policyholder A might have one form of life insurance and Agent B might convince Policyholder A to purchase a different type of policy that has fewer benefits. Agent B might have been able to collect more commissions on the newer policy—which was his primary motivation.

Twisting is performed by unethical agents or brokers in an effort to benefit themselves personally, such as when they are able to collect more commissions on policies through deceptive practices with their clients.

## Unfair Claims Practices

Within the Unfair Trade Practices Act, a few sections pertain indirectly to claims handling in general, but there is nothing about specific deceptive acts that, if performed, would be found in violation of specific language within the statute. The Unfair Claims Settlement Practices Act, adopted by many states, was promulgated to regulate insurers in their claims activities with consumers. The act can also apply to agents who adjust losses. The employees of an agency are acting on behalf of the insurer and paying policyholders on drafts provided by the insurer to the agency. If the agent does not handle a claim properly or fairly with a customer, the agent could be found in violation of any number of specific sections of the act. Chapter 3 in this textbook describes the Unfair Claims Settlement Practices Act in detail.

# Consumer Impact

What an agent, broker, or other individual acting in the capacity of an agent says or does with regard to insurance will have a great impact on consumers.

Consumers receive protection for a vast array of loss exposures through insurance policies. Many consumers do not understand the nuances of the insurance they purchase, never mind all the complicated pages of language and their possible interpretations.

The laws and regulations described in this chapter assist in protecting the insurance consumer against fraudulent or unlawful activities stemming from agents' and other insurance professionals' behavior. By licensing agents and brokers and subjecting them to continuing education requirements, insurance departments protect consumers and assure that they will receive proper information regarding the purchase of insurance.

When agents and brokers are aware of their legal responsibilities toward consumers, the consumers are going to be more adequately protected. The protection comes in the form of the consumer receiving appropriate coverage for his or her needs and receiving satisfactory customer service. Good service at the time of sale, during the term of the policy, and during a claim is all part of the package overseen by various forms of regulation.

Insurance consumers are entitled to receive accurate and adequate information about their insurance purchases. Much of this information is provided to them through agents and brokers, often verbally. This is the main purpose for the regulation of agents' and brokers' activities through licensing. In addition to regulating the activities of insurance professionals, though, the industry, consumer groups, and each state provide educational materials to consumers free of charge.

An abundance of pamphlets and informational brochures is disseminated to consumers in an effort to keep them advised of insurance issues that may affect their insurance needs. These brochures and pamphlets are issued by a number of groups, insurers, and other organizations.

For example, an insurance company published the pamphlet entitled "Five Reasons Auto Insurance Costs So Much And What We Can Do To Fight Back!" as shown in Exhibit 7-4. This pamphlet provides consumers with reasons for problems with auto insurance premiums, including that people have a lot of accidents. It offers solutions for reducing accidents, such as the

**Exhibit 7-4**
Insurance Company Pamphlet

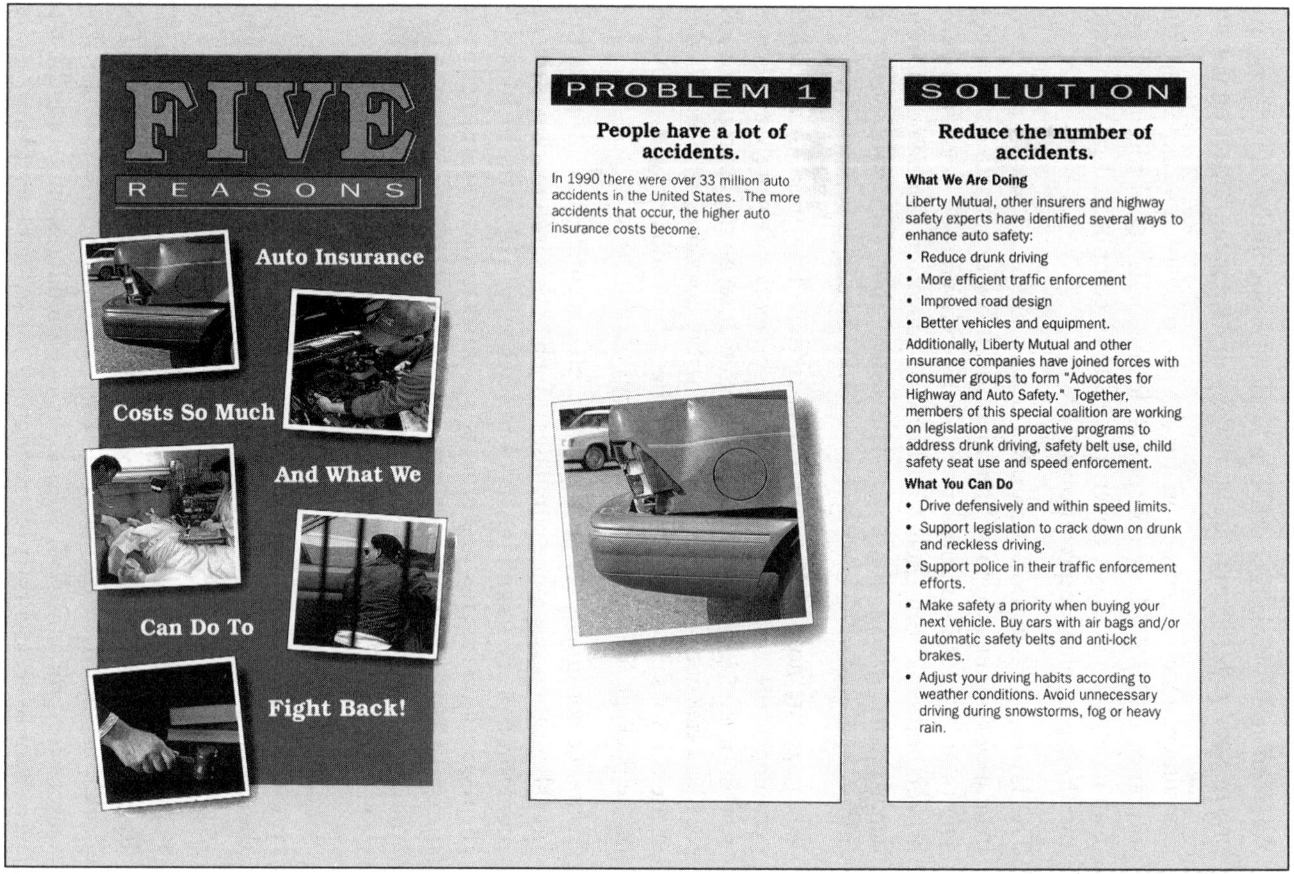


Source: Liberty Mutual Insurance Group/Boston (September 1992).

**Exhibit 7-5**
Massachusetts Informational Pamphlet

Source: Massachusetts Division of Insurance (October 1993).

reduction of drunk driving and improving road designs. It offers solutions that the consumer can assist with, which include driving defensively within the speed limits and making safety a priority when buying the next vehicle.[46]

Pamphlets are printed by several state insurance departments on subjects such as auto or homeowners insurance. For example, Massachusetts has been sending pamphlets like the one depicted in Exhibit 7-5 to its consumers explaining its auto insurance for many years. Most other states disseminate auto and homeowners booklets and guides to their consumers as well.

Insurance trade associations, such as the CPCU Society or the Independent Insurance Agents of America (IIAA), offer books and pamphlets designed for educating consumers. Often, insurance agents or brokers do not individually author these booklets, but the agents and brokers are key distributors of the information.

# Summary

Agents and brokers are the primary contacts for most consumers, and as a result, their activities are heavily regulated. Regulations are developed and altered periodically as needs dictate. Most of the regulation has come about in an effort to protect the insurance consumer against fraud and deceptive practices by the industry in general.

Agents and brokers operate in a similar manner while selling insurance, advising clients about coverage, servicing the accounts, and in other activities. Agents differ from brokers in that they enter into contracts with insurers and, as a result, receive responsibilities and benefits from the insurers. In areas of dispute, agents are viewed as legally representing insurers, while brokers are viewed as legally representing policyholders most of the time.

Licensing regulations and procedures are promulgated at the state level. Most states follow the NAIC Model Acts as they relate to agents and brokers licensing and continuing education. The commissioners of each state determine specific issues to be addressed in the laws.

Because of the nature of the relationship between agents with insurers and brokers with policyholders, a fiduciary responsibility on the part of the insurance practitioners exists. Agents and brokers are placed in a position of trust, and regulations are developed to ensure that the trust is not abused.

Each state has adopted Unfair Trade Practices Acts, which closely follow the language of the NAIC Model Act. Unfair practices such as misrepresentation, rebating, twisting, and even unfair claims activities are described in many of the regulations.

Proposals have been made to nationally regulate the activities of agents and brokers, particularly in the licensing area, for various reasons. The main argument for this proposed regulation is to establish uniformity among the states. This way, agents and brokers who wish to obtain licenses in several states will not have to file different forms, carry different titles, and comply with separate regulations. This uniformity arguably would help the agents and brokers better comply with the laws and serve the insuring public more professionally and competently. Moves are already underway to nationalize the licensing forms, with several states having implemented the standard form in 1994.

# Chapter Notes

1. NAIC, *Model Laws, Regulations and Guidelines*, vol. IV, p. 210-2.
2. NAIC, *Model Laws, Regulations and Guidelines*, vol. IV, p. 210-2.
3. *Rhode Island Insurance Licensing Examination Candidate Handbook*, Assessment Systems, Inc., p. 1.
4. 641 F. Supp. 297, 303 (E.D. Pa. 1986), aff'd, 833 F.2d 307 (3d Cir. 1987).
5. 654 F.2d 218, 220 (3d Cir.), *cert. denied*, 454 U.S. 1092 (1981).
6. 104 Minn. 76, 80-82, 116 N.W. 221, 223-24 (1908).
7. 62 Cal. App. 3d 108, 117, 132 Cal. Rptr. 796, 802 (2d Dist. 1976).
8. Barry Ostrager and Thomas Newman, *Handbook on Insurance Coverage Disputes*, 5th ed., p. 617; 394 F. Supp. 558, 564-65 (W.D. Mo. 1975).
9. Morrison Mahoney & Miller, *Defense Counsel*, vol. 6, no. 2, June 1994, Cover Page; 656 F. Supp, 753 (D. Conn. 1987).
10. *Rhode Island Insurance Licensing Examination Candidate Handbook*, Assessment Systems, Inc., June 1994, p. 1.
11. NAIC, *Model Laws, Regulations and Guidelines*, vol. IV, p. 210-4.
12. *Texas Department of Insurance Licensing Information Bulletin*, Insurance Testing Corporation, p. 1.
13. *Rhode Island Insurance Licensing Examination Candidate Handbook*.
14. *Rhode Island Insurance Licensing Examination Candidate Handbook*, p. 6.
15. *Texas Department of Insurance Licensing Information Bulletin*, p. 36.
16. NAIC, *Model Laws, Regulations and Guidelines*, Agents and Brokers Licensing Model Act, July 1990, pp. 210-8, 210-9.
17. *Best's Review*, January 1994. Arkansas, California, Colorado, Connecticut, Delaware, Florida, Georgia, Idaho, Illinois, Indiana, Iowa, Kansas, Kentucky, Louisiana, Maine, Maryland, Massachusetts, Michigan, Minnesota, Mississippi, Missouri, Nebraska, Nevada, New Hampshire, New Jersey, New Mexico, New York, North Carolina, North Dakota, Ohio, Oklahoma, Oregon, Puerto Rico,

Rhode Island, South Carolina, South Dakota, Tennessee, Texas, Utah, Virginia, Washington, West Virginia, Wyoming.

18. NAIC, *Model Laws, Regulations and Guidelines*, Agents Continuing Education Regulation, p. 215-2.
19. *Texas Department of Insurance Licensing Information Bulletin*, Insurance Testing Corporation, p. 2.
20. Agents and Brokers Licensing Model Act, *Model Laws, Regulations and Guidelines*, vol. 1 (Kansas City, MO: NAIC, July 1990), p. 210-11.
21. *Rhode Island Insurance Licensing Examination Candidate Handbook*, p. 1.
22. *Deskbook Encyclopedia of American Insurance Law*, 3d ed., Data Research, Inc., pp. 63, 64; 473 So.2d 1319 (Fla. App. 1st Dist. 1985).
23. *Deskbook Encyclopedia of American Insurance Law*, p. 64; 670 S.W.2d 94 (Mo. App. 1984).
24. *Massachusetts Insurance Law Digest: Agent License Training, Pictorial 1989*, p. 18.
25. *Deskbook Encyclopedia of American Insurance Law*, p. 64; 454 So.2d 31 (Fla. App. 1st Dist. 1984).
26. 329 S.E.2d 900 (Ga. App. 1985).
27. *Deskbook Encyclopedia of American Insurance Law*, p. 65; Caribbean Ins. Servs. v. American Bankers Life Assur. Co. of Florida, 754 F.2d 2 (1st Cir. 1985).
28. NAIC, *Model Laws, Regulations and Guidelines*, vol. IV, p. 210-2; 417 F.2d 471, 473 (10th Cir. 1969); 281 F.2d 871, 874 (10th Cir. 1960).
29. 401 F.2d 650, 657 (3d Cir. 1968), *cert. denied*, 393 U.S. 1050 (1969).
30. Ostrager, pp. 626, 627; 192 F. Supp. 879 (W.D.Wash. 1961).
31. 294 S.E.2d 336 (S.C.1982).
32. *Deskbook Encyclopedia of American Insurance Law*, p. 66; 754 F.2d 145 (4th Cir.1985).
33. *Rhode Island Insurance Laws, Agents, Brokers, Solicitors*, Chatsworth, CA: NILS Publishing Company, March, 1994, pp. 66, 67.
34. The filing is titled Senate Bill 94-S 3168 Sub A.
35. *Rhode Island Independent Agent*, May/June 1994, pp. 8-27.
36. *Deskbook Encyclopedia of American Insurance Law*, p. 56; 502 So.2d 93 (Fla. App. 5th Dist. 1987).
37. *Deskbook Encyclopedia of American Insurance Law*, p. 58. Case Fidelity & Cas. Co. of N.Y. v. Bordelon, 428 So.2d 1162 (La. App. 5th Cir. 1983).
38. NAIC, *Model Laws, Regulations and Guidelines*, vol. IV, pp. 880-2, 880-3.
39. NAIC, *Model Laws, Regulations and Guidelines*, vol. IV, p. 880-1.
40. NAIC, *Model Laws, Regulations and Guidelines*, vol. IV, p. 880-3.
41. NAIC, *Model Laws, Regulations and Guidelines*, vol. IV, p. 880-4.
42. NAIC, *Model Laws, Regulations and Guidelines*, vol. IV, pp. 880-4, 880-5.
43. *Deskbook Encyclopedia of American Insurance Law*, pp. 50, 51; 719 S.W.2d 634 (Tex. App. 1986).

44. *Deskbook Encyclopedia of American Insurance Law*, pp. 51, 52; 425 So.2d 1181 (Fla. App. 1983); see Todd v. Malafronte, 484 A.2d 463 (Conn. App. 1984) and Nat'l Old Line Ins. Co. v. Lane, 323 S.E.2d 707 (Ga. App. 1984) for similar findings.

45. NAIC, *Model Laws, Regulations and Guidelines*, vol. IV, pp. 880-4, 880-5.

46. Liberty Mutual Insurance Group, "Five Reasons Auto Insurance Costs So Much and What We Can Do To Fight Back," Boston, printing 9/92B.

# Chapter 8

# Regulating Insurer Insolvency

Ask an insurance regulator why insurance is singled out for special regulatory attention. There is a very good chance that the first thing mentioned will be *maintaining solvency*. The early detection and correction of financially troubled insurers are core duties of an insurance regulation. Protecting the public from insolvent insurers is one of the principal goals of an insurance department.

The mid-1980s ushered in a new era in solvency regulation. The number and cost of insurance company failures since then have brought new, and often uncomplimentary, attention to insurance regulation. In addition, the pace of change in insurance markets, financial methods, and information technology have forced regulators to rethink the old ways of monitoring and controlling solvency. Regulators needed new tools. Take, for example, the bulky yellow property-liability insurer and blue life and health insurer "blanks" that detail the financial condition of insurers. They covered the desks of financial examiners each spring at the filing deadline. Now this information is available at the click of a computer mouse on the examiner's desktop.

For decades, insolvencies were relatively infrequent and made up less than one percent of all insurers. Nevertheless, most insurance department staffs are preoccupied with trying to deal with that one in a hundred that will fail. Commonly, over half the staff in an insurance department is directly involved with financial regulation. In addition, those few insolvent insurance companies consume an inordinate amount of time from an insurance commissioner and senior insurance department staff.

Solvency regulation involves more than the early detection of problems. Remedial action—knowing when and how to apply authority—is the hallmark of good regulation. This chapter will discuss three forms of intervention into the affairs of insurers: *supervision*, *rehabilitation*, and *liquidation*. They are the three phases of regulatory response to the deteriorating financial condition of an insurer.

The insolvency of an insurance company is treated differently from the bankruptcy of most other businesses. Unlike other businesses, a failed insurance company is not handled by a federal bankruptcy court. If a commissioner can convince a state judge that the company is insolvent, state law governs the orderly liquidation of the insurer. This chapter discusses the relationships among the management of the troubled insurer, the court, and other state regulators.

Insurance guaranty funds are another peculiarity of the insurance industry. Few industries pay for the debts of their bankrupt competitors as do insurers through guaranty funds. This chapter introduces the role and functions of insurance guaranty funds. It explains their origins and the financial effect of guaranty funds on consumers and other insurers.

Critics of state regulation within Congress and the insurance industry have proposed legislation to change the system of state regulation of insurer liquidations. This legislation has attracted more industry support than have past attempts to involve the federal government in the regulation of insurance. This chapter will discuss why these critics are displeased with the current approach to solvency protection. The final section also reviews three avenues for reforms, which have applications to other areas of regulation.

# Trends in Insurer Insolvencies

This section reviews trends in the number, nature, and cost of insurance company insolvencies since 1969. That year was a milestone for solvency regulation because it marked the advent of NAIC models for insurance company liquidation laws and insurance guaranty funds. The dramatic changes in insurer solvency shown here help to explain the unprecedented changes in the NAIC and state insurance departments.

## Number of Insolvencies

Exhibit 8-1 traces the history of property-liability and life and health insolvencies since 1969. During the period from 1969 to 1983, the number of insolvencies seldom exceeded twenty in any one year. The insolvency rate (insolvencies per licensed insurer) generally was less than 0.5 percent per year.

**Exhibit 8-1**
Number of Insurer Insolvencies by Year

| Year | Property & Casualty | Life & Health | Year | Property & Casualty | Life & Health |
|---|---|---|---|---|---|
| 1993 | 43 | 27 | 1980 | 5 | 9 |
| 1992 | 56 | 52 | 1979 | 10 | 7 |
| 1991 | 46 | 58 | 1978 | 7 | 11 |
| 1990 | 32 | 41 | 1977 | 9 | 6 |
| 1989 | 39 | 42 | 1976 | 8 | 5 |
| 1988 | 35 | 19 | 1975 | 29 | na |
| 1987 | 19 | 20 | 1974 | 9 | na |
| 1986 | 25 | 14 | 1973 | 7 | na |
| 1985 | 49 | 9 | 1972 | 4 | na |
| 1984 | 26 | 11 | 1971 | 14 | na |
| 1983 | 11 | 20 | 1970 | 11 | na |
| 1982 | 8 | 10 | 1969 | 6 | na |
| 1981 | 9 | 8 | | | |

Sources: National Committee on Insurance Guaranty Funds; National Organization of Life Guaranty Associations.

Then, in 1984, an avalanche of property-liability insolvencies began. By 1992 the number of property-liability liquidations reached fifty-six, a high-water mark for the industry. As discussed below, not all financially troubled insurance companies are put into liquidation. Often the best regulatory response to impending failure is to broker a merger or acquisition with a sound insurer or investor. Exhibit 8-2 shows that the number of voluntary retirements and mergers of property-liability insurers also increased from 1987 through 1993. Most of these retirements and mergers were motivated by the financial weakness or insolvency of the insurers.

Life and health companies set their own records for insolvencies. In 1991, fifty-eight life and health insurers were involuntarily liquidated, just over 2.0 percent of all life and health insurers. This is compared to a pre-1989 average insolvency rate of just under 0.5 percent per year.

## Size, Age, and Premium of Insolvent Insurers

New and small insurance companies made up about two-thirds of all insurer insolvencies between 1970 and 1990. This is predictable since new companies

**Exhibit 8-2**
Retirements of Property-Liability Insurers by Year

| Year | Involuntary | Voluntary | Mergers |
|---|---|---|---|
| 1993 | 43 | 21 | 24 |
| 1992 | 56 | 13 | 17 |
| 1991 | 46 | 13 | 17 |
| 1990 | 32 | 6 | 9 |
| 1989 | 39 | 11 | 13 |
| 1988 | 35 | 11 | 10 |
| 1987 | 19 | 5 | 8 |

Source: A.M. Best, *Best's Review.*

have less experience and are less diversified. Often these small insurers serve difficult markets, such as pollution liability, commercial auto, or medical malpractice, which makes these insurers even more prone to fail. However, the succession of record-breaking insolvencies in the mid-1980s included large and established property-liability insurers, such as the Mission Group, Transit Casualty, Ideal Mutual, and American Mutual. The American Mutual failure was unusual since it was one of the oldest property-liability insurers in the United States. Executive Life, First Capital, and Mutual Benefit Life were exceptionally large life insurers that became insolvent in the early 1990s. Mutual Benefit Life, the largest insolvent insurer in history, had $14 billion in assets.

These large-scale insolvencies are the exception and not the rule. For most of the past twenty years, insolvent companies were responsible for less than 0.25 percent of industry premiums written in any year. During 1985, the premium of insolvent insurers reached about 1 percent of all written premium in the property-liability industry. This was three times the previous percentage record set in 1977.

## Deficits of Insolvent Insurers

Insolvent insurers leave behind unsatisfied debts and obligations. The gap between the debts of failed insurers and available assets has widened. This growing cost of insolvencies has been largely borne by the remaining financially healthy insurers.

Of particular concern to regulators were the massive failures that began in the late 1980s. Exhibit 8-3 shows the estimated cost of the ten largest property-liability insurer insolvencies since 1969. All occurred since 1984.

**Exhibit 8-3**
Projected Costs of Top Ten Property-Liability Insolvencies
(years 1969–1989)

| Insolvent Insurer | Year of Insolvency | Projected Cost ($ millions) |
|---|---|---|
| Mission Insurance Co. | 1985 | $458.6 |
| Integrity Insurance Co. | 1986 | 322.7 |
| Transit Mutual Insurance Co. | 1985 | 307.9 |
| Ideal Mutual Insurance Co. | 1984 | 274.5 |
| Midland Insurance Co. | 1986 | 271.7 |
| Champion Insurance Co. | 1989 | 180.9 |
| Enterprise Insurance Co. | 1985 | 150.3 |
| Iowa National Mutual Ins. Co. | 1985 | 128.4 |
| Carriers Insurance Co. | 1985 | 122.9 |
| American Mutual Ins. Co. | 1989 | 111.0 |

Source: National Conference of Insurance Guaranty Funds.

As huge as the insolvencies of the 1984-1992 period were, they did not directly hurt most policyholders or third-party loss claimants. Guaranty funds, discussed later, stood in for the failed companies and paid the vast majority of covered claims. However, as also discussed later, the losses paid by guaranty funds are shifted to other insurers, their policyholders, and taxpayers.

## How Bad Is the Industry Record?

The failure of an insurer is not necessarily bad. In the economy at large, thousands of companies, large and small, go out of business each year. Compared with this commonplace churning among businesses, how much damage is done by insurer insolvencies? As discussed later in this chapter, because of *guaranty funds*, relatively little *direct* harm has been done to consumers. However, indirect effects must be considered. Does guaranty fund protection make consumers too relaxed about selecting financially strong insurers? Is the pressure on regulators to shut down weak insurers diminished? How much of the cost for guaranty fund protection is shifted to policyholders and taxpayers?

In 1990, the report released by the House Oversight and Investigations Subcommittee of the House Committee on Energy and Commerce, "Failed Promises," received widespread attention. The report documented spectacular cases of poor regulation. "Failed Promises" served as a wake-up call for insurance commissioners and the NAIC. In 1989, a torrent of reforms began. The NAIC adopted a number of new or improved regulatory models addressing solvency, and many states incorporated these solvency standards into their insurance codes. Many organizational improvements were also made within the NAIC.

The critics still argue that these reforms are too late. In fact, "Wishful Thinking," the 1994 sequel study by the House Oversight and Investigations Subcommittee of the House Committee on Energy and Commerce, saw little to be optimistic about. It contended that efforts by the NAIC and state regulators were inadequate and that a major collapse of the insurance industry was a possibility.

Insolvencies and near insolvencies reached unprecedented levels from 1984 through 1993. However, this spike is traceable to a set of factors that have been corrected, either by reform legislation (such as tougher capital requirements) or by market forces (for example, the improving market for commercial real estate investments). The extreme underwriting cycle (discussed in Chapter 4), which bottomed in late 1984, contributed greatly to the property-liability failures. While the underwriting cycle has not been tamed, that particular cycle was unusually sharp. Improved financial regulations are now in place to detect and mitigate problems like those that arose during that cycle—for example, better controls on the accuracy of loss reserves reported on Annual Statements.

The rash of life insurer insolvencies was largely associated with ill-conceived investments. Life insurers have reverted to their conservative investment holdings and less risky product offerings. They have enjoyed strong premium growth and good profit margins in the early 1990s. The economic conditions and insurance investment policies that caused this problem are not likely to be repeated soon.

As shown in Exhibit 8-4, the problems of the insurance industry are dwarfed by the losses of commercial banks and savings and loan (S&L) institutions. The cumulative losses of defunct S&Ls and commercial banks over the period from 1983 to 1993 have been much higher than losses from failed property-liability insurers.

For the 1980-1990 period, the number of bank and S&L failures was ten times more frequent than property-liability insurer failures. Moreover, the asset values of failed property-liability insurers were a small fraction of the asset values of the failed banks and S&Ls.[1]

How good is the record of state regulation? By some measures insurer solvency—while rocked with troubles in recent years—is good. Since 1989, state

**Exhibit 8-4**
Cost of Failed Property-Liability Insurers Compared to Other Financial Institutions (billions of dollars)

| Year | Savings & Loans[1] | Commercial Banks[2] | Property-Liability Insurers[3] |
|---|---|---|---|
| 1993 | 47* | 0.6 | .5 |
| 1992 | 90* | 4.7 | .4 |
| 1991 | 34.4 | 6.7 | .4 |
| 1990 | 37.5 | 2.6 | .5 |
| 1989 | 5.4 | 6.3 | .7 |
| 1988 | 31.2 | 6.7 | .4 |
| 1987 | 3.7 | 2.0 | .9 |
| 1986 | 3.1 | 1.7 | .5 |
| 1985 | 1.0 | 1.1 | .3 |
| 1984 | 0.7 | 1.5 | .1 |
| 1983 | 0.3 | 1.4 | .04 |

* Estimated, Congressional Budget Office

1. Sources: U.S. Treasury Department; Resolution Trust Corporation.
2. Source: FDIC.
3. Source: National Council of Insurance Guaranty Funds.

regulators, working through the NAIC, have passed more reform legislation than at any other period in that organization's history. Some entirely new approaches to regulation are in use, such as accreditation of state insurance departments and risk-based capital requirements.

In addition, the NAIC has greatly increased its staff and scope of activity, including establishing a sophisticated database and information system and creating a new financial analysis office. However, there is no assurance that there cannot be a repeat of the "failed promises." The next regulatory crisis may come from a new and unanticipated breach in the regulatory defenses.

A very low rate of insolvency is not the only benchmark of industry or regulatory performance. Another standard might be the extent to which regulation increases expenses and restricts product offerings. In an extreme case, regulators could become so restrictive on risky products (long-term-care insurance or medical malpractice insurance) that the supply of these products would disappear. Similarly, requiring too much surplus decreases profits of insurers and can restrict entry to the market or increase prices. Regulators should strive—along with insurers—to maintain balance between risk and reward.[2]

Insolvency only becomes a regulatory failure if insurance consumers or claimants are injured by the failure. The regulator's job is to make sure that the net worth of the company never falls below the level needed to ensure that policy claims can be paid when due. Claims of general creditors and owners are subordinate in law and regulatory attention to the claims related to the insurance contract itself. The greatest regulatory dereliction is to allow liabilities, excluding the claims of owners, to go unmatched by assets to pay for them. Executive Life, Carriers, Mission, and Transit collapsed with billions of dollars of net losses—to insureds, other claimants, and the taxpayers.

## Why Insurers Become Insolvent

Policyholders have a vital interest in an insurer's ability to keep its promises. The management and employees of insurers are obviously concerned with the solvency of their employers—their livelihoods and way of life depend on it. Though less personally poignant, investors and lenders have huge amounts riding on good regulation. Armies of actuaries, accountants, and financial analysts make their living out of finding cracks in the financial bulwarks of insurers. Finally, state regulators are concerned because their mission is to prevent insolvency and because the system of state regulation is threatened by insurers' financial instability and a loss of confidence by the public.

Why do insurers fail? Usually, no single event or mistake causes an insurer to become insolvent. Rather, a collection of management blunders and adverse events is necessary. Following are some factors that experts have identified as most frequently contributing to insolvencies:

- Rapid premium growth
- Inadequate rates and reserves
- Out-of-line expenses
- Lax controls over managing general agents
- Reinsurance uncollectible
- Fraud[3]

Poor management decisions are the root of most of the problems cited above. A combination of inadequate rates and lax underwriting starts a deterioration in a book of business.[4] If these problems are not promptly detected and corrected, the decay in the quality of the business accelerates.

Rapid premium growth precedes nearly all of the major failures. Rapid growth is not harmful, per se. However, rapid premium growth reduces the margin for error in the operation of insurers. Moreover, rapid growth is usually a strong indication of bargain-basement rates and lax underwriting standards. If rates are inadequate and losses understated, the net losses and deterioration of capital rise faster than management can handle.

Losses from natural catastrophes were not implicated in many of the failures occurring in the late 1980s. However, the string of record-setting catastrophic losses from 1989 through 1992 reawakened insurers and regulators to the threat that storm and earthquake disasters pose to insurer solvency. In the first hundred years of U.S. insurance history, large catastrophic losses were the leading cause of multiple insurer failures. The fact that few property-liability companies failed despite record-breaking hurricane and earthquake losses from 1989 through 1992 is testament to an improved spread of risk and largely adequate reinsurance. In principle, insurers can effectively immunize themselves financially from having their surplus wiped out by record-setting natural disasters. Ensuring that primary writers arrange adequate reinsurance with financially strong reinsurers is an ongoing concern of insurance regulation.

One problem that analysts have in identifying the causes of insurer failure is the difficulty of determining when a company is financially troubled, or even when it is insolvent. A thinly capitalized insurer could have its admitted assets fall below liabilities if a regulator wished to make more conservative judgments than management's about the admissibility of certain assets or how its loss reserves would develop over time.[5]

Mergers and acquisitions are a discreet way for a weak company to cease to exist or to be saved without the world's knowing how bad its condition was or how it became that way. Capital infusions by parent companies or outside investors also clear the slate of past management sins without the event's being seen as a financial failure or insolvency. Omaha Indemnity, held up as an example of mismanagement in "Failed Promises," was saved from insolvency by capital infusions of over $300 million by its parent insurer. The NAIC's Supervision, Rehabilitation and Liquidation Model Act recognizes the need for discreet intervention.[6] Thus, the insolvencies shown in Exhibit 8-1 probably miss a number of forced mergers and acquisitions of insurers quietly arranged by insurance commissioners. Ensuring that primary writers arrange adequate reinsurance with financially strong reinsurers is an ongoing concern of insurance regulation.

# Regulatory Control

The regulator is expected to take whatever steps necessary to require the insurer to protect its claims-paying ability. A wide range of types of intervention is possible, depending on the source of the problem. If the problem is poor operating controls, the regulator might demand a business plan for correcting them. If the problem is fraud or abuse by a managing general agent, that relation might be severed and funds recovered.

The first form of regulatory intervention is usually fact finding on site or by written reports. If the commissioner finds that the company might be "hazardous to the policyholders or the general public," he or she may issue the following types of orders:[7]

- Increase the level of reinsurance.
- Reduce, suspend, or limit the volume of business being accepted or renewed.
- Reduce general or specific company operating expenses.
- Increase the insurer's capital or surplus.
- Suspend or limit dividends to stockholders or policyholders.
- Limit or withdraw from certain investments.
- Document the adequacy of rates.

These orders might be made after a public hearing or can be made on an emergency basis if the commissioner has good cause for believing the company is in immediate danger of collapse. Often a commissioner negotiates voluntary compliance with informal directives to avoid potentially ruinous publicity for the insurer. Orders, like other interventions discussed here, are subject to judicial review.

Public intervention with a nondomiciled company is likely to draw criticism from that company's domiciliary regulator. The domiciliary regulator is likely to contend that he or she is handling the situation and is working to correct the problem. Any intervention by nondomiciliary regulators would damage these efforts, or so it can be argued.

A notorious case that illustrates the conflict that often arises among regulators occurred when a large group of commissioners met at a December 1990 NAIC meeting to address the financial concerns associated with Executive Life. Commissioners throughout the United States were keenly aware of Executive Life's overinvestment in junk bonds and collectively discussed means to correct the company's hazardous financial condition without panicking policyholders. The following resolution passed, admonishing the Commissioner of New Jersey for demanding a $500 million security deposit for the then tottering-but-not-fallen Executive Life Insurance Companies.

> NOW, THEREFORE BE IT RESOLVED that the NAIC believes that the action taken by the New Jersey Insurance Department is irresponsible and contrary to the best interests of New Jersey policyholders and all policyholders of Executive Life Companies. . . .[8]

If informal supervision or "orders" constraining business practices fail, the regulator can seek court authority to formally take control of the management of the insurer. This is called **rehabilitation**. The duties, objectives, and problems of rehabilitating an insurer are discussed later in this chapter.

Regulators approach the courts cautiously, since they do not want to preempt the possibility of management's correcting the problems or of another entity's purchasing the insurer or the troubled book of business. (A regulatory system that mistakenly identifies an adequately financed company as weak can trigger the system's own demise.)

Since insurance is a business that depends on consumer trust, the regulator-rehabilitator is challenged to maintain the loyalty of an insurer's customer and agent base. Policyholders begin to surrender policies or drop coverage if other viable insurers are available. Agents avoid submitting applications. Creditors and reinsurers are cautious in the terms they extend in future dealings with the insurer under regulatory control. When the problems are seen to be beyond repair, the commissioner is obliged to petition a court for authority to shut down the insurer and begin the liquidation process. Most regulators, if they attempt rehabilitation at all, are forced by the deterioration of the company to rapidly move from rehabilitation to liquidation.

Financial regulation involves coordinating the efforts of many stakeholders in the financial condition of insurers. Regulators from several states often join together to examine and evaluate potentially troubled insurers (under the association examination discussed in Chapter 6). The NAIC plays an increasingly central role as a data coordinator and technical resource.

The line between a sound and an unsound insurer is not always clear. It takes seasoned judgment and finesse to know when and how strongly a regulator should intervene. Financial indicators, like IRIS and FAST ratios (discussed in Chapter 6), cannot consistently identify insurers in need of regulatory intervention. Moreover, financially sound insurers sometimes fail to meet these computerized bench marks.

Insurers file between 100 and 500 pages of financial reports with insurance regulators each year. The reports grow more detailed and frequent if the regulator sees a pattern of financial problems. Using these reports, a trained examiner can pick out companies that bear close scrutiny.

Knowing when to take over the supervision of the affairs of an insurer requires financial and administrative judgment. Some key issues are the following:

- How accurate are loss reserves?
- If assets were liquidated quickly to meet current creditor demands, what would the proceeds be?

- Has management enacted tough enough measures to stem the operating losses (underwriting, rating, expenses)?
- Is the company's reinsurance adequate and collectable?

### Role of Actuaries and Accountants

Actuaries and accountants are engaged by insurer management to assist in preparing, evaluating, and auditing financial records and reports made to regulators and others. Historically, the relationship between these professionals has excluded any duty to regulators. This has changed a great deal in the last few years.

The NAIC has promulgated standards for accountants to certify that they know and understand the regulatory requirements of any insurer they are engaged to audit. As a condition of being accepted as an insurance auditor, a CPA firm must agree to report certain classes of financial problems to the board of the insurer and to the appropriate regulators.

Actuaries also support the process of regulation. Insurers must obtain an opinion of the adequacy of reserves from a qualified actuary as part of their Annual Statement filing requirements. The NAIC hopes that this will substantially improve the adequacy of reserves and hence reduce the number of surprise deficiencies in the capital of insurers.

### Need for Coordination

In the past, regulators who learned of the severe weakness of an insurer might have been discouraged from publicly taking action against the company by the domiciliary commissioner. In some instances, the domiciliary commissioner was concerned with the local effect (such as the number of jobs lost) of an insurer liquidation. More often, the domiciliary commissioner wanted to preserve his or her discretion to handle the problem in his or her own way. This "home state first" attitude and lack of coordination have been largely superseded by coordinated intervention into troubled companies by the NAIC. The NAIC has built up its own staff expertise to analyze the condition of weak insurers and to recommend follow-up actions to the Financial Analysis Working Group (FAWG, discussed in Chapter 6). FAWG ensures that domestic regulators are effectively dealing with financially troubled, nationally significant insurers.

## Insurance Receiverships

Since the turn of the century, insurance commissioners have been given a special role in handling financially troubled insurers. This section explains that role from a legal and administrative perspective. Receiverships are extraordinarily complex activities, involving shared responsibility among receivers, courts, and guaranty funds.

This section discusses the duties described in the NAIC Insurers Rehabilitation and Liquidations Model Act. The liquidation of an insurance company can involve billions in assets, hundreds of products, and thousands of policyholders spread over the world. Complex issues and deep conflicts of interests can arise. Receivers have their own individual styles of managing these issues, which can cause conflict between receivers and with other stakeholders. Little wonder exists that a vast case law has emerged to govern every phase of receivership.[9]

## Rehabilitation

Rehabilitation is generally a prelude to liquidation. Saving an insurer once it is in receivership is difficult. A realistic goal of rehabilitation is to stabilize the company while a more permanent solution is explored and implemented.

The rehabilitator is commonly a retired industry executive or experienced insurance attorney. The rehabilitator's first challenge is to stabilize the company's cash flow and protect its assets from the claims of creditors.

Once stabilized, the crux of the receiver's problem is this: are the assets of the company, if reasonably managed, sufficient to meet policy claims and other liabilities? This seems straightforward. However, the rehabilitator must puzzle through many complications, including the following:

- How will loss reserves develop?
- Can expenses be trimmed, and how fast?
- How far are rates from being actuarially adequate to meet costs?
- Can rates (usually inadequate) be raised without destroying the company's ability to market to its desired market segment?

Usually the interval from receivership to **liquidation** is only a few months. Following is the report resulting from an Illinois liquidator's futile attempt to rehabilitate a company:

> Security Casualty Company. . .was placed into rehabilitation by court order entered on August 17, 1981. Extensive efforts were made to rehabilitate Security Casualty Company through the transfer of the company's various books of business to new carriers and through the investments of new assets. The company's in force business in Florida was sold to Wausau Underwriters of St. Louis in November 1981. The company's Canadian book of business was also sold.
>
> On December 4, 1981, the Circuit Court of Cook County, Illinois issued an Order of Liquidation. . . .[10]

## Liquidation

When an insurer is clearly beyond rehabilitation, the commissioner should petition a state court for a finding of insolvency and direction to liquidate the company. State laws allow a commissioner to appoint a special deputy liquidator to act as his or her agent in the day-to-day business of winding down the insurer. The liquidator has broad powers to seize and dispose of the insurer's assets, hire and discharge personnel, enter contracts and lawsuits, and manage the affairs of the insurer. In essence, the liquidator has two tasks:

- Freeze and quantify the insurer's liabilities
- Marshal the assets and convert them to cash

It is best for most parties with a stake in the insurer that liabilities be frozen quickly. To do this policies must be canceled (usually with 60 to 120 days' notice) and deadlines established for filing proofs of loss. Along with this, the assets of the insurer—from desks to reinsurance receivables—must be sold or collected.

The first few months of a liquidation are busy—sometimes chaotic. During that time the liquidator must, among other things:

- Give notices of liquidation to creditors and policyholders and inform them of their rights to file claims
- Cancel policy coverage
- Notify agents of their duties in the liquidation
- Identify, sell, and collect assets (investments, reinsurance recoverable, and so forth)
- Recover any improperly transferred assets
- Establish a procedure for receiving and adjudicating claims
- Make personnel decisions regarding the insurer's staff and hire outside help, as needed

These functions are fraught with controversy, so a liquidator is often in court. Lawsuits commonly involve claimants, reinsurers, and former management. Conflicts also arise with other state regulators and guaranty funds, typically concerning the rights of one state's citizens over those of another state. Liquidating a large interstate insurer—like Executive Life or the Mission Group—involves the use of many highly compensated actuaries, attorneys, and accountants. Thus, the administrative expenses of the liquidation process can seriously erode the assets of the insurer. So complex is management of liquidations that at least ten states have set up separate liquidation bureaus, some with hundreds of employees.

Years later, after all claims have been filed and adjudicated and all assets reduced to cash, the liquidator can petition the court to distribute assets to creditors according to a specific "order of distribution" enumerated in the law. The usual priority classes of distribution are:

1. The costs and expenses of administering the liquidation
2. Partial payment of debts to employers for services rendered within one year of the order for liquidation
3. All claims for policy losses incurred
4. Claims for unearned premiums and claims of general creditors

While guaranty funds typically get an early release of some assets to help pay for policy claims, this final distribution usually takes a decade or more from the court's declaration of insolvency. Furthermore, in the typical payout of assets, each class must get full payment of its claims before the court can allow payments to a lower class. Seldom do general creditors receive full (or even partial) payments of losses.

# Guaranty Funds

This section discusses the purpose and operation of property-liability guaranty funds (also called associations). Guaranty funds were established to protect policyholders from the inability of an insolvent insurer to pay its policy claims when due. They are a comparatively new institution—Wisconsin established the first fund in 1967. Since then, property-liability guaranty funds spread to all fifty states and the District of Columbia. Most of the laws establishing these funds follow the "Post-Assessment Property and Liability Insurance Guaranty Association Model Act" developed by the NAIC. This model is based on a **post-insolvency assessment** approach to funding claims. Under this approach, the fund estimates the claims it must pay after an insolvency and issues assessments to solvent insurers operating in that state for this obligation. New York is the only state that assesses to prefund a reserve for insolvencies. Guaranty funds also exist for life and health insurance. By the nature of some life products, their coverages and operating procedures are sometimes quite different from property-liability funds.

## Purpose

Guaranty funds are organized to pay most claims that would have been due under the policies written by insolvent insurers. Funds also repay a portion of unearned premium of insolvent insurers. Each fund commonly covers the property claims of its own residents and liability claims arising within that state, regardless of the residency of the third-party claimant. Following are some of the additional limitations on fund coverage in addition to the terms of the policy:

- *Lines covered.* Most direct property-liability policies if issued by insurers licensed to transact insurance in that state. Title, credit, mortgage, and ocean marine are almost always excluded. All reinsurance and surplus lines contracts are excluded.
- *Refunds of unearned premium.* Most states cover return of unearned premium, often with a $10,000 limit per policy.
- *Maximum covered claim (cap).* The model calls for limit of $100,000 per policy claim, except for workers compensation, which provides unlimited statutory benefits. However, many states have $300,000 caps.
- *Claim deductibles.* The NAIC model, followed by most states, requires a $100 deductible per covered claim. This is over any policy deductibles.
- *Large net worth deductible.* Many states have adopted a special deductible for insureds with large net worth ($10-15 million). Such companies face a claim deductible of up to 10 percent of their net worth.
- *Trigger of coverage.* For most states, fund coverage only becomes available for an insurer after a court has found it to be insolvent and has put it into liquidation.

The original role of property-liability funds was paying relatively small claims, which generally arose out of homeowners or auto policies. After the failure of large commercial lines insurers beginning in 1984, funds found themselves paying for the claims of sophisticated corporate policyholders. The special net worth deductible was added to many fund laws to remove coverage for firms with $10 million or more in net worth.

The NAIC model also describes a role for guaranty funds in preventing insolvencies. The guaranty fund board can make recommendations to the commissioner on insolvency protection and participate with the commissioner in the correction of a financially hazardous member company.

## How Funds Are Operated

A guaranty fund is a nonprofit, unincorporated entity established by a special provision of state law. All insurers selling lines of insurance covered by a fund automatically become members of the association. Unlicensed insurers, such as excess and surplus lines insurers, are not covered by guaranty funds.

The members elect a board of directors, usually subject to the approval of the commissioner. Beside the veto authority of the commissioner, some funds allow greater public control by adding *public* members. These directors have broad authority to organize the fund through a *plan of operation* to meet its legal purposes. The commissioner typically exercises some veto power or control over the content of the plan and has the right to examine the records of the fund.

Most of the staff expertise in a fund lies in the adjudication of claims. The fund stands in the place of the insolvent insured. Thus, every policyholder or third-party claimant must cooperate with the fund the same way he or she would have to cooperate with the insurer. Because of the specialized nature of claims adjudication, funds frequently contract for third-party experts (in some cases, the employees of the insolvent insurer) to process claims. Claims covered by an insurance policy, but not covered by a guaranty fund (due to caps, deductibles, and exclusions), might be asserted against the liquidator of the insolvent insurer.

Paying for guaranty funds has become very costly for their members. Exhibit 8-5 shows that the assessments authorized by all post-insolvency guaranty funds reached an all-time high of $903 million in 1987. The assessment is offset by recoveries from the estates of insolvent insurers. The law gives guaranty funds priority treatment in recovering their costs from the insolvent insurer. Still, the annual net assessments for all post-insolvency property-liability funds averaged about $431 million between 1990 and 1994. Assessments are commonly made on the basis of premiums written for separate "accounts" divided along lines of insurance, such as workers compensation, auto, and all other covered property-liability insurance.

From time to time, critics question the ability of post-insolvency funds to pay for catastrophic losses. In most states, annual assessments cannot exceed 2 percent of premiums written in the state and account subject to assessment. This percentage of premium cap is occasionally reached for a short time, as with the Florida fund after paying for insolvencies caused by the record high claims following Hurricane Andrew. However, studies by the industry and the NAIC have found that state funds generally have ample capacity to meet any reasonably foreseeable insolvencies. The total assessments for all post-insolvency guaranty funds have averaged about 4 percent of industry net written premium since 1986.

To the extent that they are not reimbursed from the estate of the insolvent insurer, insurers can attempt to pass on the cost of their assessments to their policyholders in their rates. In addition, many states allow some form of credit for assessment against premium taxes owed by members of guaranty funds. As a result of these two actions, guaranty fund assessments can be shifted in whole or part to the public.

## Effect on Consumers

Consumers with claims obviously benefit from guaranty funds. Instead of

**Exhibit 8-5**
Post-Insolvency Guaranty Fund Assessments, 1980 to 1994

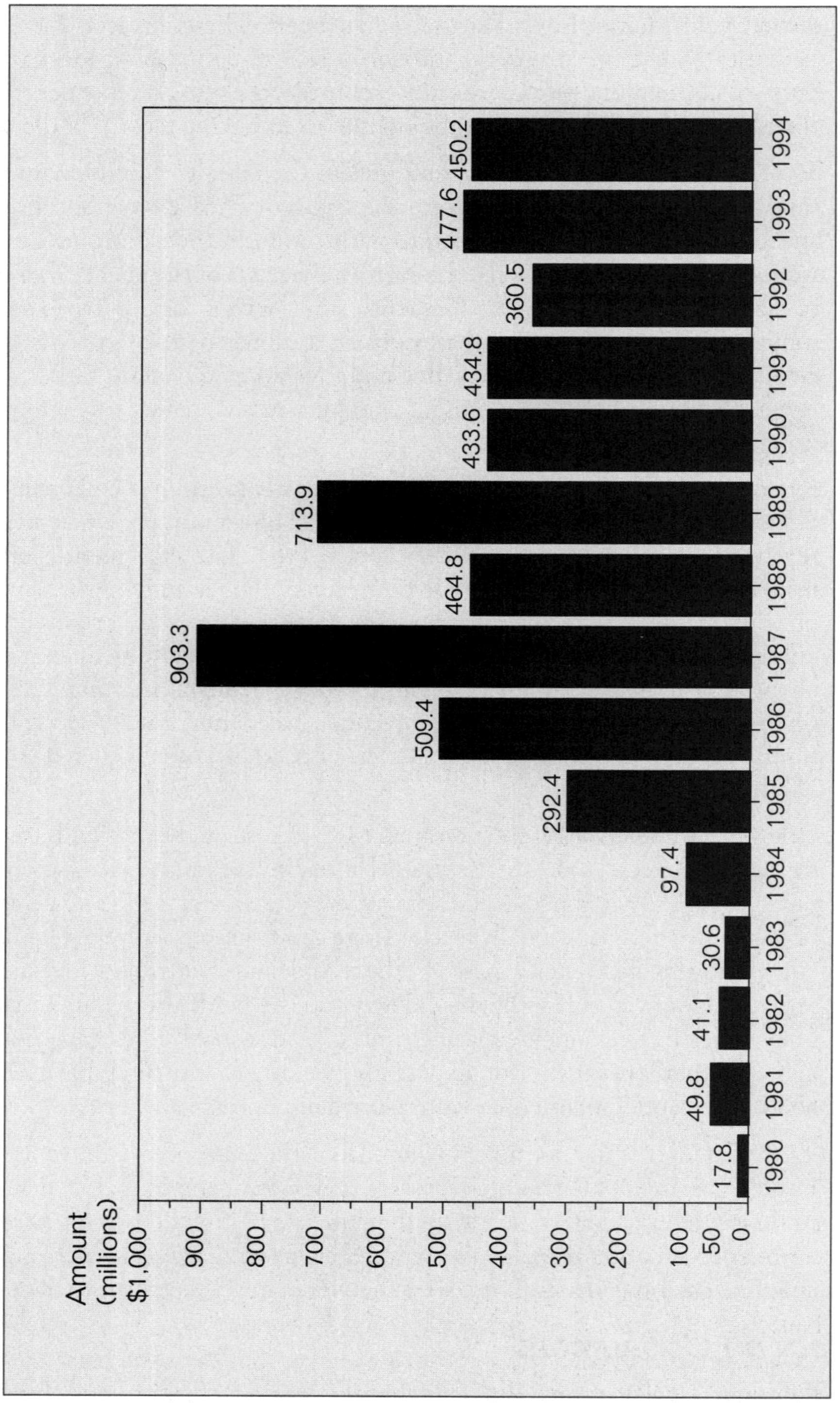


Source: National Committee on Insurance Guaranty Funds.

waiting in line for a fraction of a dollar, as takes place under federal bankruptcy laws, they get the total value of most claims paid promptly. The indirect cost of funds on consumers is hidden but real. First, the cost of guaranty funds is partly passed back to consumers in the form of higher insurance rates.

Second, insurance markets are distorted. Recently some writers have criticized state guaranty funds for removing the incentive for consumers to "shop the market" for financially sound insurers.[11] According to this line of reasoning, consumers and regulators tolerate poorly managed insurers too long. Also, insurers that engage in excessively risky behavior are tolerated because consumers are immunized from losses and, for some products, gain better dividends or rates from the higher yields of those insurers investing in high risk-high yield assets.

Consumers are willing to go along with risky underwriting by insurers because as customers they are immunized from policy losses. Some consumers are direct beneficiaries of risky underwriting behavior, for example, the high-risk driver who obtains insurance at standard rates from an insurer aggressively seeking to expand. Similarly the owners of annuities or variable life products tend to enjoy better earnings if the life insurer invests in riskier portfolios.

These behaviors can provide increased benefits for both insureds and insurers. Yet by the nature of risk, these behaviors also can result in insolvency and large costs to guaranty funds. The most spectacular example of this is Executive Life, which left guaranty funds across America holding a $1.5 to $2.0 billion tab for the company's aggressive investments in junk bonds.

## Effect on the Insurance Industry

The high costs of paying for insolvencies through guaranty funds motivate insurers to promote strong financial regulation. The price for insolvencies is high for two reasons. First, insurers are directly assessed for the operation of guaranty funds. Between 1969 and 1993, insurers paid out $4,619 million in net assessments for post-insolvency guaranty funds—for property-liability insurance alone. Over 80 percent of this net cost occurred after 1986.[12]

Second, competition is distorted. Insurers that can aggressively market or loosely underwrite can gain a greater share of the market compared to more conservatively managed insurers.

Insurers want regulators to monitor their competitors and remove the derelict carriers. The industry is on record promoting strong financial regulation. This support is shown in unequivocal statements from trade associations such as the National Association of Independent Insurers[13] and the Professional Insurance Agents Association. It is also evidenced by industry support for increased staffing of regulatory departments and the NAIC.

# Brief Assessment of the System for Dealing With Insurer Insolvencies

This section provides a critique of the current system of seizing and liquidating troubled insurers and the guaranty fund mechanism. It reviews comments by industry critics and defensive reactions by state regulators.

In the 1970s, insolvencies were confined mostly to intrastate or regional personal lines carriers. Then, the rehabilitation and liquidation of insurers could be conducted by each state in an insular fashion. The needs for interstate coordination were modest. The growing complexity of the process has prompted calls for reform. The basic issue concerns how the activities of funds and agencies in fifty states can be coordinated to reduce unnecessary work and improve the consistency of treatment to policyholders.

Three remedies have been suggested. They are worth comparing not only for their application to liquidations and guaranty funds but also because similar reform options are being debated for other aspects of insurance regulation.

## NAIC Reforms

The first option is to continue the process of reform from within the NAIC. This process is incrementally addressing some issues by promulgating better uniform procedures. For example, the NAIC promulgated uniform data reporting standards from guaranty funds to liquidators. The weakness of this approach is that no state can be compelled to adopt the uniform procedure laws. Moreover, the implementation of even the model act can be different from state to state.

## Interstate Compacts

The weakness of the NAIC process is the inability to produce conformity. States seldom pass the NAIC models verbatim. Many state legislatures prefer to tailor the laws to meet state interests. In addition, there are persistent concerns about the mechanism for coordinating the work of liquidators and funds.

Interstate compacts can be used to force a higher degree of binding uniformity. **Interstate compacts** are binding agreements among states (subject to Congressional approval) that subordinate individual state lawmaking to the compact authorities acting in their scopes of responsibility. Over 150 such compacts are in use, controlling such activities as pollution, ports, and parental responsibility. A consortium of industry, regulatory, and legislative leaders is studying the formation of compacts to solve the problems of interstate liquidation of insurers.[14]

### Federalization

Ever since McCarran gave state regulation preeminence over federal law, Congress and federal agencies have tried to regain that authority. For example, the Federal Trade Commission challenged the title insurance industry for price fixing. Members of Congress periodically introduce legislation to control various elements of the insurance industry or state regulation such as the Risk Retention Acts of 1981 and 1986. The willingness of Congress to intervene is tied to public displeasure over some aspect of insurance industry conduct, such as during the hard markets for commercial liability insurance in 1985 and 1986.

## Summary

Beginning in the mid-1980s, an alarming increase in the number of insurer insolvencies occurred. The shortfall in assets over obligations to creditors, especially policyholders, has grown from an average of a few hundred million dollars per year industry-wide to over $2.5 billion in a single liquidation. The financial strains caused by these insolvencies, particularly coming at about the same time as the savings and loan and the banking crises, produced controversy over the way insurers were regulated. Out of these concerns came sweeping changes in solvency regulation.

Regulators want to detect insurers headed toward an unacceptably weak financial condition as soon as possible. The ability of regulators and private rating agencies (such as A.M. Best) to predict financial problems has been limited. In fact, both regulators and rating agencies sometimes fail to detect companies that are currently operating near the point of insolvency. Usually, though, regulators are aware of the fundamental problems causing the decline of an insurer. Only skilled management by seasoned insurance professionals can save a company once it deteriorates to a level severe enough to invite regulatory intervention.

Once a potentially weak company is detected, the regulator engages in a variety of activities to clarify the company's financial condition. As a clear picture of the company's balance sheet and operating experience emerges, the regulator must select one of three courses of action: (1) formal or informal supervision, (2) court-ordered rehabilitation, or (3) court-ordered liquidation.

Of the regulator's three choices, supervision is most frequent and covers the broadest range of activities. Supervision can be as informal as asking management to supply a business plan for correcting financial problems. At the other extreme, it could include orders to limit or change business practices.

Rehabilitation is intended to salvage a financially weak insurer. Since the purchase of insurance is built on trust in an insurer's ability to pay for its promises, regulatory control severely weakens the ability of an insurer to maintain a market for its products. As a result, many rehabilitators end up stabilizing a company, selling some of its good business, and preparing it for liquidation.

Liquidation is ordered once a company is beyond saving. State law names the insurance commissioner as the liquidator for insolvent insurers. The regulator-liquidator conducts two prominent functions: (1) marshaling the assets of the insurer in liquidation and (2) freezing and quantifying liabilities. Once the final liquidated value of the insurer's estate is known, remaining assets are distributed according to a statutorily defined formula.

Guaranty funds were established to protect insureds and third-party claimants from insurance company insolvency. The popularity of funds is attested to by the fact that every state has enacted a fund to cover the majority of business written by licensed insurers.

Guaranty funds are administered by member insurers. The funds act in place of the defunct insurer and pay covered claims. The cost of these payments is initially paid for by assessments against the remaining solvent insurers in the state. Ultimately the fund tries to recoup its payments from the liquidated estate of the insurer responsible for the losses. Also, in many states, tax credits and write-offs allow insurers to shift part of the cost of their assessments to other taxpayers.

Guaranty funds protected most claimants during the surge of insolvencies that began in the mid-1980s. They appear to have ample capacity to pay for reasonably foreseeable insolvencies. However, these funds have been criticized for reducing consumer incentives to pay attention to the financial condition of their insurer.

Over the past several years, a variety of proposals has been advanced to reform the receivership and guaranty fund mechanisms. Three remedies have been proposed: (1) establishing a federally run receivership and guaranty fund mechanism for large interstate companies, (2) establishing an interstate compact to streamline and regulate the operation of interstate liquidations and fund coverage, and (3) reforming the existing system incrementally, within the framework of the National Association of Insurance Commissioners.

# Chapter Notes

1. This point was stressed in: NAII Task Force on Improved Solvency Regulation, *A Call for Balance in Structuring Insurer Solvency Regulation*, Des Plaines, IL: National Association of Independent Insurers, 1992, pp. 7-8.

2. The need for balance was stressed by the NAII Task Force, pp. 3-4.
3. There are a number of studies on the causes of insolvency. While they use different classification systems, they are in general agreement. NAII Task Force on Improved Solvency Regulation, cited above; A. M. Best Company, *Best's Solvency Study, Property/Casualty Insurers 1969-1990*, Oldwick, NJ: A. M. Best Company, Inc., 1991; Stewart Economics, Inc., "Managing Insurer Insolvency," presentation at the National Association of Insurance Brokers, 1988; Dan R. Anderson and Roger A. Formisano, "Causal Factors in P-L Insolvency," *Journal of Insurance Regulation*, vol. 6, pp. 449-461.
4. This process is well described for property and casualty insurance business in Stewart Economics, Inc., "Managing Insurer Insolvency," National Association of Insurance Brokers, 1988. A similar process exists for unprofitable life and health products.
5. A senior financial examiner once confided to the author that a company she examined would have had negative net worth if she used conservative loss development factors for its long-tail liabilities. Today, that company is A+ rated. This type of close brush with statutory insolvency occurs more often than is generally understood, even by insurance professionals.
6. Spencer L. Kimball, "Introductory Comment," *Reference Handbook on Insurance Company Insolvency*, 2d ed., Chicago, IL: American Bar Association, 1989, p. 52.
7. See National Association of Insurance Commissioners (NAIC), "Model Regulation to Define Standards and Commissioner's Authority for Companies Deemed To Be in Hazardous Financial Condition," *Model Laws, Regulations, and Guidelines*, vol. 2, October 1992, pp. 385-1 to 385-4.
8. This is graphically described in *Wishful Thinking*, U.S. House of Representatives, Subcommittee on Oversight and Investigations, Committee on Energy and Commerce, October 1994, p. 22.
9. An excellent digest of the case law is contained in "Tort and Insurance Practice Section," *Reference Handbook on Insurance Company Insolvency*, 2d ed., Chicago, IL: American Bar Association, 1989, pp. 127-372.
10. Kimball, p. 404.
11. Robert Klein and Michael Barth, "Solvency Monitoring in the Twenty-First Century," *Journal of Insurance Regulation*, vol. 3, no. 3, Spring 1995, pp. 256-301.
12. National Conference of Insurance Guaranty Funds, *Property/Casualty Guaranty Association 1993 Assessment and Financial Information Summary*, Indianapolis, IN: September 1994.
13. NAII Task Force on Improved Solvency Regulation, cited above.
14. Jones Schact and Peter Gallanis, "The Interstate Compact as an Effective Mechanism for Insurance Receivership Reform," *Journal of Insurance Regulation*, vol. 12, no. 2, Winter 1994, pp. 188-219; John Manders, Theresa Vaughan, and Robert Myers, Jr., "Insurance Regulation in the Public Interest: Where Do We Go From Here?" *Journal of Insurance Regulation*, vol. 12, no. 3, Spring 1994, pp. 285-340.

# Chapter 9

# Insurance Regulation in Practice

This chapter presents a series of case studies that apply the information contained in previous chapters. The use of case studies helps to bring regulation to life and allows readers to better understand how the subject matter of the previous chapters fits into the system of state insurance regulation.

Four case studies are included in this chapter. They roughly follow the organization of the text, beginning with the formation and licensing of an insurance company and ending with the receivership of an insurance company. Between these two end points are a market conduct examination case and a financial examination case. The cases are purposely abbreviated to fit the needs of the course. In real life, the aspects of insurance regulation dealt with in the case studies can be extremely detailed and time-consuming for both insurers and regulators.

Throughout the chapter are questions to focus readers on the cases and guide the reader through the issues involved in each case. The questions can also be used by readers to test their knowledge and understanding of the issues involved in general and for each case in particular.

## Case 1: The Formation of an Insurer

> What issues should the promoters consider?

A group of ten insurance agents (the promoters) decided that they wanted to form an insurance company that offered the coverages needed by their clients. They dealt with the following formation issues:

- The company will be named We-Cover-You Insurance Company (WeCYIC). The promoters have done a name search, and currently no insurance company exists under that name.
- The promoters have selected the state in which they want WeCYIC to be domiciled. The state provides certain business incentives and is in a location central to the home states of the various promoters.
- WeCYIC will sell property and liability insurance to small businesses that cannot find desired coverage at reasonable prices in the geographical area. As insurance agents, the promoters know the territory well and have identified several types of insurance needs that are not being met by the insurers in the area. Therefore, the promoters believe they have a ready market.
- The initial minimum capital and surplus requirements to become licensed in the state are $1 million in capital and $500,000 in free surplus. The promoters believe they can manage to meet these minimums.
- The promoters have identified two reinsurers that would probably be willing to assume some of the risk that the new company underwrites—ABC Reinsurer and CVO Reinsurer.
- The promoters will organize WeCYIC as a stock insurer. They believe that, in so doing, they will encounter less trouble raising the capital and surplus needed to meet the minimum requirements for their chosen state of domicile.
- The promoters have identified four individuals who might be willing to serve as company officers and eight individuals who might be willing to serve as the company's directors. In addition, the promoters have identified several key personnel–an actuary, an underwriter, a corporate attorney, and an accountant–who are willing to work for the new insurer.
- The promoters, through their business experience in the insurance industry, have come to know several key outside individuals who could serve as advisors and experts in various ways.

The promoters hired Smith, Inc., to conduct a feasibility study of their proposal to determine whether the plan of operation they outlined was viable. Smith, Inc., determined that the plan of operation, as outlined by the promoters, was viable.

| |
|---|
| Are there any additional issues the promoters should consider? |

## The Application

> What information and which forms are usually necessary?

The promoters then put together the following information required for incorporation as a stock insurer in the domiciliary state selected:

- An application for Certificate of Authority
- A power of attorney
- A business plan
- A feasibility study
- Pro forma financial statements
- Articles of incorporation and bylaws
- Biographical affidavits of directors, officers, and key personnel
- An application fee

Prototypes of insurance policies and rate materials were not required by the state. The state insurance department preferred to have these documents filed once the proposed company had been approved for incorporation as a stock insurer.

> How might another state differ concerning policy and rate prototypes?

### Application for Certificate of Authority

> What information is usually included in an application for Certificate of Authority?

The application for Certificate of Authority requires that the promoters indicate the name of the insurance company and the lines of business it proposes to write. The statement must be signed by an officer of the proposed insurer and be notarized. Furthermore, the application fee must be paid when the application is submitted. These details are shown in Exhibit 9-1.

### Power of Attorney

> What purpose is served by the power of attorney?

The power of attorney grants authority to an executive of the state's insurance

**Exhibit 9-1**
Application for Certificate of Authority

## APPLICATION FOR CERTIFICATE OF AUTHORITY
### ADMISSION TO THE STATE

*To The Insurance Commissioner of the State:*

The undersigned Insurer hereby applies for a Certificate of Authority under Article X, Chapter Y, Part 2, Division 1 of the Insurance Code of the State, for the transaction in the State of the following classes of insurance:

Fire, Marine, Plate Glass, Liability, Boiler and Machinery, Burglary, Sprinkler, Automobile

*(Here insert classes of insurance as defined in the sections of the Insurance Code printed on the back hereof)*

and certifies that said classes of insurance are all the classes of insurance transacted by it in any jurisdiction, if not an alien insurer, or in the United States, if an alien insurer, except as follows:

None

(Name classes of insurance as defined in the section of the Insurance Code printed on the back hereof—If none, write "none")

and further certifies that it has corporate powers to transact such classes of insurance, is not in arrears to said State or to any county or city therein for fees, licenses, taxes, assessments, fines or penalties accrued upon business transacted in said State, has complied and will comply with all of the present and future laws of such State regarding the governmental control of such insurance by said State, and believes that it fully complies with all of the requirements and has done all the matters and things necessary to entitle it to receive such Certificate of Authority.

Dated February 17, 199X

We-Cover-You Insurance Company
(Give full and exact name of Insurer)

(Seal)

By Lisa Lee

Title Vice President

State of State
County of County } ss.

Lisa Lee, being duly sworn, deposes and says: That XX/she is the Vice President of the Insurer making the foregoing application for Certificate of Authority and that all the statements contained in said application are true.

Lisa Lee
(Signature of Insurer's Officer who signed foregoing application)

Subscribed and sworn to before me this 17 day of February, 19 9X.

L Jones
Notary Public

FEE: $1,000

FORM CS-7

department to accept service on WeCYIC's behalf with respect to lawful process and legal process against WeCYIC. As shown in Exhibit 9-2, WeCYIC's power of attorney designates the state insurance commissioner as this executive.

**Exhibit 9-2**
Power of Attorney

**APPOINTMENT OF COMMISSIONER OF INSURANCE AS ATTORNEY**

KNOW ALL MEN BY THESE PRESENTS

That the We-Cover-You Insurance Company an insurer in State, now authorized or having applied for authority to do an insurance business in State, hereby appoints the Commissioner of Insurance of State, his successors in office, and any deputy superintendent, its true and lawful ATTORNEY, in and for State, upon whom all lawful process against said insurer may be served in any action or proceeding in State, subject to and in accordance with all the provisions of the Insurance Law of said State in force at the time of such service. This appointment shall be binding upon any successor acquiring the assets and assuming the liabilities of such insurer by merger or consolidation, and shall not be terminated so long as there are in effect any contracts, or liabilities or duties arising out of contracts, which were issued or delivered by such insurer in this State.

IN WITNESS WHEREOF, the said We-Cover-You Insurance Company in accordance with the resolution of its Board of Directors duly passed on the 20th day of February, 19 9X, has to these presents affixed its corporate seal, and caused the same to be subscribed and attested by its President and Secretary, at the City of Anytown, in State, on the 20th day of February, 19 9X.

WE COVER YOU INSURANCE COMPANY

President

Secretary

## Business Plan

What is typically included in a business plan?

Excerpts from WeCYIC's business plan are shown in Exhibit 9-3. WeCYIC's business plan sets out for the state insurance department the characteristics of the proposed insurance company. The business plan describes why the promoters (referred to as the investor-agents in the business plan excerpts) desire to establish such an insurance company and how they plan to proceed.

**Exhibit 9-3**
Excerpts From WeCYIC's Business Plan

**Mission:** The fundamental mission is to provide a stable and profitable agency-based market for coverages needed by small businesses that are not available in the existing market.

**Business Overview:** The small businesses in State do not have access to many of the coverages they need to operate on a financially sound basis. As agents in State, the investor-agents regularly must tell prospects that no coverage is available at prices they can afford. Therefore, to meet the needs of these small business owners, the investor-agents will establish a property-liability insurer to provide the coverages that are currently not available.

**Corporate Structure:** The insurance company will be incorporated as a State domiciled stock insurance company. The bylaws and articles of incorporation will allow the State insurance department to license the insurance company as a property-liability insurance company.

**Financial Support:** The investor-agents have located six financially-sound entrepreneurs who are willing to provide between $150,000 and $175,000 each as financial backing for initial capitalization. In addition, the investor-agents are willing to invest an additional $1 million. With the available financing, the insurance company will be able to meet the minimum requirements of the state for capital and free surplus.

## Feasibility Study

Of what use is a feasibility study in the application process?

Smith, Inc., evaluated the feasibility of WeCYIC's operators if organized according to its business plan. Smith, Inc., was specifically directed to establish the appropriate funding level and corresponding capital contributions necessary for WeCYIC to be financially sound.

The data used by Smith, Inc., was primarily provided by WeCYIC. In addition, an advisory organization provided supplementary insurance industry data. The data included expected losses and loss adjustment expenses, sales figures for coverages, and lag times between report data and settlement dates, among other sources.

A simulation analysis was performed by Smith, Inc., on the data. The recommended capitalization level was $1,750,000, which could be achieved with financing generated by the promoters. Thus, the feasibility study indicates that the proposed insurer could prosper if organized and operated according to the proposed business plan.

## Pro Forma Financial Statements

> What purpose do pro forma financial statements serve in the application process?

The pro forma statements for WeCYIC are shown in Exhibit 9-4. As required by state law in the state in which the promoters want to locate as a domestic, five years of financial data are estimated. The pro formas are based on the business plan and the results of the feasibility study. The pro formas indicate that, based on its business plan and feasibility study, WeCYIC will be profitable and maintain sufficient surplus during its first few years of operation.

## Articles of Incorporation and Bylaws

> What types of information are included in the articles of incorporation and the bylaws?

Excerpts from the proposed articles of incorporation and the bylaws for the company are depicted in Exhibits 9-5 and 9-6. The articles of incorporation establish that WeCYIC will be a stock insurer as indicated in the business plan. The bylaws indicate the powers that WeCYIC's officers and directors, both individually and collectively, will have over the company's operations. The articles of incorporation and bylaws were developed to comply with the requirements of the proposed state of domicile.

## Biographical Affidavits

Biographical affidavits are required for each of the proposed directors, officers, and key personnel. Exhibit 9-7 supplies certain information about the proposed officers for WeCYIC. That is included in each officer's biographical affidavit. Similar information has been gathered for WeCYIC's directors and key personnel and reported to the state insurance department on biographical affidavits.

## Application Fee

To apply for incorporation and domestic license, the promoters must pay an application fee of $1,000. This was indicated at the bottom of the application for the Certificate of Authority in Exhibit 9-1.

**Exhibit 9-4**
Selected Pro Forma Financial Data for WeCYIC (000 omitted)

| Income Statement Data | Year 0 | Year 1 | Year 2 | Year 3 | Year 4 | Year 5 |
|---|---|---|---|---|---|---|
| Written premium* | 0 | $1,500 | $1,514 | $2,519 | $3,008 | $3,743 |
| Earned premium | 0 | 900 | 1,508 | 2,117 | 2,812 | 3,449 |
| Net investment income | 0 | 210 | 315 | 398 | 524 | 643 |
| Total revenue | 0 | 1,110 | 1,823 | 2,515 | 3,336 | 4,092 |
| Incurred losses & LAE | 0 | 338 | 903 | 1,359 | 1,848 | 2,348 |
| Other underwriting expenses | 0 | 480 | 484 | 806 | 962 | 1,198 |
| Total underwriting expenses | 0 | 818 | 1,387 | 2,165 | 2,810 | 3,546 |
| Net income before taxes | 0 | 293 | 436 | 349 | 526 | 547 |
| Income taxes (assume 30%) | 0 | 88 | 131 | 105 | 158 | 164 |
| Net income | 0 | $ 205 | $ 305 | $ 244 | $ 368 | $ 383 |
| **Balance Sheet Data** | | | | | | |
| Total admitted assets | $1,750 | $2,622 | $3,113 | $4,031 | $4,964 | $6,110 |
| Reserves for losses and LAE | 0 | 68 | 248 | 520 | 890 | 1,359 |
| Unearned premium | 0 | 600 | 605 | 1,008 | 1,203 | 1,497 |
| Other liabilities | 0 | 198 | 200 | 333 | 397 | 494 |
| Capital & surplus | $1,750 | $1,757 | $2,260 | $2,504 | $2,871 | $3,254 |

*Assuming no reinsurance

## Meeting With Representatives From the State Insurance Department

Why should the promoters meet with state insurance regulators?

After filing their application, the promoters scheduled a meeting with staff from the state insurance department to discuss the application. The promoters wanted to be sure that the application was in order and to ensure that the staff had a chance to meet with the promoters. Discussing the application face to face allows both parties to resolve issues in a time-efficient manner.

## Organizational Examination

The state insurance department wanted to verify certain information about WeCYIC's application for incorporation and licensure that was not addressed in the meeting with the promoters. For example, the regulators needed to

**Exhibit 9-5**
Excerpts from the Articles of Incorporation of WeCYIC

. . .

FIRST

The name of the Corporation is We-Cover-You Insurance Company.

. . .

THIRD

The purpose of the Corporation is to engage in any lawful act or activity for which corporations may be organized under the General Corporation Law of Anystate.

FOURTH

The total number of shares of stock which the Corporation shall have authority to issue is 10,000 shares of common stock with 50 cents par value . . . .

FIFTH

In furtherance and not in limitation of the powers conferred by statute, the Board of Directors of the Corporation is expressly authorized:

(1) To make, alter, or repeal the bylaws of the Corporation; and

(2) To provide for the indemnification of directors, officers, management, employers, and agents of the Corporation, . . . to the full extent permitted by the General Corporation Laws of Anystate. . . .

SIXTH

Elections of directors need not be by written ballot unless the bylaws of the Corporation shall so provide.

. . .

NINTH

The personal liability of the directors of the Corporation is hereby eliminated to the fullest extent permitted by . . . the General Corporation Law of Anystate . . . .

make sure that the capital and surplus were deposited in an approved financial institution and to visit the home office to make sure that the management team was ready to begin the company's operation. Therefore, examiners from the insurance department visited the site of the home office and met with the company officials to clear up any unanswered questions involved with the application.

## State Insurance Department's Decision

The state officials determined that the company could be incorporated

**Exhibit 9-6**
Excerpts from the Bylaws of WeCYIC

ARTICLE I
NAME
The Name of the Company is
We-Cover-You Insurance Company

ARTICLE II
LOCATION

. . .

Section 1. ANNUAL MEETING. The Annual Meeting of the Shareholders shall be held within 180 days after December 31 of each year at such time and place as may be determined by the Board of Directors, for the purpose of election of Directors and for transaction of such other business as may properly come before the meeting.

. . .

SECTION 4. CHAIRMAN. The Chairman of the Board of Directors shall preside at all meetings of the Shareholders; in his absence the Vice Chairman of the Board of Directors shall preside, or if neither is present, the Shareholders shall elect their own Chairman.

. . .

ARTICLE IV
DIRECTORS

SECTION 1. DUTIES. The business of the Company shall be managed and controlled by a Board of Directors which may do all such lawful acts and things as are not by statute, or by the Articles of Incorporation, or by these By-laws directed or required to be exercised or done by the Shareholders.

. . .

SECTION 5. VOTING. Each Director present shall be entitled to cast one vote on all questions coming before a meeting of the Board of Directors or any committee thereof, and all questions unless otherwise provided herein shall be decided by a majority of the votes thus cast.

. . .

ARTICLE IX
FISCAL YEAR

The fiscal year of the Company shall begin on the first day of January in each year and end on the thirty-first day of December in each year.

. . .

**Exhibit 9-7**
Biographical Information for WeCYIC's Officers

| Name | Ed Donnelly | Lisa Lee | Dot Canelli | Ray Wojorski |
|---|---|---|---|---|
| **Company Position** | President | Vice President | Secretary | Treasurer |
| **Education** | B.S., M.A. | B.S. | B.S., M.S. | B.S., Ph.D. |
| **Ownership of WeCYIC stock** | 1% | 2% | 0% | 1% |
| **Employment** | Currently Vice President of ABC Insurance Company | President of own agency | President of own agency | President of consulting firm |
| **Professional Licenses** | None | Licensed P/C agent | Licensed P/C agent | None |
| **Criminal Record** | None | None | None | None |

according to the application submitted by the promoters. However, the company's domestic license would be withheld pending approval of insurance policy forms, rate manuals, and rates by the insurance department.

# Case 2: Investigating an Insurer's Conduct in the Marketplace

> Why might insurers be examined for market conduct?

Smith Insurance Company (SIC) is a regional provider of personal auto insurance, homeowners insurance, and related lines, that is licensed in five states, including its state of domicile. The company was targeted for a market conduct examination by its domiciliary state insurance department. A complaint analysis revealed that the state insurance department had received a large number of complaints (when compared to premium volume) concerning SIC. The complaints alleged unfair discrimination and unfair claims settlement practices primarily in the area of personal auto insurance. In addition, one of the other states in which SIC operates notified the domiciliary state insurance department of an increased number of complaints alleging similar unlawful behavior as suspected by the domiciliary state insurance department.

> Which areas of the insurer might be examined during the market conduct examination?

Wendy Dalton, Dwayne Redmund, and Ed Granger were assigned to investigate the insurer's market conduct in the areas of personal auto insurance underwriting and claims through a field examination at the insurer's home office. Wendy was appointed as the examiner-in-charge for SIC's market conduct examination.

## Notification

> Who should be notified of a market conduct examination? When?

Wendy sent the CEO of SIC a letter notifying him about the pending market conduct examination scheduled one month from the date of the notice. In her letter, Wendy stated that SIC had been named in an unusually large number of complaints to the state insurance department as a percentage of its premium volume, especially with respect to unfair underwriting and unfair claims settlement in its personal auto insurance line. The insurance department, therefore, had determined that a market conduct examination should be conducted to investigate SIC's personal auto insurance underwriting and claims settlement procedures and practices of the previous six months. Wendy requested that the CEO designate a person in the home office to act as the company's examination coordinator and provide her with the coordinator's name, title, mailing address, and telephone number within twenty days of receipt of the notification. She also advised the CEO that the examiner team was available to visit the company for a pre-examination meeting with the insurer's examination coordinator and the heads of the underwriting and the claims departments. Wendy asked the CEO to provide her (within twenty days) with the name, title, and address of the person to whom the billings for the costs incurred during the exam would be sent since the insurer was required to pay the costs of the exam.

In her letter, Wendy also requested that she be provided with the following information within twenty days:

- The name of all insurers with which SIC was affiliated
- The addresses of all offices in the state where policy files contain underwriting and claims information

Wendy notified the NAIC and the other four states in which SIC does business that a targeted market conduct examination of SIC was to take place on the specified date. Wendy noted that the examination targeted the insurers' underwriting and claims settlement activities.

## Coordinator's Packet

Upon receiving the information concerning SIC's examination coordinator, Wendy sent the coordinator a packet of information that described the role of an examination coordinator. The packet is designed to acquaint the coordinator with the examination process and what he or she is expected to do during the process. Included in the packet were the following pieces:

- A chronology of the examination with a brief description of each step of the process. The chronology included steps concerning the insurer's recourse in the event it was found in noncompliance.
- A projection of the time to conduct the examination.
- An estimate of staff and dollar resources expended by the insurer for the market conduct exam.
- A list of the office equipment and supplies required by the examiner team.
- A description of the information and data required by the examiner team at the start of the exam.

## Pre-Examination Meeting

> What is the purpose of a pre-examination meeting? Of what benefit is it to the insurer?

The examiner team was asked to meet with the exam coordinator and the vice presidents of claims and underwriting. The meeting was scheduled for a week before the actual examination was to begin.

> What types of information is the examiner team likely to look at?

At the pre-examination meeting, the examiner team described the examination procedure for the vice president of underwriting, the vice president of claims, and the examination coordinator for SIC. The reasons for the examination and the period to be examined were discussed. Wendy explained that the insurer would be required to provide the examiners with a work area separated from the insurer's staff. She requested that SIC provide access to telephones, computers, and other necessary office supplies that had been outlined in the coordinator's packet. Wendy also requested copies of previous market conduct examinations and audit reports. The examination coordinator and the examiner team also discussed the following information assembled and available for the examiner team on the date the examination was set to begin:

- A description of the market distribution systems or production methods SIC used to generate personal auto insurance business
- A listing of all of SIC's personal auto insurance producers appointed in the domiciliary state, indicating the distribution by ZIP Code within each office's county
- A copy of SIC's organizational chart for the entire region and for the domiciliary state, showing the primary reporting relationships
- A listing and description of all the quality control programs used by SIC to monitor SIC's application of its rates, rules, forms, underwriting standards, and statistical plans and to monitor SIC's claims settlement practices, particularly with respect to its personal auto insurance program
- A listing and description of the underwriting rules, rate manuals, and claims settlement guidelines for personal auto insurance written in SIC's domiciliary state, including manual pages for all revisions adopted during the period under examination
- A description of the insurer's affiliation with insurance organizations, such as rating bureaus, advisory or statistical organizations, auto insurance plans, and so on
- A listing of all current personal auto policies written or renewed, and all personal auto policies canceled by the insurer and by the insured in the domiciliary state within the period of examination, with sufficiently detailed information to allow random selection of policies for review, including the premium for each policy
- A listing of all personal auto claims files, categorized as follows: claims open; claims closed with payment by category (such as collision, medical payments, and so on); claims denied; claims closed without payment; and subrogation claims, with the data detailed enough to allow random selections of files for review

Wendy emphasized that the exam coordinator was the examiner team's contact person and should be authorized to provide any information requested by the team. Wendy also noted that the exam coordinator and the vice presidents of claims and underwriting would be able to visit with the team during the examination process so that they remained informed of the process and the findings of the examiners.

## Department Document Review

> What does the examiner team do to prepare for the market conduct exam?

During the time between the notification and the examination date, Wendy reviewed the insurance department records on SIC. The domiciliary state insurance department had examined SIC's market conduct five years ago and its financial condition four years ago. In both examinations, only minor violations were detected and SIC was required to pay a small amount in fines.

However, sixteen months ago, one of the other states in which SIC operates had conducted a market conduct examination of SIC that concluded that the company was engaging in unfair discrimination. In that state, SIC had included ambiguous terminology in its underwriting guidelines, inconsistently applied its underwriting requirements, and showed inconsistency in the use of its underwriting guidelines among branch offices. The company was ordered to correct its problems and was fined $100,000. The other three states in which SIC was licensed did not have examination data more recent than that of the domiciliary state.

The NAIC had records of the increased number of complaints in the domiciliary state and the state that had similar findings. The NAIC also indicated that the market conduct exam done sixteen months earlier was the most recent exam of the company and the only exam to report such violations.

## Additional Pre-Examination Activities

After her review of the departments' and the NAIC's information regarding SIC, Wendy decided that the market conduct examination of the insurer should concentrate on the following:

- SIC's personal auto insurance underwriting guidelines and their application to a sample of risks on a company-wide basis and by branch office and agency
- SIC's personal auto insurance claim settlement guidelines and their application to both first- and third-party claims on a company-wide basis and by branch office and agency

Wendy met with Dwayne and Ed to review the purpose and scope of the market conduct examination of SIC. Wendy related her document review results and asked Dwayne and Ed to provide comments and suggestions about the examination's scope. Wendy, Dwayne, and Ed then discussed their respective responsibilities during the on-site exam. Finally, Wendy emphasized the need to maintain adequate working papers so that they would have supporting data for their conclusions and recommendations. Analyses and factual support, including worksheets that identified individual file data, were necessary as supporting information.

With the examination team's plan determined, Wendy returned to SIC to meet individually with the examination coordinator, the vice president of underwriting, and the vice president of claims two days before the exam was to begin. With the examination coordinator, Wendy reviewed the scope and likely duration of the exam process and made sure that the work area and supplies were available and that the data she had requested would be available for the exam. Wendy also told the coordinator that the examiners would need to visit the company's four branch offices in its domiciliary state, so she and the coordinator established a schedule for those visits. During her visits with each vice president, Wendy reviewed the examination procedure and her expectations of support from his or her departments.

The day following her visit to the company, Wendy met with her supervisor, the department's chief market conduct examiner. Wendy informed the chief examiner of the current status of the project and provided an overview of the exam details.

> How can these meetings help to improve the market conduct examination process?

## The Examination Process

Upon arriving at SIC on the first day of the exam, the examiner team first met with the examination coordinator to go over last minute details. The coordinator showed the team to its work area and made sure that all of the supplies and space requirements were met. The team reviewed the information provided to ensure that each of the items requested at the pre-examination meeting had been supplied. The examiner team then began the examination.

### Underwriting Examination

> What steps are taken to examine the insurer's underwriting practices?

Personal auto underwriting was the first area examined. Wendy reviewed the company's underwriting guidelines, underwriting bulletins, and declination procedures. Dwayne looked at the agency agreements and the insurer's correspondence with producers and branch offices. Ed studied the company's interoffice and interdepartmental memos and the minutes of executive meetings. The results of the team's investigation were discussed by the exam team members and with the vice president of underwriting; they were then recorded. (They are discussed later in this case.)

When the team members had completed their review of the underwriting guidelines and other written information, they turned to how the personal auto underwriting guidelines were applied to the risks assumed and declined by SIC. The personal auto insurance files were divided into five categories: policies written during the exam period, policies renewed during the exam period, policies terminated during the exam period, policy applications declined during the exam period, and policies remaining in force during the exam period. A random sample from each category was selected and statistically analyzed for underwriting accuracy in the compliance with state statutes and regulations and manual rules and the assignment of proper coverage. The results were discussed by the examiner team and the vice president of underwriting and were then recorded. (They are discussed later in this case.)

The categories were then stratified into subgroups by agent and by branch office. Statistical tests were conducted to determine whether statistically significant differences in the application of underwriting guidelines occurred among agents and among branch offices. As with the above statistical results, the examiner team and the vice president of underwriting discussed the stratified statistical results, which were recorded by the team members. (They are discussed later in this case.)

During the underwriting examination, the examiner team checked with the state insurance department section that reviews rates and forms to ensure that SIC's records concerning products and prices were accurate. Rates and forms used by SIC were checked to see whether they had been filed and approved, as required by state law.

## Claims Examination

> What steps are taken to examine the insurer's claims settlement practices?

Following their examination of SIC's personal auto insurance underwriting procedures and practices, Wendy, Dwayne, and Ed studied SIC's personal auto insurance claims settlement procedures and practices. They first considered the company's claims settlement procedures and policies. Ed reviewed SIC's personal auto policy forms to become familiar with the coverages provided and the exclusions contained in the policies and to confirm compliance with statutory provisions. Dwayne reviewed SIC's methods for processing personal auto first- and third-party claims, from the time the claim was reported to the time the claim was settled. Wendy reviewed with the vice president of claims the company's procedures for maintaining claims records, providing draft and settlement authority, and enforcing the claims procedures manual, including involvement in subrogation and salvage activities. The examiner team and the vice president of claims discussed the findings, and the team recorded the results. (They are discussed later in this case.)

Wendy, Ed, and Dwayne then conducted statistical tests to determine how SIC applied the claims settlement procedures the examiner team had studied. The examiner team had received the categorized list it had requested that divided the company's claims within the examination period into the following categories: claims open; claims closed with payment; claims denied; claims closed without payment; and subrogation claims. The team performed each of the following statistical tests:

- Using randomly selected samples from the open and closed claims to determine whether the company had unfairly delayed claims settlement and to determine whether the company conformed to its policy language
- Using a randomly selected sample from closed claims to determine whether the company's handling of each claim was documented sufficiently
- Using a randomly selected sample from the subrogation claims to determine whether the company had fulfilled its duties to the policyholders and claimants, such as reimbursing claimants for the deductibles recovered

The examiner team discussed its observations with the vice president of claims and then recorded the results. (They are discussed in the next section of this case.)

## The Examination Findings

The examiner team, upon completing its examination of SIC's personal auto underwriting and claims settlement procedures and practices, met with the company's CEO, examination coordinator, and vice presidents of underwriting and claims to explain precisely how the team had conducted the examination and to discuss the team's findings. The results of the examination are discussed below.

### Underwriting Examination Results

The examiner team identified two deficiencies of SIC's underwriting practices:

- *The company used ambiguous terminology in its underwriting guidelines.* For example, one guideline required that high-risk drivers be denied coverage.

However, the factors that distinguished a high-risk driver were not identified.

- *The company inconsistently applied its underwriting requirements.* The examiners found evidence that the decision to accept or deny a particular high-risk driver depended on the underwriter who made the decision. For example, some drivers with two points were denied coverage while other drivers with two points were accepted. In all respects the drivers accepted and the drivers denied coverage were equivalent risks. The only difference was the underwriter who made the decision.

Wendy believed that the inconsistency in applying the underwriting requirements was due, primarily, to two issues:

1. The ambiguous terminology in the underwriting guidelines
2. The training and experience of the underwriting staff

## Claims Examination Results

The majority of SIC's problems stemmed from the company's claims settlement practices. The examiner team identified the following deficiencies of the company's claims settlement practices:

- *The company did not promptly investigate and settle claims.* The laws in the state required insurers to investigate and settle first-party property claims within forty days of receiving the claim, on average. SIC's claims settlement average was forty-five days. In addition, state laws required insurers to investigate and settle third-party property claims within ninety days, on average. SIC's third-party average was 100 days.
- *The company did not make equitable and fair settlements.* Evidence indicated that claims adjusters delayed payment, with the approval of supervisors, to get claimants to settle for less than they were due under policy terms.
- *Some of those producers given limited claims settlement authority had abused their privileges.* The claims review procedures of the company were not adequate. Producers, in some cases, had filed fraudulent claims through their respective offices and settled them to their own benefit. The company had not detected the fraud and had continued to approve the producer's claims.
- *Upon completion of subrogation, the company did not promptly reimburse insureds' deductibles and other expenses paid by the insureds during and arising from their claims settlement.* The company had taken, at times, up to three months to reimburse insureds for amounts that the insureds had paid but that the company had received through subrogation.

## The Examination Report

The examiner team, once it had completed its examination of SIC's personal auto underwriting and claims settlement procedures and practices and discussed the results with the company's officials, drew up a report that recorded its observations and conclusions concerning the company's market conduct activities in those examined. The report included the following sections:

- A *summary* of the examination, including the major problems identified
- A *background section* providing a brief statement about the company—its state of domicile, its state of incorporation, and the date of its last examination by the state insurance department
- A *methodology section* outlining, in detail, the means by which the exam was conducted, including how the files were selected, the number of files per sample, the number of files from which the samples were drawn, and the percent of the total represented in each sample
- A *findings section* outlining, in detail, the problems identified by the examination
- *Technical appendices*, including the warrant for the examination, the certification of the examiner-in-charge, and a disclaimer that advised any insurers that they could not use the report for advertisement purposes

The report was submitted to the Commissioner of Insurance for his review. He approved and signed the report. A copy of the final report was then sent to SIC.

## Regulatory Action

Given the examiner team's findings, what regulatory actions might be taken?

Once a final report for a market conduct examination is filed, the insurance department can issue the necessary regulatory actions based on the examination findings. When the company received the final report, it had ten days to request a hearing on any or all of the subject matter included in the report. If no hearing is requested, the report is filed. SIC chose not to request a hearing, and the report was filed.

The findings indicated that SIC had violated several state laws. The primary concern of the insurance department, however, was the fact that policyholders and claimants of SIC had been treated unfairly. SIC was ordered to correct its problems in accordance with the following suggestions:

- Develop definite underwriting guidelines and apply them consistently.
- Develop and implement a thorough training program for underwriters and claims adjusters that includes knowledge of ethics and of state laws, regulations, and rules that apply to both positions.
- Develop and enforce a claims review system that is designed to detect fraud by producers.
- Shorten the time taken to adjust and settle property claims. In addition, shorten the time period to reimburse insureds following successful subrogation.

In addition, because the problems identified were not isolated incidents, SIC was fined $250,000. Another targeted market conduct exam was scheduled one year from the date on which the final report was filed and the current market conduct examination was closed.

The results of the examination were forwarded to the NAIC and to the state insurance departments in the four other states in which SIC does business.

# Case 3: An Insurer's Financial Examination

> For what reasons might an insurer be subjected to a financial exam?

All-Safe Insurance Company (ASIC) was scheduled for a financial conditions examination. It had undergone a change in management control two years ago. The insurance commissioner in ASIC's domiciliary state believed that it should be examined because, since that change, the financial condition of the company had appeared to deteriorate. Since ASIC is a large, regional insurance company with more than $1 million in premiums written in the NAIC Western Zone, it falls under the zone (or association) examination process.

## Calling the Zone Examination

Forty days before the examination was to begin, the domiciliary insurance commissioner entered the notice of examination into the Examination Tracking System (ETS) as required for zone examinations. States in which ASIC does business in the zone, the zone secretary, and the NAIC Examination Services Office (ESO) were notified through the NAIC Examination Tracking System (ETS) *examination call letter* that provided the following information:

- The name of the contact person: Jack Simpson was named as the examiner-in-charge by the domiciliary state insurance department.
- The company to be examined: ASIC.
- Information about the proposed examination: a financial examination, which would require six months to complete, was set to begin in forty days, at ASIC's home office.
- Zones invited to participate: only states in the Western Zone, since ASIC conducts business only in the Western Zone.

The states in the Western Zone received the notification through the ETS, and five states indicated their desire to participate in the examination. Those states notified the zone secretary through the ETS with an *intent to participate letter*. Each state's letter identified the examiner whom it would assign to the examination.

The zone secretary reviewed the letters from the five states and selected an examiner, Tom Wisener, to represent the zone during the financial conditions examination of ASIC. In the state that Tom represented, ASIC had its highest volume of premiums written (with the exception of the domiciliary state in which ASIC writes most of its premiums). Using an *examination participation letter*, the zone secretary notified Tom's state, the domiciliary state, and the ESO of Tom's selection as the zone representative for the examination.

## The Examiner Team

As indicated in the examination call, Jack Simpson was named examiner-in-charge by ASIC's domiciliary state, and Tom Wisener was selected as the examiner to represent the zone. The examiner team was rounded out by appointing two additional examiners from the domiciliary state—Maureen Turner and Leo Artini.

As examiner-in-charge, Jack served as team supervisor. Among his duties, Jack had the following authority and responsibilities:

- Develop the initial plan for the examination and update it periodically to reflect the exam's current status
- Inform each of the other three examiners of current exam developments
- Discuss problems involved during the examination with each of the other three examiners

- Manage the activities of the other three examiners—assign them work, review their work, ensure their professional conduct, and monitor their general progress during the exam
- Keep ASIC's management informed of the progress of the examination

As zone representative, Tom served as liaison between the examiner team and the zone secretary, the other zone state insurance commissioners, and the ESO. Tom was to voice any dissent he might have when the final exam report was prepared and to make sure his dissenting views, if any, were included in the final report.

Maureen and Leo were to serve as staff examiners under Jack's direction. For the purposes of the financial conditions examination of ASIC, Jack was their supervisor.

## Planning and Conducting the Examination

What steps are taken to conduct a financial examination?

As indicated above, Jack was primarily responsible for planning the examination. The planning phase provided Jack with the opportunity to become acquainted with ASIC's operations and areas of solvency risk. The better prepared Jack is before the start of an examination, the more effective and efficient the exam can be. Thus, in planning ASIC's financial conditions examination, Jack strove to achieve the following three objectives:

1. Identify ASIC's key solvency risk areas so that analysis could be more focused on those areas and less focused on other areas with less solvency risk
2. Increase his understanding of ASIC's management and operations so that he could better supervise Maureen, Leo, and Tom while at ASIC and so that he could better evaluate the area's ASIC's key solvency risk
3. Improve the documentation of ASIC's key solvency risk areas and the extent of the examination in each area so that the quality of the examination could be improved and regulatory action could be more appropriate than before

The ultimate goal of the planning process was to establish a schedule and format for the examination that responded to the unique characteristics of ASIC.

## Review and Analysis

> What can be accomplished by review and analysis before the on-site exam begins?

In order for Jack to become familiar with the company's management, products, and operations, and with the insurance department's perception of the company's activities, he reviewed and analyzed the following documents:

- ASIC's general correspondence and other files to evaluate the impact of significant events on account balances and future operations
- The Financial Analysis Annual Statement Review Package, including ASIC's profile report, Financial Analyst Workpapers, IRIS ratios, risk-based capital results, and other financial results since the last financial examination to identify significant or unusual solvency results or trends
- Work papers and reports from work performed in prior periods to assess the overall scope of the work performed, the perceived risk areas, and the findings with respect to key solvency trends and results

Jack also held discussions with ASIC's management to better understand the significant changes that had occurred since the company had undergone its change in management and to identify other significant changes that had recently taken place.

Jack asked Maureen and Leo to participate in the review and analysis of the company. Given Maureen's expertise as a financial analyst, Jack asked her to make a more in-depth analysis of the Financial Analysis Annual Statement Review Package. Jack asked Leo to become familiar with the ways in which the company conducted its business and to evaluate the industry conditions that could adversely affect the company's solvency.

## In-House Planning Meeting

> What purpose is served by an in-house planning meeting?

Following their review and analysis of ASIC, Jack, Maureen, and Leo met with their insurance department's examination supervisor and Tom to discuss the results. Maureen reported on the company's prior financial condition and on the current indications of ASIC's financial standing, including the company's most current risk-based capital level, IRIS ratios, financial statements, and key solvency risk factors. Leo explained the structure of ASIC, its key markets and product lines, and its key customers and major competitors. Leo also discussed the business and economic trends, the competitive environment, and the regulatory changes that might affect ASIC's solvency. Jack then summarized his understanding of the company and his ideas for the examination's focus:

- The primary reason for calling the examination was ASIC's change in management two years ago. Since that change, several financial factors had begun to indicate financial trouble, especially in the areas of surplus management and premium volume.
- Because of indications that the insurer's overall financial condition was taking a turn for the worse, a full scope examination of the company's financial operations might be in order. This would involve analysis of each of the following for ASIC:
    - Management
    - Plan of operation
    - Corporate records and accounts
    - Financial statements
    - Business in force
    - Loss experience
    - Reserves
    - Asset quality
    - Use of reinsurance
- The period examined would be the second six months of ASIC's most recently ended year of operation.
- Given the scope of the proposed financial examination, the team might need six months to complete the examination.

## Final Plan

Having reached a general consensus at the in-house planning meeting, Jack, Maureen, Leo, and Tom continued to develop the examination plan. The team outlined the scope of the analysis to be accomplished for each account it planned to examine. The tests to be performed and their scope were also outlined. The level of analytical review and the types of analytical review procedures were also outlined.

For example, the team concluded that an analysis of the insurer's investments was necessary to determine whether fluctuations in the value of ASIC's investments were partly responsible for the insurer's surplus decrease. The team decided to calculate several ratios to evaluate the investment performance and compare those ratios to results from prior periods, to forecasted results, and to industry and competitor data. Those ratios included the following:

- *Individual invested assets to total assets*, to better understand ASIC's investment philosophy and liquidity and to evaluate its compliance with statutory requirements
- *Investment yield*, in total and by category, to determine investment performance
- *Bond maturity schedule*, to determine ASIC's liquidity position
- *Ratio of market value to book value of stocks*, to measure those stocks' market performance

Based on the team's outlines, Jack was able to develop work assignments and a work schedule for the team members.

To ensure that the team had completed all the details and acquired all the necessary documentation, Jack filled out an Examination Planning Questionnaire. The questionnaire, an excerpt of which is shown in Exhibit 9-8, asked Jack about the various areas of the insurer's operations. For the examination of ASIC, Jack needed to fill out the entire questionnaire. By doing so, Jack was able to determine whether the team had considered all of the pertinent information and circumstances for the examination process and to determine whether the scope of the analysis, tests, and analytical review were appropriate. Jack was also able to make sure that the workloads and schedule he had developed were viable.

Jack then put together a planning file that included all of the documents and supporting work papers that had been compiled. The file was forwarded to the domiciliary insurance department's examination supervisor for approval.

## Final Planning Meeting

Once the file had been reviewed by the examination supervisor, Jack met with him to discuss the plan. The meeting provided an opportunity for the supervisor and Jack to discuss the examination approach and reach an agreement about how the exam would proceed. The supervisor approved the plan, and Jack was able to implement it.

## Conducting the Examination

| |
|---|
| What will the examiner team consider in the financial examination process? |

**Exhibit 9-8**
Excerpts from the Examination Planning Questionnaire

. . .

III. INTERNAL AUDIT ACTIVITIES AND INTERNAL CONTROLS

Is an internal audit department used?

A. Do internal auditors prepare and follow written audit programs? Is the scope of internal audit activities planned in advance with:

Senior management?
Board of directors?
Audit committee?

B. In a separate memorandum, describe the normal duties of the internal auditors including extent of financial audits and operational audits.

Indicate the following:

Size and organization of the staff (including ratio of supervisors to staff);
Prior experience of the staff members;
Number of CPAs and CIAs; and
Scope restrictions.

C. Do internal auditors have direct access to:

Senior management?
Board of directors?
Audit committee?
Appropriate executives?

Are responses to recommendations documented?
Is implementation of internal audit recommendations monitored?

Are there training programs for internal auditors?
Describe the training programs.
Describe any established continuing education requirements.

Are any internal auditors or members of their families related to other employees?

IV. MONITORING PROCEDURES

BUDGETS

A. Does management develop an annual budget and financial plan based on corporate goals and objectives?

Are budget expectations communicated to those affected?

B. Are estimates included in financial data and statements reviewed by knowledgeable persons independent of the estimation process? Who performs the review?

Are the entries supported by explanation and/or documentation?

C. Are financial performance and status of the company's financial condition periodically reviewed and/or compared to the plan? Are variances between

*Continued on next page*

performance vs. plan explained by management? How often are these analyses performed?

D. Do budgeting procedures cover all subsidiaries and departments? Do budgets and forecasts cover:

Premium income by line of insurance?
Policy benefits by line of insurance?
General expenses?
Investments (allocation of investable funds, and income and expenses)?
Statutory surplus?
Federal income taxes?
Cash flow?

E. Does management use financial and other informational reporting to gauge accomplishment of plan and to maintain a controlled environment? Is assessment made of:

Profitability?
Business growth?
Investment of funds, including liquidity?
Direct expenses?
Capital expenditures?

FINANCIAL PLANNING AND REPORTING

F. In a separate memorandum, summarize the qualifications of key employees responsible for preparation and issuance of financial statements. Include names, titles, job responsibilities, background, and number of years in present position.

G. Are financial statements submitted at regular intervals to operating management?

To the board of directors?
To the audit committee?

Are they accompanied by analytical comments? Do they show comparisons with:

Prior periods?
Budgets or forecasts?

H. Who reviews and approves financial information for public distribution (e.g., press releases, filings with regulatory bodies, and policyholders' or shareholders' reports)?

Chief executive officer?
Chief operating officer?
Chief financial officer?
Chief actuary?
Board of directors?
Audit committee?

. . .

Jack and his team of examiners arrived at ASIC on the date the examination was scheduled to begin. They were shown to a private office area that had been set aside for them, with the supplies required for their tasks. The team then began its examination of ASIC's financial condition.

For example, as part of the examination of ASIC's stocks and bonds, the examiner team verified securities through the following steps:

- They studied the custodial agreement between ASIC and the trust company used as a depository for ASIC's securities to ensure that the agreement included certain safeguards and provisions, such as the trust company's obligation to indemnify ASIC for any loss of the insurer's securities where such loss was caused by the negligence or dishonesty of the trust company.
- They physically inspected, counted, and identified the securities as the ones specifically acquired by ASIC.
- They confirmed that the securities were legally owned by ASIC by studying a sample of such items as private placements, affidavits from custodian officials, and ASIC's log entries.
- They contacted the NAIC's Securities Valuation Office (SVO) to determine whether ASIC had correctly valued several of the securities it held.

Jack supervised the process. He reported on the progress of the examination to the domiciliary insurance department's examination supervisor. He kept ASIC's management informed of the requirements and process of the examiner team. He assisted where needed in the examination process and coordinated the work of Maureen, Leo, and Tom. As zone representative, Tom kept the zone supervisor informed of the progress of the examination.

## Examination Results

Following the completion of the examination, Jack put together the examination report that included all of the procedures involved and the findings from the examination of ASIC's financial condition. As deemed appropriate, the report focused on the problem areas that were of regulatory concern:

- The company's new management was not as knowledgeable about ASIC's operations as the former management had been. The company had therefore suffered under the new management. The new management philosophy was not conservative, and the company's investments and loss reserves reflected the liberal style of the new management.
- Recent, more risky investments, with the downturn in the economy, had begun to lose significant value. This had an adverse effect on policy-

holders' surplus and the insurer's profits. In addition, the insurer had not valued certain investments in accordance with the *Securities Valuation Manual*.

- The loss reserves and loss adjustment expense reserves had fallen below the minimum levels allowed under statutory accounting procedures, yet the company had not established the required excess of statutory over statement reserves.

In total, because of the new management philosophy, the insurer was heading toward financial hardship and regulatory intervention.

Maureen, Leo, and Tom agreed with Jack's report and signed off on it. The domiciliary state adopted the report and mailed a copy of it to each of the states in which ASIC does business, the NAIC, and the NAIC's Financial Analysis Working Group (FAWG). The company also received a copy of the report.

ASIC requested a hearing on the issue of reserving assumptions. ASIC's management did not agree with the findings that the company had violated the statutory requirements for establishing loss reserves. By ASIC's calculations, the minimum levels of reserves had been met.

The domiciliary insurance commissioner called a hearing and requested that Jack, Maureen, Leo, and Tom be present. The commissioners of those states that had participated in the exam and the zone secretary were also invited. The hearing was held within ninety days of the company's request, and the findings were that the examiners made a correct assessment of the company's reserving practices.

## Correcting the Problems

> Given the results, what corrections are likely to be required by the examiners?

The examiners' report recommended that ASIC's management become better acquainted with insurance company management procedure and the laws, rules, and regulations that govern the financial conduct of insurance companies. It was also suggested that ASIC hire an experienced actuary and an accountant who could help the company correct the problems associated with investment asset valuation and with loss and loss adjustment expense reserves estimation.

Periodically, the domiciliary insurance department made inquiries to determine whether ASIC was working to correct the problems identified in the financial conditions examination. The insurance department also scheduled a limited scope examination of the insurer for the following year. If the company fails to correct those problems identified, the domiciliary insurance department has threatened to charge the directors and officers with mismanagement of the insurer and intervene in the company's management.

# Case 4: Dealing With a Financially Troubled Insurer[1]

> What types of indications warn regulators of an insurer's financial trouble?

Oh-No Insurance Company (ONIC) is a property-liability insurance company that does business in two states. ONIC has been trying to increase its market share in nonstandard auto insurance. It has experienced rapid premium growth in the past two quarters and has a history of underreserving. The line of insurance it sells, in conjunction with these two factors, has caused extreme volatility in its reported loss reserves.

## The Problems

ONIC increased its premium writings far in excess of what its surplus could support at the same time it reduced its rates to inadequate levels. A financial conditions examination by the domiciliary insurance department also revealed other threats to the insurer's solvency:

- Significant benefits—much greater than what the company could reasonably afford or justify—were paid to several company officers who were also shareholders.
- An agreement with an affiliated company stated that the affiliate would provide ONIC with investment management advice for a fee. However, although the fee was paid, the employees of ONIC actually performed the investment work. The fee appeared to go directly into the pockets of ONIC's officers.
- A significant adjustment was needed to increase ONIC's reserves to adequate levels.
- Long claims settlement lags caused loss adjustment expenses to be high and resulted in an underreserving of claims.

## Correcting the Problems

> Given these problems, what can be done to rehabilitate the insurer?

ONIC faced insolvency, which required that the domiciliary insurance department act immediately. Past experience of the company and the insurance department's past dealings with the company's management indicated that informal action would not be effective. Therefore, to protect ONIC's assets and stabilize the situation, the insurance department did the following:

- Ordered ONIC to immediately stop writing insurance coverage until the problems identified could be corrected.
- Assigned one of its full-time staff members to monitor ONIC's operations in the company home office and to oversee all money matters. Disbursements, withdrawals, and payments could not be made without the regulatory staff member's approval.
- Instructed all investment personnel not to release funds or securities without notification to and approval from the insurance department.

Once the insurance department was sure that the problems facing ONIC could not get worse, it began to develop a plan of corrective action, which was implemented in the following steps:

1. ONIC's rates were raised to adequate levels, and agents' commission rates were reduced.
2. ONIC reentered the market with a limit on the amount of business it could write for any given period.
3. ONIC implemented more selective underwriting standards and upgraded its book of business.
4. ONIC was required by the insurance department to terminate an agreement with an affiliated law firm to handle claims settlements and to hire additional in-house claims adjusters to speed up the claims settlement process.
5. Claims files were continually monitored to ensure that reserves were adequate.
6. The agreement for investment management services was terminated, and company officers were ordered to return the fees paid to them under the agreement to ONIC.
7. The guilty officers were required to resign.

The result of these actions on ONIC's financial statements was negative. Surplus was decreased by the increase in loss reserves. The reduction in premium volume increased ONIC's cash-flow problems. To alleviate these pressures on ONIC's financial statements, the insurance department helped ONIC arrange reinsurance to provide a temporary gain in surplus.

After getting ONIC to a level of operation that was acceptable to the insurance department, the insurance department backed away from overseeing the day-to-day operation of the insurer. However, ONIC was required to develop and submit a long-term business plan with specific goals and a timetable for returning to a position of financial strength and sound operations.

# Summary

The cases provided in this chapter were designed to draw together insurance regulatory issues that have been discussed in previous chapters of this text. The cases should have provided some insight into the regulatory process as it applies to the various situations discussed.

The first case dealt with what an insurer goes through to incorporate. The second case illustrated a targeted market conduct examination. The third case detailed a full scope financial conditions examination. The final case described the process of rehabilitating a financially troubled insurer.

# Resources

Laucher, Joel K., and Khanh LeCong. *Market Conduct Examinations* (California Department of Insurance, 1995).

National Association of Insurance Commissioners (NAIC). *Financial Examiners Handbook* (Kansas City, MO: NAIC, 1994).

National Association of Insurance Commissioners (NAIC). *Troubled Insurance Company Handbook* (Kansas City, MO: NAIC, 1989).

Wulf, Donald M., and Frank Weaver. *Market Conduct Examinations in Illinois: A Twenty Year Evolution* (Illinois Department of Insurance, 1994).

# Chapter Note

1. This case is based on Case 2 in the *Troubled Insurance Company Handbook* (Kansas City, MO: NAIC, 1989).

# Bibliography


Actuarial Standards Board. "Statement of Principles Regarding Property and Casualty Insurance Ratemaking." Washington, DC: 1988.

All-Industry Research Advisory Council. *Special Investigative Units: Surveys on Insurance Company Use of SIUs for Fraud Investigations*, AIRAC, Oakbrook, IL: 1984.

American Arbitration Association. *Facts About the American Arbitration Association.* New York, NY: American Arbitration Association, October 1989.

Anderson, Dan R., and Roger A. Formisano. "Causal Factors in P-L Insolvency." *Journal of Insurance Regulation*, vol. 6, pp. 449-461.

*Auto Insurance Report*. Laguna Niguel, CA: Risk Communications, June 13, 1994.

Barclay, Lee D. "Rate Regulation for Solvency." *Journal of Insurance Regulation*, vol. 8, 1990, p. 316.

*Best's Solvency Study, Property/Casualty Insurers 1969-1990*. Oldwick, NJ: A. M. Best Company, 1991.

Block, Stanley B., and Geoffrey A. Hirt. *Foundations of Financial Management*. 6th ed. Homewood, IL: Irwin, 1992.

*CalJur: Insurance Companies to Insurance Contracts and Coverage*. Vol. 39, 3d ed. San Francisco, CA: Bancroft-Whitney Co., 1977.

*Couch on Insurance*, 2d ed. (rev. ed.). Rochester, NY: The Lawyers Cooperative Publishing Co., 1984.

D'Arcy, Stephen P., and Neil Doherty. *The Financial Theory of Pricing Property-Liability Insurance Contracts*. Philadelphia, PA: Wharton School, University of Pennsylvania, 1988.

*Deskbook Encyclopedia of American Insurance Law*. 3d ed. Egan, NY: Data Research, Inc., 1989.

"Five Conn. Agencies Accused of Diverting Premiums." *Insurance Times*, May 31, 1994, p. 1.

"Florida Charges 87 Agents of Metropolitan with Fraud." *Best Week*, March 14, 1994, p. 6.

Gaunt, Larry D., et al. *Commercial Liability Underwriting*. 3d ed. Malvern, PA: Insurance Institute of America, 1990.

Glendenning, G. William, and Robert B. Holtom. *Personal Lines Underwriting*. 3d ed. Malvern, PA: Insurance Institute of America, 1990.

Haggerty, Alfred G. "3 Pru Agents in Arizona Sued for Misleading Policyholders." *National Underwriter* (Life-Health ed.). June 6, 1994, p. 3.

Harrington, Scott. "The Impact of Rate Regulation" and "Prices and Uncertainty Results in the Property-Liability Insurance Industry: A Survey." *Journal of Risk and Insurance*, December 1984, pp. 577-619.

Harrington, Scott, and Helen Doerpinghaus. "The Economics and Politics of Automobile Insurance Rate Classification." *Journal of Risk and Insurance*, vol. 60, no. 1, 1993, p. 59.

Hartz, Douglas A., and David John Masini. "Financial Strength." *Property-Casualty Insurance Accounting*. Durham, NC: Insurance Accounting and Systems Association, 1994.

Hines, Bernard L. *Arbitration and Mediation*. Washington, DC: Colortone Press, 1988.

Hubbel, Michael R. and Mary Lanning, "Tackling the Burden of Continuing Education." *Best's Review*. Oldwick, NJ: A.M. Best Company, January 1994, pp. 58-61.

Insurance Fraud Bureau of Massachusetts, 1993 Annual Report.

"Kansas Strengthens Insurance Fraud Law." *Taylor's Insurance Digest*, March 12, 1994, p. 34.

Kertesz, Louise. "Oregon's SAIF Anti-fraud Effort Recovers Millions." *Business Insurance*, May 23, 1994, p. 15.

Kimball, Spencer L. "Introductory Comment." *Reference Handbook on Insurance Company Insolvency*. 2d ed. Chicago, IL: American Bar Association, 1989.

———. "The Meaning of the McCarran-Ferguson Act Today." *Journal of Insurance Regulation*, vol. 10, no. 1, Fall 1991, pp. 5-22.

Kimball, Spencer, and Barbara Heaney, *Basic Source Materials on the American Regulation of Insurance*. Kansas City, MO: The National Association of Insurance Commissioners, 1995.

Klein, Robert, and Michael Barth. "Solvency Monitoring in the Twenty-First Century." *Journal of Insurance Regulation*, vol. 3, no. 3, Spring 1995, pp. 256-301.

Klein, Robert W. "Solvency Monitoring of Insurance Companies: Regulators' Role and Future Direction." In Edward I. Altman and Irwin T. Vanderhoof, eds. *The Financial Dynamics of the Insurance Industry*. New York, NY: Irwin Professional Publishers, 1995.

Knowles, Robert J. "Alabama Jury Slams Pru for $25M Over Agent's 'Fraud.' " *National Underwriter* (Life-Health ed.), April 18, 1994.

Krohm, Gregory. "The Implications of ISO's Change to Loss Cost Filing for Rate Regulation." *Journal of Insurance Regulation*, vol. 8, 1990, p. 316.

Launie, J.J., et al. *Principles of Property and Liability Underwriting*. 3d ed. Malvern, PA: Insurance Institute of America, 1986.

Liberty Mutual Insurance Group. "Five Reasons Auto Insurance Costs So Much and What We Can Do To Fight Back." Boston, MA: printing 9/92B.

Malone, Elizabeth, and Jim Rose. "NAIC: Regulatory Systems Perspectives, Solvency Surveillance Tools." Presentation at the A.M. Best Users' Conference, September 1, 1992.

Manders, John; Theresa Vaughan; and Robert Myers, Jr. "Insurance Regulation in the Public Interest: Where Do We Go From Here?" *Journal of Insurance Regulation*, vol. 12, no. 3, Spring 1994, pp. 285-340.

Markham, James J., et al. *The Claims Environment*. Malvern, PA: The Insurance Institute of America, 1993.

"Maryland Legislature Passes Bill to Make Insurance Fraud a Felony, Expands Definition." *Insurance Advocate*, April 23, 1994.

*Massachusetts Insurance Law Digest: Agent License Training*. Indianapolis, IN: Pictorial, 1989.

McLeod, Douglas. "State Seeks to Recover Funds." *Business Insurance*, May 16, 1994, p. 2.

Meier, Kenneth J. *The Political Economy of Regulation: The Case of Insurance*. Albany, NY: State University of New York Press, 1988.

———. *Defense Counsel*. Vol. 6. no. 2, June 1994, cover page.

"Michigan's Proposed Antifraud Legislation Pro-Consumer." *Taylor's Insurance Digest*, June 4, 1994, p. 77.

Morrow, Glen J. "Regulatory Environments: Do They Matter?" *Journal of Insurance Regulation*, vol. 11, no. 1, Fall 1992, pp. 19-52.

Murrey, Joe H., and John Von Fenstermaker. "Long-Run Profitability of Fire and Marine Insurance Companies: A 100-Year Study of Boston Insurers." *Journal of Insurance Regulation*, vol. 9, no. 2, Winter 1990, pp. 259-273.

NAII Task Force on Improved Solvency Regulation. *A Call for Balance in Structuring Insurer Solvency Regulation*. Des Plaines, IL: National Association of Independent Insurers, 1992.

National Association of Insurance Commissioners (NAIC). "Financial Analysis and Solvency Surveillance," a supplementary publication to *Services to NAIC Members*. Kansas City, MO: NAIC, 1994.

———. *Financial Condition Examiners Handbook*. Kansas City, MO: NAIC, 1994.

———. *Financial Regulations Standards and Accreditation Program*. Kansas City, MO: NAIC, 1994.

———. *Market Conduct Examiners' Handbook*. Kansas City MO: NAIC, 1994.

———. *NAIC Model Laws, Regulations and Guidelines*. Vols. 1, 2, and 4. Kansas, City, MO: NAIC.

———. *Risk-Based Capital Requirements for Insurers: A New Solvency Tool for Consumer Protection*. Kansas City, MO: NAIC, 1994.

———. *Troubled Insurance Company Handbook*. Kansas City, MO: NAIC, June 1989.

———. *Using the NAIC Insurance Regulatory Information System*. Kansas City, MO: NAIC, 1993.

National Conference of Insurance Guaranty Funds. *Property/Casualty Guaranty Association 1993 Assessment and Financial Information Summary*. Indianapolis, IN: September 1994.

*New York Insurance Regulations*. Chatsworth, CA: NILS Publishing Company, July 1993.

Niose, David A. "Legal Dimensions: Supreme Court RICO Decision to Impact Professional Malpractice Liability." *The Standard*, October 23, 1992, pp. 8-10.

"OAL Approves DOI's Fraud Detection Standards." *Smart's Insurance Bulletin*, May 20, 1994, p. 3.

Ostrager, Barry, and Thomas Newman. *Handbook on Insurance Coverage Disputes*. 5th ed. Englewood Cliffs, NJ: Prentice Hall, 1992.

Outreville, J. Francois. "Underwriting Cycle and Rate Regulation in Automobile Insurance Markets." *Journal of Insurance Regulation*, vol. 9, no. 2, Winter 1990, p. 274.

*Rhode Island Independent Agent*, May/June 1994, pp. 8-27.

*Rhode Island Insurance Laws, Agents, Brokers, Solicitors*. Chatsworth, CA: NILS Publishing Company, March 1994.

*Rhode Island Insurance Licensing Examination Candidate Handbook*. St. Paul, MN: Assessment Systems, Inc., June 1994.

"RICO: Can a Good Law Still Have Some Bad Side Effects?" *Journal of American Insurance*, Second Quarter, 1995, p. 1.

Schacht, Jones, and Peter Gallanis. "The Interstate Compact as an Effective Mechanism for Insurance Receivership Reform." *Journal of Insurance Regulation*, vol. 12, no. 2, Winter 1994, pp. 188-219.

*The Standard*. January 25, 1994, p. 15.

*State of Massachusetts Insurance Licensing Examination Candidate Handbook*. March 1992.

State of New York Insurance Department Circular Department Circular Letter No. 7 (1993). New York, NY: State of New York Insurance Department, July 15, 1993.

Stewart, Barbara, et al. *A Brief History of Underwriting Cycles*. Kansas City, MO: National Association of Insurance Commissioners (NAIC), 1991.

Stewart Economics, Inc. "Managing Insurer Insolvency." A presentation at the National Association of Insurance Brokers, 1988.

*Texas Department of Insurance Licensing Information Bulletin*. St. Paul, MN: Insurance Testing Corporation, 1994.

Thorness, Bill. "The New SIU Team." *Claims Magazine*, September 1994, p. 53.

"Three Sent to Jail for Louisiana Fraud." *National Underwriter* (Property-Casualty ed.), September 13, 1993, p. 6.

"Tort and Insurance Practice Section." *Reference Handbook on Insurance Company Insolvency*. 2d ed. Chicago, IL: American Bar Association, 1989.

U.S. House of Representatives, Subcommittee on Oversight and Investigations, Committee on Energy and Commerce. *Wishful Thinking*. October 1994.

Ward, William D. *Property-Casualty Insurance Accounting*. 6th ed. Durham, NC: Insurance Accounting and Systems Association, 1994.

Williams, Penny. "Hancock Fined for Misleading Agency Sales Practices in RI." *Insurance Times*, April 19, 1994, p. 5.

———. "Maine Worker Gets Jail for Workers Compensation Fraud." *Insurance Times*, November 16, 1993, p. 6.

# Index

## A

## D



## E

## F



## G

## H



## I

## N



## O



## P



## Q

# R

## S

## T



## U

## V



## W



## Z